Transgressing Frontiers:
Shifting Rhetorics in Linguistic and Literary Discourses

Edited by

Kelvin Ngong Toh

Langaa Research & Publishing CIG
Mankon, Bamenda

Publisher:
Langaa RPCIG
Langaa Research & Publishing Common Initiative Group
P.O. Box 902 Mankon
Bamenda
North West Region
Cameroon
Langaagrp@gmail.com
www.langaa-rpcig.net

Distributed in and outside N. America by African Books Collective
orders@africanbookscollective.com
www.africanbookscollective.com

ISBN-10: 9956-551-45-7

ISBN-13: 978-9956-551-45-3

© Kelvin Ngong Toh 2021

All rights reserved.
No part of this book may be reproduced or transmitted in any form or by any means, mechanical or electronic, including photocopying and recording, or be stored in any information storage or retrieval system, without written permission from the publisher

About the Authors

Blasius Agha-ah Chiatoh is Associate Professor of Linguistics and Head of Department of Linguistics at the University of Buea. Specialised in literacy, he has over the years developed special bias for language planning, bi-multilingual education and sociolinguistics.

Eunice Fonyuy Fombele is Lecturer in the English Department the University of Buea. Her main area of research is Gender and Cultural Feminist Studies. Her other research areas revolve around Narrative Ethics, the Womanist Ethics of Care, Conceptualizing the Family and the Emerging Adult Studies, Studies in Coloniality and Decolonial Ethics, Ecocriticism and Studies in Marginality.

Eunice Ngongkum is presently Professor of Postcolonial African Literature and Ecoculture in the Department of African Literature and Civilisations at the University of Yaounde 1. Her articles on these subjects have appeared in scholarly journals both at home and abroad.

Fonka Hans Mbonwuh is an Assistant Lecturer of Sociolinguistics in the Department of English at the University of Bamenda. He has published in the areas Contact Languages especially Cameroon Pidgin-creole, Varieties of English, English in Education, Language and Communication and Spoken English.

Henry Kah Jick is Associate Professor of African Literature and Orature. He has published articles in scholarly journals in Cameroon, Nigeria, Britain, India and the United States. His affiliation is the Department of English at the University of Buea. He is currently Head of Division for Cooperation in the Department of Academic Affairs at The University of Bamenda.

Joseph Nkwain is currently an Assistant Lecturer in the Department of English at the University of Maroua. He has published extensively locally and internationally. His research interest include: Sociolinguistics, postcolonial pragmatics, New Englishes and Discourse Analysis.

Kiwoh Terrence Nsai is an Assistant Lecturer in the Department of English at the University of Buea. His research interest is on Contact Linguistics, Language Policy, and Language Management.

Mbuh Tennu Mbuh is Associate Professor of British Literature and Postcolonial Studies in the Department of English at the University of Yaounde 1. His research areas include: African Literatures and cultures, Comparative Religions, Multiculturalism, British literature and 'De-writing'.

Miriam Ayafor is Associate Professor of English Language at the University of Yaounde 1, Cameroon. She is holder of a BA (Yaounde), MA (Leeds) and PhD (Ulster at Coleraine) all in English Language Studies. Her research interests include the grammar of New Englishes and Sociolinguistics, with emphasis on Pidgins and Creoles.

Peter Foinjong Awoh is Assistant Lecturer of British Literature in the Department of English, Higher Teacher Training College at The University of Bamenda. His areas research interest are Multiculturalism, interdiciplinarity, Cameroon Anglophone Literature and global literatures in English and Creative Writing. He is currently the Coordinator of Civics and Ethics at The University of Bamenda.

Rosalyn Mutia is an Associate Professor of American Literature in the Department of English at the University of Yaounde 1, Cameroon. Her interest include gender studies and multiculturalism. Presently she is an Officer in Charge of Special Duties at the Prime Minister's Office in Cameroon.

Kelvin Ngong Toh is Associate Professor of African and Comparative Literatures. He teaches in the English Departments at the University of Buea and the University of Bamenda. His areas of research are the black diaspora literatures and cultures, literature of the African continent and cultures, political philosophy, music and film studies as well as literary and cultural theory.

Table of Contents

Introduction 1
Kelvin Ngong Toh

Section I: Creating the Self, Dismantling the Other

Chapter One: Each Other's Other, or Not at All: Ideological Barriers and Literary Iconoclasm in J. M. Coetzee's *Foe* 11
Mbuh Tennu Mbuh

Chapter Two: A Language of their Own: Feminist Poetry and Linguistic Experimentation 39
Rosalyn Mutia

Chapter Three: Transgressing Otherness through Marvellous Realism and Negotiating Self/Space in Maryse Condé's *I, Tituba, Black Witch of Salem* 65
Eunice Fonyuy Fondze-Fombele

Chapter Four: Signature and the Self-Other Dialectic in the Poetry of Robert Graves 87
Peter Foinjong Awoh

Chapter Five: Globalization, Information Communication Technologies and African Narratives: Reading Chimamanda Ngozi Adichie's *The Thing Around Your Neck* and *Americanah* 111
Eunice Ngongkum

Section II: Linguistic Shift and Accommodation

Chapter Six: Towards a Policy of Linguistic Freedom in Cameroon 133
Blasius Agha-ah Chiatoh

Chapter Seven: Justice Across Linguistic Frontiers: Preserving Second Official Language Rights in Cameroon Law Courts 153
Kiwoh Terence Nsai

Chapter Eight: Voices Behind Writings on Walls: Effective Communication or Not? 169
Fonka Hans Mbonwuh

Chapter Nine: An Emic Reading of Taxicab Inscriptions in Cameroon 189
Joseph Nkwain

Chapter Ten: Euphemism Versus Blunt Language in Linus Asong's *The Crown of Thorns* 209
Miriam Ayafor

Section III: Displacement and Recognition

Chapter Eleven: Displacement and the Quest for Self in Amos Tutuola's *The Palm-wine Drinkard* 235
Henry Kah Jick

Chapter Twelve: Rape and the Nation in Edwidge Danticat's *Breath, Eyes, Memory* 251
Kelvin Ngong Toh

Introduction

Kelvin Ngong Toh

Discourse on frontiers or borders is becoming complex, ambiguous and overlapping by the day. In this complexity of epistemic constituencies, frontier discourse sways between the acceptance and rejection of the border, especially in the 21st century characterised by physical and ideological movements (Lagios, Lekka & Panoutsopoulos 2018). However, the crossing and crisscrossing of people, spaces and discipline continues to make frontier discourse relevant in interpreting and articulating the world during this century (Marden 2000). While discussing the polarity that has come to characterise frontiers discourse, it seems clear today that movements of ideology and people constitute the force in the (re)territorialisation of communities and disciplines. Lucy Bond and Jessica Rapson (2014: 2) submit that 'the process of *reterritorialization* has not only involved the physical transportation of the objects, but a corresponding *remediation* of their meaning.' As such, present day 'bordering' and the conversation around it is conditioned by 'the burgeoning literature on globalization' that is 'highlighting the shifting boundaries of identity and the final annihilation of space' (Marden 2000:53). Yet the annihilation of space does not completely destroy spaces as crossing enables communities, ideologies and disciplines to be reconstructed, thereby building a 'new internationalism' (Bhabha 1994). Today, frontiers have become so porous that efforts made by nation-states, ideologies and disciplines to contain crossing seem increasingly ineffective as movements proceed with uncontrollable speed.

The focus of this book is to assess, through language and literary studies in interpretation, the epistemic representation of frontiers in it shifting and fixing categories. In this collection, the different researchers stress on the fact that crisscrossing has taken its toll on communities and disciplines and that hegemonic positions are becoming more and more redundant and provocative. Frontier discourse is therefore, a socio-political and culturally oriented discourse. Importing it to language and literary studies also shows that literary circles like language are also shifting and erasing borderlines. As Angela Noella William argues, 'literary theory [including language theories] and criticism have been moving away from essentialist approaches to race, gender and ethnicity, [so that] essentialism has found new life in the logic of how many of our curriculums and syllabi are designed' (William 2003 :126). In the different chapters of this book, the authors have shifted from the dominant frontiers of the disciplines and have tackled issues that crisscross temporal/spatial and epistemological spaces.

Sarah Nutall in 'Flatness and Fantasy: Representation of Land in Two Recent South African Novels' affirms that the frontier is a political construct whose fundamental goal is to own and to demarcate. Such markers or objective for mapping frontiers also fosters difference and an enablement for the 'self' and 'other' binaries. Nutall finds this binary not only in geopolitics and cartographical science but also as epistemological and ontological. While Nutall focuses on the construction of frontiers, Mary Douglass focuses on the absorbency of borders. She maintains that '[a]ll margins are dangerous. If they are pulled this or that way, the shape of fundamental experience is altered. Any structure of ideas is vulnerable at its margins' (Nutall 1996:121). Recent events in the Middle East, Europe and the Mediterranean show that the frontiers can never be firm in this age of globalism as people cannot be stopped from migrating especially when their safety is at stake; not even with contemporary Trumpism and Johnsonism that clamour strongly for foundationalism and nationalist-centricism.

The chapters in this book discuss crisscrossing of frontiers both as geography and epistemology. This is in line with the new cultural ontology that opens up new interpretations and shifts from previous ones in the disciplines of Language, Linguistics, Arts and Literature. The book pulls together a wide range of issues based on a plurality of theoretical assumptions. However, for the purpose of organisation, the issues presented are grouped into three broad sections. Section one looks at the creation of the self as a way to dismantle the other. In section two, the focus is on linguistic shifts and the fact that all languages need space in multilingual societies. Lastly, section three shows how people travel out of their homelands to seek comfort.

Creating the Self, Dismantling the other

The self and other binaries are major ideological positions that have come to be the focus of a lot of research. In as much as it seems over trodden as Mbuh Tennu Mbuh expounds in this section of the work, we argue that in terms of cultural and epistemological discourse, the barrier between the self and the other continue to dominate human life and reactions. This section discusses the other as a cultural frontier that the chapters here interrogate with the general goal to dismantle and blur the barriers. It is in dismantling that the other begins to create the self. One thing that dominates discussions in this section is the fact that barriers of self and other are fluid and unstable, an argument long posited by Hegel, Marx and later Derrida and Foucault. Mbuh Tennu Mbuh's arguments that barriers are constructed with the instinct to dominate the other sets a strong starting point in this section. Interestingly, the quest to 'own' and to dominate others cut across all cultures, religions, races and genders so much so that much of the blocks are constructed by consent.

The issue of cultural frontiers, as part of the binary construct which Mbuh qualifies as historically constructed, has over the years been driven by the idea of 'sameness' which Mbuh argues that it only underscores the victim/authority binary. The victim/authority binary is also articulated from the perspective of gender constructs as

Rosalyn Mutia and Eunice Fonyuy Fondze-Fombele discuss in their essays. Nevertheless, all three authors herald a shifting trend to 'fixed' spaces (Bhabha 1994) with Mutia discussing 20th century Anglo-American poetesses as transgressing by claiming poetic voices – creating an enabling environment; which was Virginia Woolf's disparate call.

Fombele argues that people that are othered should consciously engage themselves in a de-othered agenda that will blur borders and build new co-operative identities in an already difficult global world.

In the project to create the self, the personae becomes relativized. Peter Foinjong Awoh, from a purely Hegelian perspective, argues that the self and othered spaces are in themselves infinite categories that mutate and create new categories. In this case, Awoh discusses the idea of the split personality as a process of blurring and de-confinement.

Eunice Ngongkum celebrates the encounter between Africa and the rest of the world as a part of creating new identities and creating new centres for the African as they become global figures and personalities. Ngongkum holds that the legitimization of knowledge from a clearly Lyotardian perspective is central for the Africans effort to create new centres. Mbuh terms it the digi-modernist world for Africans as they create new selves.

Linguistic Shift and Accommodation

This section focuses on the mutating positions that scholarship in language and linguistic studies has undergone especially in Cameroon and Africa at large. John Leavitt (2015: 18) contends that 'the diversity of languages was one of the central facts about human beings and potentially, at least, had implications for conceptualization of natural and social institutions'. This submission enhances the fact that there is need to respect linguistic difference which is referred to as the 'principle of linguistic relativity'. Hence, Blasius Agha-ah Chiatoh and Kiwoh Terence Nsai in their chapters focus on the consequences of language or linguistic rights and abuse. Chiatoh's arguments are that in multilingual setups, language accommodation and recognition is important because the consequence of any form of linguistic domination is protest. Using the contexts of Cameroon, Chiatoh opts for a redefinition of linguistic policies – those which are more englobing.

Kiwoh makes the same points as Chiatoh referring to dominance and abuse of linguistic rights in Cameroonian courts before the Cameroon-Ambazonia war escalated in 2017. In fact, Kiwoh's chapter simulates one of the immediate causes of the war with Anglophone Cameroonian lawyers taking to the streets to protest on the francophonisation of the judiciary system. Kiwoh submits that the dominance of French as a legal language frustrates the justice of clients who do not identify with that language. Thus, there is the need to use the language of the clients in their courts.

With regard to linguistic relativity, Fonka Hans Mbonwuh, Joseph Nkwain and Miriam Ayafor all state that there is no universal way of using language. Thus, language use is determined by the individual and their context. Mbonwuh takes his arguments to a very formal setting with strict roles – the school setting. His findings evince that the walls and toilet spaces become avenues of speaking by students whose messages cannot be accommodated in the centre space. Nkwain pushes on the same idea but shifts from purely formal settings like schools to writings on taxicabs where he studies the way language is used and the messages that are communicated in the writings. He argues that the language use transgresses dominant forms and creates new avenues for the authors to express themselves. Ayafor, while arguing that there is euphemistic and blunt language in literary productions maintains that the borders between the two is fluid and can hardly be static. Ayafor further stresses on the relativity of language as she argues that different contexts and ideologies determine what is blunt and what is euphemistic.

Displacement and Recognition

In the last section of the book, the chapters focus on the physical movements of people. As the chapters indicate, movement is both voluntary and involuntary and in the age of globalisation and the increase rates of movements, borders have become more porous (Toh 2015). Henry Kah Jick's chapter hinges on the journey motif ideology in orature in which he shows that movement can change and transform one's perception. His reading of Tutoula's *The Palm-Wine Drinkard* reveals that if the drinkard does not go out, he cannot improve on himself and his community. This is the same orientation that Kelvin Ngong Toh takes while discussing the relationship between the West and the Third World. However, Toh seems not to celebrate the West as an abode for migrant Caribbeans but shows how new centres and diasporic identities are constructed because of movements.

Bibliography

Bhabha, H. K., (1994). *The Location of Culture*. London and New York: Routledge.

Bond, L. & Rapson, J., (2014). *Media and Cultural Memory/Medien und Kulturelle Erinnerung*. Berlin: De Gruyter.

Douglass, M., (1966). *Purity and Danger*. London and New York: Routledge.

Freire, P., (2000). *Pedagogy of the Oppressed*. New York and London: Continuum.

Lagios, T., Lekka, V & Panoutsopoulos. , (2018). *Borders, Bodies and Narratives of Crisis in Europe*. London: Palgrave Macmillan.

Leavitt, J., (2015). Linguistic Relativity: Precursors and Transformations. In *The Routledge Handbook of Language and Culture*. London and New York: Routledge, pp. 18-30

Nutall, S., (2000). The Geopolitics of Sovereignty, Governance and

Citizen. In: *Migration, Globalisation and Human Society*. London and New York: Routledge, pp. 47-69.

William, A. N., (2003). Border Crossing: Filipino American Literature in the United States. In: *Beyond Borders: American Literature and Post-Colonial Theory*. London: Pluto, pp. 122-134.

Toh, K.N., (2015). Black Diasporic Nationalism: A Reading of Edwidge Danticat's *Breath, Eyes, Memory* and Fatou Dime's *Le Ventre de L'Atlantique*. In *Recreating Centers and the Politics of Nationalism: Reading Across Cultures*. Saabrucken: Lambert Academic Publishing, pp. 108-128.

Section I:
Creating the Self, Dismantling the Other

Section 2

Competing Selfishness and the Crisis

Chapter One

Each Other's Other, or Not at All: Ideological Barriers and Literary Iconoclasm in J.M. Coetzee's *Foe*

Mbuh Tennu Mbuh

Introduction: When were we Other (ed)?

Located at the crossroads of globalisation and multiculturalism today, otherness is both a contested and over-diluted concept that almost renders itself unnecessary in analysing the manner in which identities are affirmed and preyed on. While the instincts to dominate and resist such domination remain preoccupying in a world where boundaries are supposed to be collapsing, it is important to note that the ability to other or be othered depends on ideological positions that repeatedly assert themselves based on respective emotions of authority and victimhood; and as we shall see, no one is othered who does not participate in the process. Drawing then on Daniel Defoe's classic text in cultural othering, *Robinson Crusoe*, this chapter contends that otherness depends ironically on a mutuality between the belligerent forces; and that J. M. Coetzee's version of the Defoe novel, *Foe*, exposes the limiting, if not irrelevant, nature of ideologies that construct historical and cultural temporalities within which both the authoritative and victimised personalities are imprisoned. What emerges in the end is a metafictional utopia in which hegemonies are dissolved in the interest of wo/man living in the vital space of a functional moment.

In this regard, I engage this chapter against a developing background of being 'persecuted' (however convivially) by Christian enthusiasts, due to my growing conviction that the sacred mystery of the Christian era—camouflaged as 'Current Era' in Christian hermeneutics and representing an AD timeframe— coming to an end, thanks to disciplines like Egyptology, Cultural Studies, Bioethics, etc., and is being replaced by a frantic celebrity *staging* of God and the divine essence. The alternative fields of critical evaluation have significantly revived the debate over the positive values of pre-western civilisations, intervening at a moment when a neo-Thomas and social media, evidence-crazy generation privileges Android iniquities to Holy Ghost 'certainties'. However, even at the risk of being accused as an othering agent myself, it must be said that ignorance can indeed be blissful especially because Christian history of stigmatisation relies on its own functional convenience to evolve; and also on a significant element of ignorance which is synonymous with 'faith', on the part of the unquestioning parishioner, who is then expected to prefer Oscar Wilde's 'exotic fruit' (of knowledge?) whose bloom remains a mystery, untouchable.

Even with its contested historicity, we can begin by suggesting that the Bible is the watershed of the discourse of othering. The monocultural outlook of its formatted myth explains the privileged position of Adam and Eve in the ancestry of humans. While biblical scholars have described the eventual multicultural outlook of Israel in terms of how 'Jews themselves conceived the shaping of their nation in combination with gentiles' (Gruen 2011:288), it will be interesting to consider the nature and impact of dissent within that pioneer family at that initial moment in order to understand how the notion of the Other was formalised. Perhaps the most popular example is the dispute between Cain and Abel, which results in the murder of the latter. When God seeks to know from Cain about the fate or whereabouts of Abel, Cain declares arrogantly in Genesis 4:9: 'Am I my brother's keeper?' I suggest that the breakdown of the family bond here can mark the formal start of othering in especially western consciousness, based on paradigms of possession and dispossession, the favours and/or disfavours that are associated with these, and the formative base of what would eventually emerge as capitalist instincts associated with the collusion between wealth, power, and the authentication of selfhood. The Bible's controversial outreach logically develops from this split, especially when perceived good and evil are racialised according to whose voice is proclaimed and listened to. Cain, the bad son, is othered into exile, while his brother is hailed, even in death, as the personification of moral authority by which other standards are valuated. This biblical background generally accounts for the manner in which otherness was to be constructed and justified in the Anglo-Saxon tradition of which Coetzee (as we will see) is a composite continuation.

In exploring 'the history of the construction of a British identity 'in context' … as an *intersubjective* linguistic event occurring on a specific terrain' in *British Narratives of Exploration,* Frederic Regard wonders: 'Was the Other always bound to be the dead corpus of the ethnographer? Or did this muted Other's corpse manage to resist objectification, resurrect from the table, and become a haunting presence, preventing both the explorer and the explored from resting in peace?' (Regard 2009: 6). Even with the histo-colonial/exploration context of this statement, it is obvious that the notion of the Other here relates to the animosity that usually gathers around postcolonial scholarship from the western academy, with an attempt to rationalise nascent colonialism. Considering E. S. Burt's view in *Regard for the Other* that '[o]ne can hardly envision the self without the other against which it is defined' (Regard 2009: 1), it is necessary to insist that far from constituting a 'dead corpus' and the remnants of a 'muted … corpse' that should surrender to 'objectification', the Other and its varied discourse necessarily 'resurrects' today as an analogous intertext in the variegated world of digimodernist multiculturalism within the same personality or mutual contexts. The overlapping conceptual terms here signal the point where condescending notions of the Other are redundant and have to be reconsidered afresh in line with the amazing mutations in change around us. This is the general context in which Rita Bernard locates Coetzee's work in *Apartheid and Beyond: South African Writers and the Politics of Place* as innovative in postcolonial theory, highlighting its 'critique of the Enlightenment project as manifested in colonial exploration, its deconstruction of binary oppositions like 'civilisation' and 'barbarity', its subversion of British canonical texts like *Robinson Crusoe*, and its rigorous investigation of the ethics of representation' (Bernard 2007: 4). One of Coetzee's greatest contributions to the debate, I think, is the suggestion in his work that the Other cannot be objectified; and a further invitation for us to see an exclusive binary conception or valorisation of the world as both limited and limiting. The objectifier—and Susan Barton is the ironic resurrection of colonial traces of the distorting or distorted nomenclatures—claims a false status based on a similarly falsified historiography that locates the Other at a peripheral disadvantage. In other words, there is no *genuine* Other today: it has actually never been, and we live and participate either as victims or victimisers, in this thwarted pedagogy.

Drawing on this background, my analysis is guided by views on the Other from Emmanuel Levinas and Derek Attridge, with an obvious bias for a postcolonial reading. In explaining 'the relation between the *I* and the *you*' based on the research of his predecessors, Levinas refers to 'the distance of proximity [as] the marvel of the social relation' in which 'the difference between the *I* and the other remains':

> But it is maintained as the denial, in proximity which is also difference, of its own negation, as non-in-difference toward one another. Like the non-indifference between close friends or relatives. Being concerned by the alterity of the other: fraternity. The source of the gratuitous hatred and disinterested devotion, but an affectivity distinct from the love that, like hunger, attaches itself to what can satisfy: an affectivity not to be confused with the one involving the passions of the soul, needs satisfied or unmet, nerve endings and visceral changes. (Levinas 1993: 93-94)

As we shall see, while Levinas analyses the Other as constructed or only imagined, Coetzee neutralises this abstract imposition in the

Attridgean sense of otherness as 'that which is, at a given moment, outside the horizon provided by the culture for thinking, understanding, imagining, feeling, perceiving' (Attridge 2004: 19). We will be concerned not so much with Attridge's emphasis on the encounter with textual otherness, as with the socio-cultural implications and relevance of othering or non-othering mentalities.

How then does Coetzee fit into this complex equation? This is an important question whose answer has implications for his identity as a white South African—if we restrict it to this, for now—who acknowledges but also problematises a 'white Zulu'-in-a-rainbow-nation propaganda. Relating to this, one realises that critics of South African literature have generally been polarised by the sympathies that were generated into that literature by the apartheid system. As Coetzee himself states, South African literature is unique, notably in the West, because it provides an 'inexhaustibly fertile field for writers and journalists interrogating the coloniser-colonised relationship' (quoted in Bernard 2007: 4-5). Even previous boundary-blurring works like those of Nadine Gordimer and Doris Lessing are vulnerable to this partiality mainly because personal and collective histories sneak into their narratives and often suffer from prejudicial critiques.

Perhaps we need to recall Olive Schreiner's pioneering and unequivocal representation of the racial divide in South Africa at the start of the 20th century in order to better understand our context for analysis. Her prophetic vision which is stated in the Preface to *The Story of the African Farm* denounced condescending assumptions from critics in Piccadilly or in the Strand, whose 'gift of creative imagination, untrammelled by contact with any fact' is misrepresenting. Her advice to such a critic is that he must 'squeeze the colour from his brush, and deep it into the grey pigments around him. He must paint what lies before him' (Schreiner 1953: 15-16). Writing about the South African Other as such, her authentication of place through the use of local colour was to prove vital in the evolution of South African society throughout the 20th century; and ultimately speaks to the possible neutralisation of space with which Coetzee is concerned. From Schreiner's work to Gordimer and Lessing, we see a struggle to go beyond the structured ambivalence of identity in the apartheid regime. Gordimer's representative character is '[c]aught ... between her role as coloniser and colonised, and unable to escape from her words being read neither as apologia or accusation but inevitably as a combination of both' (Kossew 2004: 8-9). Lessing, on her part, admits that the narrative of *The Grass is Singing* 'could have happened in South Africa ... and can be considered as part of the South(ern) African farm novel genre, particularly in the light of Lessing's comment that Schreiner's African Farm 'really had an enormous impact' on her' (Kossew 2004: 126). In these female writers, there is a trajectory of illusions which finally settle—and are dissolved—in Coetzee's own vision of a non-binary engagement with the society and its history. I have alluded to these three females because they clearly define the problems associated with marginalisation both as ambiguous participants within the system they set up for scrutiny and as vested critics of the inhuman rationalisation of relationships therein.

It is from this background of overlapping narrative sentiments that Coetzee fits into South Africa's literary space with metafictional ease, almost without conscious effort. This stylistic preference is reflective of his composite identity which frees him from the vested pressures of binarism that characterise the writing and reading of colonial and anti-colonial literatures. Given that these literatures authenticated questionable authority and resisted same; and also, that the colour bar largely influenced the discourses embodied in Coetzee, his writing invariably interrogates the varying voices that vie to phase out each other. Disaffected by knowledge that the colour bar could be raised or lowered depending on the reason, Coetzee can then be said to be writing himself in his work, repeatedly attempting to renegotiate the commonality of boundaries which have been polarised by dominant and subjugated identities. Coetzee finally migrated to Australia in 2002, and then acquired citizenship in 2006.

In attempting an analysis of Coetzee's perspective on otherness, then, I will argue that he rejects the background on which Daniel Defoe's *Robinson Crusoe* was written and has ever since been read generally; and then elaborate on his alternative vision of a counter-*Crusoe* otherless world. A clue to understand how and probably why man ceased being the other's keeper will necessitate answers to implied questions of who others/is othered, and why? Does the othered participate in their fate? How knowledgeable in the ideologies that guide and authorise the process of othering is the one who others? However utopian this vision of *otherlessness* may appear, this chapter concludes by reflecting on its imperativeness today and point out the link with the need for us to manage the erstwhile threats from globalisation—another frontier for constructing otherness—and the Donald Trump-inspired brand of populism. Coetzee is almost writing a moral metafictional tale about the ineffectuality of otherness in which he suggests that when wo/man ceases to be the other's keeper, relationships become tense, selfish, exploitative, and unpredictable. In his famous quote, Rousseau declares that 'Man was born free, and everywhere he is in chains. Many a one believes himself the master of others, and yet he is a greater slave than they' (Rousseau 2002: 156). Based on this, it is possible to argue that such Enlightenment challenge to biblical rationalism, for instance, is proof that man has always been each other's carer; and that crises in human history often result when this responsibility is either ignored or tampered with.

Reading Coetzee beyond Crusoe's Colonial Othering

Robinson Crusoe has generally provided a foil for critical analysis of *Foe* to the point that it can actually result in a misreading of Coetzee's text. The similarity between them, such as the reflection of *Robinson Crusoe*'s historiography in both the voice and form of *Foe* does not cancel the fact that the differences are enormous. A typical example of such reading of the two texts (to which I will return from time to time because of the significance of juxtaposing such views with mine) is provided by Jane Poyner in *J.M. Coetzee and the Paradox of Postcolonial Authorship* wherein she notes: 'In Coetzee's Robinsonade ... Cruso struggles to mould Friday into a colonial subject (he is seemingly utterly subjected), whereas Barton sets herself the task of releasing him from his bonds' (Poyner 2009: 91). If this were indeed true—that Cruso simply replicates Defoe's archetype—then Coetzee would be guilty of partiality in his characterisation, which will then undermine his 'unwriting' intentions. I use 'unwrite' as a corrective strategy which does not endorse the reactionary militancy in a 'writing back' alternative which is often used to define the relationship between *Crusoe* and *Foe*; and in fact actually affirms positive values in colonial discourse. Accordingly, Dominic Head describes Coetzee's approach in the novel as 'a postcolonial reworking' of *Crusoe*, where to 'rework' implies an amelioration of, even disclaimer to, the alternative intransigence; an approach that reflects Coetzee's 'characteristically self-conscious and ambivalent twist to this dependency' (Head 2009: 62).

Commenting on 'the ways in which Coetzee's writing puts pressure on the novel's processes of representation', Patrick Hayes sidelines the incriminating/liberating debate and instead remarks how *Foe* 'deepens [Coetzee's] exploration of the origins and legacies of the [novel] form, and does so most obviously through its allusive relationship with Defoe's *Robinson Crusoe* and *Roxana*' (Hayes 2010: 106). Defoe's background-status thus serves Coetzee's iconoclasm. Friday's terminal speechlessness is indicative of this approach, the fact of a terrible historical wrong, which Coetzee invokes, not to re-ignite debate over colonial atrocities, but to suggest how such a character problematises the contemporary debates on identity and history. Friday remains a remote site that is unknown, unexplored and possibly unexplorable. This elusiveness is a characteristic of Coetzee's writing which as Mike Marais explains in *J. M. Coetzee and the Authority of Contemporary Fiction*, connotes the fact that 'the invisible cannot be named and therefore grasped in language' (Marais

2011: 102). Friday's speechlessness is the most ambivalent articulation of consciousness, marginality, and reawakening, and in trying to rationalise these out of the dark recesses of his world, we are more or less condemned to be frustrated. Coetzee expects us to *listen* to Friday not as a textual or historical Other, but as a character whose rise above the constraining binaries offers a neutral platform for a rational and cognitive dialogue over the 'invisible'.

Coetzee's iconoclasm, which Head sees as 'challenging and elusive of interpretation' (Head 2010: 1) therefore overwrites the traditional paradigms of otherness, and there is hardly credible evidence in the text that 'Cruso struggles to mould Friday into a colonial subject', not just because Friday is not 'seemingly utterly subjected' but because if Barton 'sets herself the task of releasing him from his bonds', it is in fact a figment of her 'civilised' imagination which she has activated and is struggling to justify. Race, gender, history and ideology are just a few of these, and we need to consider how they are *unwritten* in Coetzee's innovative poetics to begin a comprehensive review of what has become a cultural given. One of the problems which Poyner seems to face in her analysis is confusing the *types* of writing which Defoe and Coetzee engage. Where the one was narrating a convenient tale of his civilisation's expansionist foundations, with individual assumptions that translate into cultural 'truths', the other exposes the insufficiency of this approach—pulling himself out of that realm psychologically—as reflected in a self-conscious style that interrogates even its own conceits. The narrative landscape in *Foe* continuously shifts and overlaps so that there is no dominant narrator—in fact the story narrates the impossibility of relying on any narrator permanently, even after the demise of Cruso who then represents a rejection of trimmed and packaged historicity. In his aftermath, Barton and Friday vie for utterance while Foe's prejudicial notions about an exotic story provide the voiced background against which the two relate.

For Poyner, 'Barton is designated the main narrator of *Foe* … whilst Cruso, the essential coloniser in *Robinson Crusoe*, is relegated to the margins of Coetzee's story: not only is he supplanted by Barton as narrator and author of the adventure, he also dies in the early stages of the narrative, never making the ideologically all-important journey home' (Poyner 2009: 92). This is clearly a questionable analysis which assumes the type of creative and critical certainty which Coetzee and his characters overwrite. I think both the designation of Barton and the relegation of Cruso are conscious manipulations of the traditional agencies by Coetzee meant to challenge colonial binaries that privilege 'home'. Cruso consciously refuses—especially after Barton joins them on the island—to perform a Crusoe-foil. Consequently, a tag like 'the essential coloniser' may insinuate unhealthy associations about a character whose withdrawal from 'civilisation' is so final that his death represents the ultimate refusal for a reunion that would transform him into a participant in the world which Barton is later embarrassed by. Poyner indicates the manner in which her embarrassment can be understood: 'it is in England that Barton will have her epiphany about her own role in Friday's 'education' and that Friday will take a stance against being incorporated into the imperialist-colonialist system of representation' (Poyner 2009: 93). This awareness is what Cruso represents in the text, a new consciousness that levels out previous barriers, and it takes Barton so long to begin realising it. What Friday does in the end is not new; it is what he had been used to with Cruso, a commonality of experience that ignores the assertion of conscious egos. Friday becomes visibly nostalgic of inexplicable sentiments only when he is in England with Barton, and begins the formal resistance that leads to her epiphanic awareness.

But Barton is not as innocent as such reading makes her to be, of colonial atrocities, if only in terms of how they installed mental shifts in perception that dislocate the native's presence in the text. Her opposition to Cruso is a vital clue to Coetzee's aesthetics with regard to an introspective survey of their dual civilization, the gender polarities within it, and how these liaise with the traditional 'Other' of that civilisation. Consequently, Cruso's death as I have suggested, is a crucial stage in the novel not only because of his emaciated state and dated ideology (which he does not endorse), but also because, in fact, he is no longer interested in building the empire the way he originally envisaged it. Poyner claims that by the time Barton 'arrives on the island in *Foe* Friday is ... enslaved, colonial violence already done, with the effect, problematically, of essentialising Friday as slave because we know nothing of his life before' (Poyner 2009: 92). A statement like this is the burden of postcolonial critique, which the novel seeks to resolve. To be enslaved and yet remain unknown to the objectifying mind is a crucial comment relating to Friday's role in destabilising the canon, because there is no indicator that the transgression on him impedes his mutuality with Cruso. The problem of essentialising his slavehood and transferring it from the possible slave masters to Cruso is one that makes us as readers, even from different backgrounds, to be guilty of toying with—and thereby reinforcing—colonial assumptions about the assumed Other.

Given that 'Friday in *Foe* is probably a black African slave' (Poyner 2009: 93), we necessarily have to compare Coetzee's approach with Pierce Brosnan's film version of *Robinson Crusoe*, another 'Robinsonade', to understand how otherness is annulled. In it, the protagonist engages in overlapping dialogues with his composite identity, and resolves matters in the end by fraternising with Friday without invoking previous power dynamics. If in Coetzee's novel Cruso's return to England (according to Poyner) is 'ideologically all-important', in terms of his 'reconstituted self that *must* return home to England to fulfil the colonising promise' (Poyner 2009: 93), then the claim or hope of unwriting the canon would have failed. Cruso goes beyond the 'colonial promise', talk less of 'fulfilling' it, and his death at the moment of 'rescue' is a protest against his return to the contested civilisation. Unable to dissolve the ideological binaries that constructed his previous personality, he has succeeded in seeing the civilisation which Barton and his rescuers represent as 'Other' to his new engagement with Friday.

Coetzee is therefore no longer interested in the unavailing debate over deconstruction, which only perpetuates difference the more it is rationalised. The polarised intersections of identity in his work offer new frontiers for creative and critical interests in managing the multicultural, globalising, and even post-human world of the twenty-first century. This is where Barton's learning process begins and becomes crucial in revaluating the novel. Although such a process is slow—because she insists on seeing Friday as savage—she is forced to rethink her stance when confronted with evidence of 'civilised' savagery in the castaway stillborn. This disrespect for the human personality—and we have to remember that she does not consider the possibility of colonial violence on Friday as the manifestation of savagery—in its formative stage complements the rate of criminality in eighteenth century England, which Defoe described so well particularly in *Moll Flanders* that he has been called its mythologist (Gladfelder 2009: 65). In addition, in the image of the stillborn, Barton realises the changing cycles of life in which she was implicated: 'Who was the child but I, in another life?' (Coetzee 2010: 105). The noble savage, which Friday represents in both the colonial and metafictional texts, is a redemptive category to 'civilized' consciousness. The redemption however has to be recognised without attempts to culture it into an 'acceptable' format. Unlike Crusoe, Cruso acknowledges this, himself already a noble savage, and the tension between him and Barton highlights the cultural gulf they now represent.

The disagreement between Crusoe and his father at the start of Defoe's novel captures the initial momentum of capitalistic otherness in England, based on the prospection of social status. Such internalised structures of social life had been determined by feudal values to the extent that a hierarchical social structure affirmed an almost deterministic lifestyle. Failure to implement this form of control, mainly because of the reforms that parliament was pressured to pass, ironically anticipated the way the discrimination was to be performed abroad as a subtext to the colonising mission, when Englishness shed its class and nationalistic differences at home, and in then bonding as a race-consciousness in the colony, also needed an ideological opposite against which to valorise its value system. This shift in consciousness camouflages the excesses of English arrogance against the Celtic fringe (which Crusoe seems to ignore in his affirmation of colonial Englishness), and will go on to gloss over the distinctive differences that defined what came to be known as Settler colonies. By defying parental expectations, Crusoe was simultaneously contradicting cultural mores and unconsciously facilitating the process of transposing the very cultural values to the exotic world. That world was in a formative process of being orientalised through a parallel project of externalising and implanting feudal hegemonies there through Middle class mediation.

In *Foe*, we relate to this charged background through a reminder of characteristic stereotypes of Africa as 'the heart of darkness'. The ship mate's description of Africa is symptomatic of this: referring to Africa as 'a great place' but wondering if Friday 'know[s] where he wishes to be set down' because '[h]e may be put ashore in Africa and still be farther from his home than from here to Muscovy' (Coetzee 2010: 109). He uses 'great' quantitatively, not qualitatively, which would have vindicated the cultural otherness of the continent. Consequently, 'One half of Africa is desert and the rest a stinking fever-ridden forest' (Coetzee 2010: 110). It is this positioned narration which *Foe* overwrites by inviting us to also nullify the discriminating opposition in the binary of Self/Other.

In Defoe, therefore, othering is a conscious process of ensuring hierarchies and inevitable control. The propaganda, which Friday resists in Coetzee's text, draws on a Hegelian assumption that a category of humans is incapable of reason and thus requires the assistance and protection of a more endowed species:

Since all mankind is naturally rational, and freedom is the hypothesis on which this reason rests, slavery yet has been, and in part still is, maintained by many peoples, and men have remained contented under it. The only distinction between the Africans and the Asiatics on the one hand, and the Greeks, Romans, and moderns on the other, is that the latter know and it is explicit for them, that they are free, but the others are so without knowing that they are, and thus without existing as being free. This constitutes the enormous difference in their condition. (Singh and Mohapatra 2008 226)

Such stigmatisation in which '[t]he Negro represents [...] natural man in his whole savageness and irrepressibility [and] there is nothing assonant with humanity ... in this character' (qtd in Laurentiis 2014: 608), complies with western othering strategy from antiquity. By the eighteenth century, this racial conceit was substituting the feudal privileges beyond Europe. Ironically, the Middle class, which emerged from the demise of feudalism, was the very agency by which the polarising ideology was exported to non-European territories. A member of this emerging class, Crusoe's potentials threaten the postcolonial subject because of an enlightenment inheritance which privileged the European-as-human, and the rest reduced to a Cartesian category of blank entities.

Foe and the Denial of Otherness

Crusoe's claim to a superior psyche is the backbone of colonial otherness, which Coetzee reassesses. As Head notes, 'Crusoe is the archetypal colonialist, enamoured of the project of taming a new world, [while] Cruso is emblematic of exhausted imperialism' (Head 2009: 63). Part II of *Foe* reflects this implied juxtaposition and ends with Barton claiming ownership of Friday the way Crusoe did in the 'original'—'I do not love him, but he is mine' (Coetzee 2010: 111)— with the only difference that she does not subject him completely to the type of physical exploitation reserved for slaves. But the psychological torture which he endures is as much a dehumanising strategy as any in formal slavery. If she betrays creatural weakness towards Friday, it is not just because she is feeling increasingly isolated and othered in her own civilisation, back in England, so that Friday—just like Cruso on the island—becomes her best risk for company; but also because the whole notion of the Other is a conceptual fantasy for class and eventually racial supremacy. Barton therefore concedes to Friday's centrality in her post-island life through whom she begins to speculate after the possibility of love. What is clear from the trajectory of her reasoning is the fact that otherness can be denied based on a new awareness which facilitates less exclusive identification. What becomes ironic as well as liberating is her realisation that she is in fact the embodiment of Self and Other, and consequently accepts what, before, she did not understand about the functional construction of otherness and how she participated in it: 'In Friday here you have a living cannibal ... If we are to go by Friday, cannibals are no less dull than Englishmen'. It is now the place of Foe to resist her new thinking by clinging to the stereotypes speculatively: 'They lose their vivacity when deprived of human flesh, I am sure' (Coetzee 2010: 127).

Based on this fluctuating indoctrination, it is clear that the possibility of textual-social distortion and renewal of meaning in Coetzee is key to a consideration that we are either each other's Other/keeper or else live in debilitating individualism. To get a clearer picture of how Coetzee's novel renews itself in meaning, and becomes a textual Other in the sense in which Attridge discusses otherness, we need to go beyond the analysis of clusters of meaning that continuously call up their own clustered meanings, often related to our respective cultural views. By the time Barton and Friday are heading to Bristol, for instance, she is convinced—and makes everybody who is interested in her conviction believe the same—that Friday 'is a slave who is now free' (Coetzee 2010: 100); or that '[h]e is a slave whose master set him free on his deathbed' (Coetzee 2010: 107). However, the deed of his freedom which she wrote is no proof (beyond its ability to generate or justify narrative duplicity, which the reader, unlike her interlocutors, understands) that he was ever enslaved by Cruso. By insisting on the fact, Barton is trying to save her selfhood from degrading into the savage primitivism with which Friday is associated; and simultaneously fictionalises the story—bearing in mind that there are several stories and storytellers in *Foe*—

in which she is a composite participant. Her encounters with people, and what she tells them, are part of the fiction; a misrepresentation that Cruso suspected, while alive, because of its ability to rationalise everything and distort as much. While Barton is already accepting a fact which Cruso laboured for her to understand, she however forgets that Friday has always been free, if only because the existentialist character he represents, cannot be constrained; his silence is proof of his freedom beyond the world of verbalised meaning, wherein such a character abhors complaints and blame.

Our background, together with Barton's as readers of a conscripting text/culture, makes our understanding of the partnership between Cruso and Friday vulnerable to atextual data. The historiography in such data is what Coetzee rejects as too consciously objectifying. To Poyner, '[b]y distinguishing Friday ... [as facially similar to a European, and pointedly not African] in *Foe*, Coetzee designates him as slave, shipwrecked en route on the Middle Passage, from Africa to the Americas. By this means, Coetzee unravels the ways in which Friday, as character, is constituted by colonialist discourse' (Poyner 2009: 93). If we accept this view, then the intertextuality on which Coetzee draws inspiringly would have served no purpose because his own narrative will still be locked in the immanence of the very 'colonial discourse'. Besides, the convenience of the Middle Passage background to Friday's condition finds no parallel with which to justify Cruso's own isolationist life on the island. In other words, as I have already suggested, in his existentialist nature Friday is more than an objectified subject; he overwrites the limiting context of culture, and his silence becomes the most *voiced* concern in an iconoclastic narrative, at once indifferent to, and aloof from, the prejudicial voice.

Elaborating on this 'voicing' possibility, Poyner argues that 'on the island, where the tools of writing have been rejected, Friday's body has been 'written upon' by colonialism and colonialist discourse since not only has he been enslaved and his tongue cut out, he may also have been castrated' (Poyner 2009: 96). This cliché-type argument relates to Barton's repeated assumption, which becomes a certainty to her following Cruso's own speculations on the mystery, that Friday 'lost his tongue to slave-catchers' (Coetzee 2010: 109); and also because of her own gender/sexual conceits towards both Cruso and especially Friday. Cruso speculates on the reasons why slave masters cut Friday's tongue and concludes: 'How will we ever know the truth?' (Coetzee 2010: 23). Perhaps truth, the way Coetzee problematises it in the novel, is not meant to be *known* because that would mean a closure which excludes new possibilities of an ever relative world in which tropes are exploited for envisaged benefits. When Kyoko Yoshida alludes to this passage and claims that '[i]t is clear from the onset who did harm to whom: the slavers to the slave', it is obvious that he too is acknowledging a possibility as truth—a trap which Coetzee tries to avoid and highlights through his intricately overlapping narrative.

This flaw in reading the text as such develops from its textualised biases in the cannibalisation of characters, where 'in Barton's mind, the idea of Friday as food is not considered at all. He is branded as the eater, which instantly transforms her into the *edible*' (Yoshida 2009: 137). If Friday's 'speech' is problematic in its exclusiveness, we should then understand that his eating habit is also speculated upon by the vindication of the assumed Self. There is, then, a suspicious certainty that cannot be rationalized as per 'civilized' assumptions, and this becomes experimental ground for Barton and Foe. Having othered Friday all this while with only flitting moments of compassion towards him, Barton and Foe begin to relate to him more philosophically, assigning for themselves the task either 'to open Friday's mouth and hear what it holds: silence, perhaps, or a roar, like the roar of a seashell held to the ear'; or 'make Friday's silence speak, as well as the silence surrounding Friday' (Coetzee 2010: 142).

Barton's 'efforts to bring [Friday] nearer to a state of speech' (Coetzee 2010: 146) are a version of colonial education which expects the purported Other to be edified while she herself is reluctant to *listen* to his voice. When she imagines that '[s]omewhere in the deepest recesses of those black pupils was there a spark of mockery' (Coetzee 2010: 146), her goodwill and frustration clash in Friday's naturalistic rejection of his being further hybridised. When Friday later draws 'row upon row of eyes upon feet: walking eyes', it is incomprehensible what he is doing, and he does not help Barton to understand. He not only refuses to hand over his 'writing' to Barton, but blots it out thereby cutting himself completely, both physically and imaginatively, from the consciousness which they wish to breed him into, in order to tap from him. Resisting the interpretive ease of the Self (even when 'row upon row of eyes upon feet' suggests the penetrating gaze and movement of expansionist colonialism), Friday simultaneously writes himself into the permanence of 'civilised' voidancy; which will also mean a predictable and possibly discriminating/discriminated personality. By blotting it out as per such consciousness, he is reminding us of his and Cruso's mutual philosophy on the island which was against permanence or the certainty of it. It is Barton who concedes in the end that '[t]here will always be a voice in him to whisper doubts, whether in words or nameless sounds or tunes or tones' (Coetzee 2010: 149).

Foe is, therefore, a metafictional narrative that reinvents the dynamics of text and meaning by challenging the art of telling a story through formal articulatory, orthographic, or cognitive means. Part of the neo-deconstruction, with which we are concerned here, relates to the creation and rejection of the Other as a tempo-spatial category, even necessity. The novel form, at least in its English version, was born out of a need to resist illogical forms of othering both in time and space. Sociocultural biases were negotiated along time frames that gained legitimacy with the eventual influence of Roman civilisation. Drawing on this mutating civilisation and destabilising it at the same time, one aspect in which Coetzee neutralises othering in *Foe* relates to the role of time as a centrist or peripheral notion. In the novel, Coetzee does this by displacing the traditional temporal frame within which otherness is authorised. The narrative relies on a momentary overlapping of time that reveals the changing mood of life in which unothered and unotherable humanity finds its freedom in the end.

In terms of spatial representation, Coetzee's conscious juxtaposition of the names 'Defoe' and 'Foe'—as metaphorical markers of the respective civilisations which he and his character's original engage—is already a signal of how his work intends to problematise the issue of an othering consciousness not in deconstructionist techniques, including those of 'writing back', but by simply transforming the narrative and its meaning into a textual disclaimer to exclusive othering. While this relates to the dynamics of literary creativity and agents, I am more concerned here with how the two collude in constructing otherness: the narrative neutralises this, while simultaneously charting a new path for participation in textual analysis. This process of denial is more than mere rejection or deconstruction in the form of 'writing back' clichés. Rather, and as I have already implied, it involves 'dewriting' the contested zones of experience and representation in non-polarising ways, possibly back to a state of mutual acknowledgement of relative culturality. Art, especially in its colonial context, has its politics and Coetzee's novel suggests that this context is intimately associated with the falsehoods of historicity, the identities that are implicated in it, and the conceit of its vision.

In contesting the parentage of the girl who has been harassing her by claiming to be her daughter, Barton is unknowingly affirming the possibility of two opposites forging a harmonious or harmonising personality in the image of the girl: 'if the girl were her father's child then her father must be my opposite, and we do not marry our opposites, we marry men who are like us in subtle ways' (Coetzee 2010: 132). However, couples who are alike hardly invent new meanings in life, just as the image of shadows and ghosts which Barton employs casually. Having already referred to Friday as her possible shadow, she now sees the girl as a ghost: 'I say to myself that this child, who calls herself by my name, is a ghost, a substantial ghost, if such beings exist, who haunts me for reasons I cannot understand, and brings other ghosts in tow' (Coetzee 2010: 132). Both unsubstantial images reflect states of relationships that define each other in opposition: Levinas 'distance of proximity' here is mental, and influential only when endorsed for vested purposes.

Eventually, Barton poses the existentialist question upon which our understanding of otherness depends: 'who am I and who indeed are you?' (Coetzee 2010: 133). Earlier in the narrative, she had reflected on this impasse, when the innkeeper where she and Friday seek lodging dismisses them with a curtly reminder that '[t]his is a clean house, we do not serve strollers or gipsies' (Coetzee 2010: 102). Served with the same drug of exclusion which she has been applying to her Others, Barton suddenly understands the condescension which she entertained against Friday when she first saw him. By softening her attitude towards him, especially in the absence of Cruso, she suggests that otherness is produced through a combination of ignorance and conceit by the assumed Self, and the acceptance of same by the imposed Other. If Cruso was Other to Barton's newly arrived sophistication on the island, she is now performing the same role of an othered category into which *her* civilization places her especially due to her partnership with Friday. Feeling the pang of exclusion from her society in the heart of winter, Barton finally understands the existentialist world in which she met Cruso and Friday, in which the need to survive does not evoke social or cultural markers: 'Feeling about in the dark, I came to a crib filled with clean hay. I stripped off my clothes and burrowed like a mole into the hay, but still found no warmth. So, I climbed out again and donned the sodden clothes and stood miserably in the dark, my teeth chattering' (Coetzee 2010: 102). She later attempts to eat acorns and even contemplate cannibalism, while making it look as if they were Friday's thoughts (remembering the stillborn and how Friday *could* prefer her, instead), in order to survive (Coetzee 2010: 105). Quoting Kilgour, Yoshida notes: '[t]he cannibal is the individual's "alien", against which [Barton] constructs [her] identity, and whose threat to that identity is represented as literal consumption' (Yoshida 2009: 147). For all her conceit, Barton is still naïve against the elemental forces which she now confronts. This explains why, in differentiating culture from nature, her views on cannibalism still uphold exclusive cultural egos.

In this discourse of othering, any doubt about one's preconceptions is the beginning of liberating self-knowledge. This dispels the arrogance of the Self and necessitates acceptance of the Other through an introspective acknowledgement of nature's embodiment. Barton experiences this change eventually in Foe's second home when, 'full of doubt', she becomes 'doubt itself', unable to define herself and environment (Coetzee 2010: 133). Her doubt dispels when she realises that 'he [Foe] and I were man and woman, that man and woman are beyond words' (Coetzee 2010: 134). Her preference for neutral terms (man and woman) as opposed to gendered alternatives (husband and wife) is a significant shift from the social context of Barton's previous Self into a new, more accommodating one.

The ghost of otherness thus disappears in the mutual fusion of the Self and the Other. Mutuality becomes the antidote to boundary-formations that keep humanity apart, together with its relation to other aspects of nature. Although Foe begins to destroy such boundaries when he kisses Barton and refers to her endearingly, (Coetzee 2010: 134), it is not clear the extent to which he is ready to bring Friday into this awareness. However, by insisting that he and Barton 'confront [their] worst fear' (Coetzee 2010: 135), it is also possible that the confrontation of personal demons is the start of destroying the constructed Other. This is the main guarantee for the retention of existential freedom, which Sisyphus clearly exemplifies from mythology, when his affinity to stone liberates him from hierarchical pressures and makes him 'superior to his fate' (Camus 1955: 76-77). Indeed, man subjected is man othered by forces that are external to his worldview. But there is no subjection that cannot be conquered by the insistence on personal freedom in mutual proximity to others, lest the individual, as already indicated, participates in their condition. The Cavalier poet Richard Lovelace was echoing this existentialist norm when he declared that 'stone walls do not a prison make/ Nor iron bars a cage' (Ferguson et al 2005: 537); and Johnny Clegg was one of the few white South Africans who saw the apartheid system as a Sisyphian jail not just to the black Other but also to the white Self; and in alluding to Lovelace's verses, he was also participating in the search for new meaning with which Coetzee was obsessed beyond a limiting binarism onto a new platform of the 'white Zulu'. Both Barton and Foe are beginning to learn a basic existentialist lesson with which Friday is familiar.

Conclusion: Otherness on the Global Stage

Foe therefore reminds us in this era of renewed global tensions in both micro and macro ideologies that the Other is us, and is also in us. The mirror of otherness is self-reflexive: to other, we violate our very being and worldview beyond personal idealism, which is central to both an enabling and accommodating lifestyle. This is the 'broader context' in which, for Head, 'the 'internationalization' of the novel is increasingly relevant to the appreciation of [Coetzee's] achievements' (Head 2009: 22). Coetzee's achievement as a writer is therefore inseparable from his insights into the limitations of analytical binarism. Failure on Barton's part to realise this, when she instead acts to justify it, leads her to indulge the erroneous belief that she can determine what constitutes the story of her life and thereby privilege certain perspectives and incidents 'according to her own desire' (Coetzee 2010: 131). Even the conditional, 'according to her own desire', is problematic because such desire and the freedom on her part to manipulate it, is locked in an othering consciousness, because she does not see 'desire' as something fluid and changing. Sameness, unlike Barton's manipulation of the term, is not a prerequisite for tolerating the other; rather, and as Attridge asserts, its relative exclusiveness can actually 'interrupt' the process of recognising the Other, which is 'a relation—or a relating—between me, as the same, and that which, in its uniqueness, is heterogeneous to me' (Attridge 2004: 33). Acceptance of this relational heterogeneity enables otherness as a necessary element in personal and cultural harmony: otherness is a natural human condition that entails a two-in-one consciousness which, if mismanaged, then spills over into a violating standard.

The imperative of 'each other's Other or not at all' in this chapter thus indicates how through such iconoclasm—subverting popular notions of the Self/Other binary—Coetzee suggests a creative and intellectual renaissance, and a new platform for global interactions in the twenty-first century. In *Elizabeth Costello*, a journalist asks the protagonist if she 'find[s] it easy, writing from the position of a man', and she replies that '[i]f it were easy it wouldn't be worth doing. It is the otherness that is the challenge. Making up someone other than yourself. Making up a world for him to move in' (Coetzee 2010: 6). Otherness is thus a double edge sword depending on who handles it, and its 'target'; a dismissal of mutual binarism or an invitational for both the embodying personality and the relating individuals within our composite universe.

In Part 3 of *Foe*, we witness Coetzee's typical concern with another perspective of othering—the problems related to writing and closure—which is not a major concern here. While *Foe* was published when apartheid stakeholders were stubbornly singing the regime's swansong, the novel—especially through Friday's characterisation— anticipates the mood of political discourse in post-apartheid South Africa. As Andre Brink notes in 'Post-Apartheid Literature: A Personal View', and describing such a process, change was perceived 'as a move inward, away from politics as drama and spectacle and social phenomenon towards internalisation and interiority' (Brink 2009: 11). This mediation—what Head again calls a 'gestural bridge to the South African context' (Head 2009: 62)—is an important remark if we have to understand the creative silence which the text dramatizes through Friday and which he in turn imposes on both the other characters and the reader. This silence is fruitful because it enhances meaning beyond its traditional site by destabilising vested assumptions and expectations of what is truth and what is not. Closure is no longer as we know it, tidying up the loose ends of the narrative; instead, it enables a new consciousness, a new beginning, to emerge from the inarticulate strands of the unconscious.

This reality explains the focus on how *Foe* envisages a world in which the notional Other responds to the imperatives of globalisation as it infiltrates cultures in even more insidious ways than Christianity and formal imperialism whence the Other was formalised. It breaks down the remaining vestiges of boundary-formation so that the Self may be threatened by the Other only when their embodiment in the same personality—or shared relationship—is denied with cultural, national, and global implications. The failure to recognise this possibility at the individual level implies that global dialogue will remain a frustratingly schematic affair. This realisation may account not just for Coetzee's later 'disgrace'-awareness, but also for his 'retreat' to the metaphorical 'Down Under' world of Australia, which D. H. Lawrence describes in *Kangaroo* as a land where socially constructed sound was absent:

There was nothing really to be said. The vast continent is really void of speech. Only man makes noises to man, from habit […] But this speechless, aimless solitariness was in the air. It was natural to the country. The people left you alone. They didn't follow you with their curiosity and their inquisitiveness and their human fellowship. You passed, and they forgot you. You came again, and they hardly saw you. You spoke, and they were friendly. But they never asked any questions, and they never encroached. They didn't care. The profound Australian indifference, which still is not really apathy. The disintegration of the social mankind back to its elements. Rudimentary individuals with no desire of communication. Speeches, just noises. (Lawrence 1980: 379)

The effort here is an attempt to narrate the primeval world which industrial capitalism destroyed in what Lawrence saw as the England of Robin Hood. His search for a utopia in the latter part of his career privileged life at the elemental level, away from a world in which 'speeches [are] just noises'. In the search for such a world where the silence of Friday speaks to us from a mutual understanding—or the need for it in the wake of the Black Lives Matter demonstrations all over the world calling for the adjustment of racist and populist instincts—the elimination of the narcissistic outlook to life will guarantee an alternative world in which the Other will be accommodated as an indispensable component of the embodied individual and our collective existence.

Bibliography

Attridge, D., (2004). *The Singularity of Literature*. London: Routledge.

Bernard, R., (2007). *Apartheid and Beyond: South African Writers and the Politics of Place*. Oxford: Oxford University Press.

Brink, A., (2009). Post-Apartheid Literature: A Personal View. In: *J.M Coetzee in the Context and Theory*. New York: Continuum, pp. 11-19.

Burt, E. S., (2009). *Regard for the Other: Autothanatography in Rousseau, De Quincey, Baudelaire, and Wilde*. New York: Fordham University Press.

Camus, A., (1955). *The Myth of Sisyphus and Other Essays*. New York: Vintage.

Coetzee, J. M., (2004). *Elizabeth Costello*. London: Vintage.

Coetze, J. M., (2010). *Foe*. London: Penguin.

Ferguson, M., Kendall, T. & Salter, M. J., (2005). *The Norton Anthology of Poetry*. 5th ed. New York: Norton.

Gladfelder, H., (2009). Defoe and Criminal Fiction. In: *The Cambridge Companion to Daniel Defoe*. Cambridge: Cambridge University Press, pp. 64-83.

Gruen, E. S., (2011). *Rethinking the Other in Antiquity*. Princeton: Princeton University Press.

Hayes, P., (2010). *J M Coetzee and the Novel: Writing and Politics After Beckett.* Oxford: Oxford University Press.

Head, D., (2009). *The Cambridge Introduction to J M Coetzee.* Cambridge: Cambridge University Press.

Kilgour, M., (1990). *From Communion to Cannibalism: An Anatomy of Metaphors of Incorporation.* Princeton: Princeton University Press.

Kochin, M. S., (2007). Literature and Salvation in *Elizabeth Costello* Or How to Refuse to be an Author in Eight or Nine Lessons. *English in Africa,* 34(1), pp. 79-95.

Kossew, S., (2004). *Writing Woman, Writing Place: Contemporary Australian and South African Fiction.* London: Routledge.

Laurentiis, A. d., (2014). Race in Hegel: Text and Context. In: *Philosophy after Kant: New Approaches to Understanding Kant's Transcendental and Moral Philosophy.* Dusseldorf: De Gruyter, pp. 591-624.

Lawrence, D. H., (1980). *Kangaroo.* Harmondsworth, Middlesex: Penguin.

Levinas, E., (1999). *Alterity and Transcendence.* London: The Athlone Press.

Marais, M., (2011). The Trope of Following in JM Coetzee's Slow Man. In: *Strong Opinions: JM Coetzee and the Authority of Contemporary Fiction.* New York: Continuum, pp. 99-112.

Poyner, J., (2009). *JM Coetzee and the Paradox of Postcolonial Authorship.* London: Ashgate.

Regard, F. (ed.) (2009). *British Narratives of Exploration: Case Studies of the Self and Other.* London: Pickering and Chatto.

Rousseau, J. J., (2002). *The Social Contract and The First and Second Discourses.* New York: Yale University.

Schreiner, O., (1953). *The Story of an African Farm.* London: Collins.

Singh, A. & Mohapatra, R. (eds.) (2008). *Reading Hegel: The Introductions.* Melbourne: Re-press.

Wilde, O., (2005). *The Importance of Being Earnest.* San Diego: CA: ICON Group International.

Yoshida, K., (2009). New York. Eating (Dis)Order: From Metaphoric

Cannibalism to Cannibalistic Metaphors. In: *JM Coetzee in Context and Theory*. New York: Continuum, pp. 135-145.

Chapter Two

A Language of their Own: Feminist Poetry and Linguistic Experimentation

Rosalyn Mutia

Introduction

The portrayal of women in literature written by men has often restricted itself to underscoring the voiceless nature of women who, in every sense, were victims of patriarchal structures. In fact, the first most widely read work on feminist literary criticism, Kate Millet's *Sexual Politics,* saw literature as a record of the collective consciousness of patriarchy which manifested the archetypal social values of capitalism, violence against women, crude sexuality, and male power in general. Female writers of the twentieth century sought to correct this image by indicating that the woman does not only have a voice but is also capable of expressing it by writing in a way that is novel and stimulating. When women entered the scholarly sphere of literature, it was therefore a kind of taking up of arms against the strictures that had held them in silence. In *Francophone African Women: Destroying the Emptiness of Silence,* Irene Assiba D'Almeida posits that feminist writing is a kind of 'taking up of arms,' as it were, against patriarchal bias in which women have forcefully broken the silence imposed on their literary voices:

> The canon does not open up voluntarily; it must be made to open. That is why I term what women have achieved in the world of letters a *prise d'écriture,* a 'taking of writing' in the sense of a militant appropriation or seizing. Indeed the term *prise d'écriture* connotes another term 'prise d'armes' (taking up arms), and though I find the military metaphor unsavoury, here to rise up in arms implies a necessary battle

for liberation. It is only by waging such a battle that a breakthrough is possible, not depending on the generosity of the dominant group, but on the deliberate action of those who take up arms to seize power. (D'Almeida 1994: 6)

For women, then, writing becomes a symbolic weapon and Mariama Bâ points out in *So Long A Letter* that 'Books are a weapon, a peaceful weapon perhaps but *they are* a weapon.' (Bâ 1968: 6)

To 'take up writing' necessitates the appropriation of language and communication. The question often asked is whether relegating women into silence presupposes that they acquired language much later than men. Eckert and McConnell-Ginet (2013) answer this question by bringing out in their research that girls speak earlier than boys and even develop linguistic complexity earlier too. Thus, taking up writing for women presupposes a re-appropriation of language. However, whether this retrieved voice is to be expressed following the conventional male establishment of the arts or to depart from it, has become a heated debate and women's venture into experimental poetics presents the answer. In the poem entitled 'The Burning of paper instead of Children,' Adrienne Rich considers the English language, 'the oppressor's language [though she] need[s] it to talk to you.' It is for this reason that Elaine Showalter opines in *A Literature of Their Own* that the central preoccupation of feminism is to expose patriarchal chauvinism, its resulting prejudices, to promote a discovery and re-evaluation of literature by women, and to examine the socio-cultural and psycho-sexual contexts of literature and criticism. This is clearly indicative of women's desire to move from the imposed silence on literary creativity and enter literary discourse. This means by-passing the subordinating gaze of the male establishment- a gaze which generates in women an intimidating fear of male criticism. For example, W.E. Farrison casts doubts on the female creative psyche concerning a stringent set of grammatical and punctuation rules that must be adhered to before writers can be trusted:

Now, as is evidenced by the long history of the art of writing, if a writer can express himself well without the aid of capitals and punctuation, he can most probably express himself better with it; and if he/she cannot express himself better with their aid it is doubtful that he can express himself better without it. (Farrison 1989: 96)

Showalter, however, considers women who write with a meticulous preoccupation with obeying the rules of grammar and punctuation, as speaking a foreign language. To her, women must use their own language; for if women continue to speak like men do when they enter discourse, whatever they say will be subdued and alienated. Rather than advocate a fundamentally new structured language with a different alphabet, vocabulary, and grammatical rules, she recommends a way of working with the existing male discourse in order to deconstruct its patriarchal biases. In this regard, she observes that the fundamental linguistic task of feminist criticism is: 'to concentrate on women's access to language, on the available lexical words which can be selected [and] on the ideological and cultural determinants of expression' (Showalter 2013: 11). To do this, women poets must get into experimentation with the existing language because poetry is essentially an artistic use of language to communicate feelings, emotions and thoughts. In patriarchal culture, poetic language has long been considered as a 'privileged metalanguage' (Kaplan 1975: 51), to which women can hardly accede. However, even though poetry is supposed to imitate this complex system of language use, it is still supposed to produce universally accepted meanings, in short, to communicate. On the other hand, much of women's poetry is ideological in its underpinnings and seeks more to pass on a message, mostly about the otherness status of women, than to play beautifully with language. So, the question arises, whether women can imbibe the language of poetic sophistication typical of patriarchal culture and still pass on an ideological message? This article seeks to find out an answer to this question. It predicates its research on the hypothetical basis that through experimentation with language, women have succeeded to write good poetry and to pass on a message about their otherness statuses.

For African American Feminists, experimentation with language is much more than a preoccupation with correct grammar and syntax. It is even more about women's literacy. bell hooks makes a cogent point of encouraging every feminist to regard literacy as an important feminist agenda: 'If we truly want to empower women and men to engage in feminist thinking, we must empower them to read and write, but I really don't see any large group of committed feminists making that a central agenda'(Olson 1994:1). Her concern is with the privileging of mainstream feminists to the disadvantage of minority feminists like African Americans by this lack of interest in promoting literacy as a feminist agenda. This is part of hooks' often repeated charge that white, liberal, and middleclass feminists have traditionally set an agenda for feminism that fails to reflect the concerns of feminists who are women of colour. The African American method of experimentation with the language is therefore quite different and for writers like hooks, it involves the notion of *praxis*, that is, of integrating reflection and action. Thus, hooks consistently integrates anecdotes and details of her personal life into her writing in order to illuminate theory. She says, 'When you tell a story about how you use an abstract idea or a bit of theory in a concrete situation, it just feels more real to people' (Olson 1994:2). As a feminist who is also concerned with issues of race, hooks re-invents language to show that in its usage, it can portray white supremacy. In general, hooks, like other African American writers like Toni Morrison and Maya Angelou, experiments with various alternatives to traditional academic prose, including interviews, self-interviews and dialogues. These are small pieces of writing, meant to be read in a little time frame and still make meaning in themselves. Also, with such a writing style, hooks says: 'I see it as a subversion of the whole sense that there was to be only one monolithic writing style that can be given scholarly legitimation in the academy' (Olson 1994:4). Other African American feminists like Neale Hurston simply revert to a novel usage which incorporates vernacular into the English language. Hurston by so doing shows the power inherent in speaking one's own language, even if it is the ruptured and broken speech of a people rendered tongue-less and dispossessed.

Women apprehend and interpret experience in some ways differently from men and since every work of art is a statement about the nature of reality, it is no wonder then that this reality in women's poetry should be stated differently in some ways from what has always been stated in poetry by men. In examining language in particular and the art-form in general of female poetry, this chapter intends to identify and explain those principles of form which recur in women's poetry and shape its vision. Because of scope, this chapter however focuses only on linguistic experimentation in the poetry of mainstream American and British feminists, Adrienne Rich and Geraldine Monk respectively.

American Women Poets and Experimentation with Language

In traditional poetry, many words and phrases have denigrated women and upheld the supremacy of men. Words such as 'effeminate' have been used to show that something is of a lower standard and therefore not good enough. However, female poets like Adrienne Rich attempt in their poetry to assume feminist associations for some phrases while at the same time give new assumptions even to quite familiar words. In this regard, Rich considers the language of female poetry as 'a language that, while freeing itself from the exclusionary dominance of patriarchy establishes a new antithetical commonality of readers, a language spoken by and for other women' (Rich 1978: 176). The lives of women have become increasingly split between an intimate and public sphere, between public and private behaviour. Modern feminist poetry has therefore been informed by these new developments. This delineation between private and public space has created a demarcation between the areas in which women must remain silent and those in which they can speak. According to

D'Almeida, silence consists of the patriarchal act of limiting women to inferior spheres. It is: 'the historical muting of women under the formidable institution known as patriarchy, that form of social organization in which males assume power and create for females an inferior status' (D'Almeida 1994: 1). This presupposes that women's voices can be heard only within the limited sphere of the inferior status to which patriarchy has restricted them. This split between spaces where women are at once comfortable and inaudible is indeed insidious. According to Norbert Elias 'it is taken so much for granted that it becomes so compulsive a habit that it is hardly perceived in consciousness,' (Elias 1994: 190). Anglo-American women have, therefore, found the need to break the blockages that have debarred them from expressing themselves in such public spheres as literature. It is in this light that the philosopher Jeff Weintraub observes thus:

> Public and private are categories posed as opposite and mutually exclusive terms. Such a formulation inevitably connotes hierarchy; one condition is evaluated more positively than the other. Within this dualism, people are limited by a falsely universal position. When they are assigned to either category, differential consequences follow in terms of power and access to resources. Such categorization marks boundaries, providing opportunity for some and restraint for others. Bounded categories tend to become metaphors and are embedded in language as images. (Weintraub 1997: iv)

Recent socio-political developments recognise 'historical transformations in the construction of the relationship between public and private spheres' and therefore between 'personal and political discourses' This transformation follows on the heels of the changes in the relationship between the public sphere of work and politics and the private sphere of personal experience and family life, which were brought about by 20th century social developments. The family as a protected unit of non-instrumental and non-rationalized relationships has increasingly been penetrated and hollowed out by the invasion of bureaucracy, mass culture and the mass media. The key to these developments is the change in the role of the mother.

In the mainstream American poetic scene, Adrienne Rich (1978 and Maggie O'Sullivan (1993) show a total rejection of patriarchal norms in its language. This rejection of that society's mores and even of its language reduces women to a state of silence. However, silence also casts its own shadow because the refusal to speak may signify the negative act of wilful withholding instead of showing the desire to escape from the structures of conventional discourse. To resolve this ambiguity, women in the poetry resort to speech. They speak not by using the victimizers' language but by creating a language of their own. A look at Rich's poetry will validate this point.

In Rich's 'Cartographies of silence,' the speaker yearns for a language that would transcend patriarchal discourse by creating its own originating presence:

> The silence that strips bare:
> In Dreyer's 'Passion of Joan'
>
> Balconette's face, hair shorn, a great geography
> Mutely surveyed by the camera
>
> If there were a poetry where this could happen
> not as blank spaces or as words
>
> Stretched like a skin over meaning
> But as silence falls at the end
>
> Of a night through which two people
> Have talked till dawn. (Rich 1978: 11)

The persona in the above poem wishes for a distinct type of language which she describes as 'not as blank spaces or as words;' but as the kind of silence which 'falls at the end/ of a night through which two people/ have talked till dawn.' Since the poet cannot even trust the words she writes, knowing that these words convey patriarchal overtones, she must resort to silence:

> Silence can be a plan
> Rigorously executed
>
> The blue print to a life
> It is a presence
>
> It has a history, a form
> Do not confuse it
> With any kind of absence.
> ('cartographies of Silence')

Silence in itself becomes a form of agency because it shuns, as it were, the danger of echoing or antithetically imitating the patriarchal voice. The persona emphasizes this by admonishing her readers not to confuse silence with absence. Silence is necessary because the climate in which women live and write has become stultifying and language as men have used it has become too tainted to be trusted. Women then relapse onto 'the silence that strips bare' which is like a face clean shaven or a great geographical space which is being quietly surveyed by the camera. However, because the poet is not unaware of the dangers inherent in silence, she yearns for a language that would be neither 'as blank spaces nor as words/ Stretched like a skin over meanings/But as silence falls at the end.' She defines this as the language *ipso facto* of women. It would be stretched like a skin over the meanings that have hitherto been attributed to feminine experience. Rich thus goes on to attempt such a language as she tries to rename the world around her, sometimes using understatement and most times writing in a deliberately fragmented manner. If the poet were to rename all around her, woman would be both the subject and the object of consciousness; but to rename necessitates the freedom of choice. This is why in the 7th poem of 'Twenty One Love Poems' she writes:

> And how have I used rivers how have I used wars to escape writing the worst things of all-not crimes of others, not even our own death, but the failure to want our own freedom passionately enough so that blighted elms, sick rivers, massacres would seem mere emblems of that desecration of ourselves? (Rich 1978: VII)

These lines reflect the conviction that only by choosing one's own life freely and by converting one's choice into language can a female poet begin to rename the things around her, and thus redefine poetry and language. At the end of the poems Rich makes an assertion which shows that she fully imbibes this conviction:

> I choose to be a figure in that light
> half blotted by darkness, something moving
> across that space the color of stone
> greeting the moon yet more than stone:
> a woman. I choose to walk here. And to draw this circle. (Rich 1978: XXI)

Feminist language, therefore, exposes a shift from the inner intimate voice of lyrics to rhetorical discourse of philosophizing, soliloquizing and questioning, which shows the need for an alternate form of power.

In 'Implosions,' Rich makes an appeal to our emotions using rhetorical discourse. This appeal seems natural and personal judging from the surface meaning of the poem:

> I wanted to choose words that even you
> would have to be changed by.
> Take the word
> Of my pulse, loving and ordinary

Send out your signals, hoist
your dark scribbled flags
But take my hand.

However, a more critical reading shows that this discourse is a political strategy dependent on identification:

My hands are knotted in the rope
and I cannot sound the bell
My hands are frozen to the switch
and I cannot throw it
the foot is in the wheel. ('Implosions')

We realise therefore that this woman who wants to write things that would inspire other women to change, is everywhere in chains. Her 'hands are knotted in the rope' and 'frozen in the switch,' while her foot is hooked to a wheel. She is therefore totally incapacitated and the poem is not just an appeal for liberation but shows the incapacitating chains under which women are wallowing in the artistic arena. From its title, we know that an 'implosion' is a violent collapse inwards. The first three lines continue to emphasize this collapse:

The world's
Not wanton
Only wild and wavering. ('Implosions')

As the poem unfolds phrases like 'All wars are useless to the dead' make readers become more convinced that its rhetoric is connected to a political demand, to a desire for change. In it, a female reader identifies with the difficulty of expressing their identity, which is the primordial essence of female voicelessness in patriarchy. The speaker desires to sound a signal for change. But almost immediately her hands become knotted in the rope with which she has to ring the bell and her fingers become numbed so that she cannot press the switch.

From this, the reader's perception of the discrimination against women is revitalized and her consciousness is re-awakened. That 'all wars are useless to the dead' is almost a political slogan pointing to women's strategy of deliberate silence. It could also be read as an outcry calling on women to hoist their flags and act now; otherwise it will be too late when they lie crushed in 'a stubble of blistered flowers'.

Even in its form, the poem is anti- representational. It has no intrinsic structure of stanzaic and rhythmic patterns. The sentences and phrases seem flung on the page at the reader and presented with such urgency, and yet such gentleness that the reader may feel like screaming.

There is also an exploration of language outside of conventional register:

> When it is finished and we are lying
> In a stubble of blistered flowers
> Eyes gaping, mouths staring
> dusted with crushed arterial blues. ('Implosions')

In this penultimate stanza, eyes are said to 'gape' and not to 'stare.' Similarly, mouths 'stare' and do not 'gape.' This unconventional register rejects patriarchal norms and portends to record the underside of events which patriarchal culture misperceives. In fact, as Maggie O'Sullivan (1993) concedes, experimental poets are interested in the primacy of language, in what can be done underneath, behind, with language. Language is used here to take up women's lives and their limitations and restrictions as a political issue, which must be brought into the limelight. The title, 'Implosions', suggests a collapse of patriarchy unto itself as a parallel of the collapse of the traditional lyrical mode. This collapse signals a resurgence of alternatives. This is echoed in the last rhetorical question in which the speaker, even through a question, makes a claim to have left a signal for change and to have even changed much by the time she would have died:

> When it is finished and we are lying…
> I' ll have done nothing
> even for you? ('Implosions')

The question presages the resurgence of a new and better represented female image both as a person and as an artist. It also emphasizes the resurgence and standardisation of radical artistic experimentalism.

In fact, this open rhetorical discourse also denotes the absence of a central poetic voice. This is not surprising, given that women live in a world which has been reinvented by the electronic media of film, video and TV and by electronic communication, making not only the personal to become public but even the public, the world at large, to become a small village. The individual voice is therefore compromised. In 'Night Break,' Rich writes in a radically fragmented manner in which the words thus fragmentally flung at the page form patterns of sound and sense:

> something broken something
> I need By someone
> I love Next year
> Will I remember what
> This anger unreal
> Yet
> Has to be gone through
> The sun to set
> on this anger
> I go on
> Head down into it
> The mountain pulsing
> Into the oildrum drops
> The ball of fire.

The words stand out almost singly as if liberated from the confines of representation. Rich uses physical space and absence of punctuation to loosen the deliberate syntactic connections between words and thus introduces ambiguities that disrupt normative forms. There is the impression of great energy behind the poem heightened by the rejection of the poetic line and by sudden instantaneous capitalizations. Sentences are broken up even on the same lines and this style foregrounds the breaking down of traditional poetics and patriarchal phallogocentrism.

The context of the poem is the Vietnam War in which America attacked Vietnam blowing up her oil wells and registering mammoth casualties:

I go on
Head down into it
The mountain pulsing
Into the oil drum drops
the ball of fire. ('Night Break')

The speaker's angry tone at this dropping of a 'ball of fire' into the oil wells captures the magnitude of the explosion and this is given more impetus as the word 'drops' stands alone and in its onomatopoeia, one can almost hear the bomb splash into the oil well. The speaker's anger is justified because international violence and the progressive feminization of poverty all take their toll on the woman. After all, after the unrest, the turmoil and the instability, women are the ones who are confronted with hungry children who must be fed:

Will I remember what
This anger unreal
Yet
has to be gone through
The sun to set
On this anger. ('Night Break')

The impact is even felt right in the home. The bedroom, the most private of the interior spaces gets invaded, as pieces of atomic bombs can be found even on beds:

> In the bed, the pieces fly together
> And the rifts fill or else
> My body is a list of wounds
> Symmetrically placed.

Villages are blown open by planes, which recess between raids. There are not enough agencies for relief and the darkness and gloom of survival becomes 'utter,' especially with famine and enormous war casualties:

> No agencies
> Of relief
> The darkness becomes utter
> Sleep cracked and flaking
> Sift over the shaken target
> What breaks is night
> not day... ('Night Break')

As seen in these lines, there is therefore a clear relation between the public sphere of work and political activity and the private sphere of individual female experience and family life.

Maggie O'sullivan (1993) in 'Another Weather System' writes using a structure which seems to follow the lure of the hawk's circling and kill with a parallel of human sickness and death:

> HUNGER
> Hooking the bill tearing the flesh lining the text.
> MARE
> SOW
> BITCH

Carrion inlets
On wire
Sky scrapping
One way.
Another
Vein lifting...

These two poems show how women use art as a liberating intellectual activity and the work of art as a means of showing in Rich's own words, how our language has trapped as well as liberated us, how the very act of naming has been till now a male prerogative, and how we can begin to see and name and therefore live – afresh.
('When We Dead Awaken: Writing as Re-vision' Gelpi and Gelpi 1993: 167)

In 'Splittings' Rich uses language in such a way as to cast retrospective and introspective glances over the roles that have hitherto limited women. In the opening stanza, the speaker's body is described as 'opening over San Francisco like the day'. This poignant metaphor underlies the poem's conviction that the body is no longer an entity to be considered in private. It is something flung open over a large expanse of public space for the whole world to see. The human body and more specifically the female body is thus re-examined in its social, cultural and psycho-sexual contexts.

It is also a kind of turn inwards for identity and the speaker realizes that as the light streams downwards upon her body which is spread over the city, each pore of her body is crying for a change. In a kind of psychological separation, the speaker believes that her body has been separated from her consciousness:

My body opens over San Francisco...
light raining down each pore crying the change of light
I am not with her. I have been waking off and on
all night to that pain not simply absence but

the presence of the past destructive…

So, the body spreads over the city, while the mind is bent on contemplating the past and all the pain of living like a woman. She wishes to be able to master this pain and address it:

> Yet if I could instruct
> myself If we could learn to learn from pain
> even as it grasps us If the mind, the mind that lives
> in this body could refuse to let itself be crushed
> in that grasp it would loosen pain pain would have to stand
> off from me and listen… ('Splittings')

In this introspection, she finds out that the pain is almost tangible and that it is a creation of patriarchy which believes that the woman's body is an object owned by a male, whether in the capacity of husband or lover. The interior mind of the woman is awakened while her body is being violated. However, as projected in this poem, interiority and the frontier of violation coalesce and yet are separated in the division between the female reawakened mind and her body. The body's male owner and violator, in this poem presented in the imagery of sunlight which shines on all and sundry in spite of whims and caprices is in an altogether different relationship to the body than its intimate occupant, the mind. It is this division that creates pain because of the woman's awakened consciousness, as the persona tells us: 'I am the pain of division creator of division'. This realization that the pain she feels is the pain of division imposed by patriarchy, makes the woman (speaker) to reject the status quo and take a resolution not to 'suffer uselessly':

> I believe I am choosing something new
> not to suffer uselessly yet still to feel…
> But we live so much in these
> configurations of the past I choose
> to separate her from my past we have not shared .

> I choose not to suffer uselessly. ('Splittings')

In the last stanza, the speaker rejects myths that have tried to define woman:

> The world tells me I am its creature
> I am raked by eyes brushed by hands
> I want to crawl into her for refuge lay my head
> in the space between her breast and shoulder. ('Splittings')

This definition, however, leads the speaker into a discovery of the awesome limitations, both cultural and political that crowd her mind:

> abnegating power for love
> as women have done or hiding
> from power in her love like a man. ('Splittings')

There is evidence that this poem makes use of language in an experimental way as it takes the female body as the locus of representation. The woman's body is indeed the focus. There is no mention of the male body. The speaker's body (the many references to the pronoun 'her' show that the speaker is a woman) is spread over San Francisco and every pore of this body is opened up to the sun's amorous invasion, as light 'rains' down on her. Later on, in the third stanza, the body is being 'raked by eyes' and 'brushed by hands.' This crude imagery of sexual activity continues to demonstrate how the woman's body has been valued over and above her intellect. Further references to her body make mention of her breasts and the spaces between her shoulders as places of solace. Nonetheless this solace-giving capacity is negative in its very nature because it is restrictive. It keeps the woman devoid of political, social, cultural and intellectual power, her only forte being emotional capability. That her body and her mind are separated from each other continues to underscore this painful division that keeps her devoid of power: 'My body opens over San Francisco.../I am not with her I have been waking off and on.' This separation emphasizes the psycho-sexual and intellectual dichotomy in which patriarchal attitude believes that woman is essentially the body – the emotion, and not the intellect. In this poem, many words referring to the body demonstrate this. More openings into her body expose her as a public not a private issue.

Hence, American feminist poetry unlike modernist and postmodernist poetry, does not, in its disparaging of interiorisation and the individual personhood, believe in total self-alienation and the absence of any form of subjectivity. The insinuation is that women must experience themselves in relation to all objects and to other women, within the matrix of all possible unforeseen eventualities. Through the language of introspection, the speaker situates the female self in a field of relationships both past and present. In a revisionist examination, the female self re-emerges stronger and alienated and it is only in this manner that it can be freed from objectification. In this freedom, we can recognize the female poets' desire to expose historical transformations in the construction of the relationship between the public and private spheres and between personal and political discourses. This relationship gives women the chance to express the personal agenda of the feminist enterprise in a male-centred discourse, using language.

Experimentation with Language among British Women Poets

In British poetry, the female poet Geraldine Monk (1987) insists on a more radical linguistic revolution which continues to show that women apprehend and interpret reality in ways quite different from men. Her poetic style seems to use formal aspects of language to question the workings of the seemingly naturalised organisation of linguistic expression. In her collection, *The Sway of Precious Demons*, the subject matter cannot be easily identified as political. Yet in terms of ideological stance, the formal experimentation with meaning involves an interplay of language, social materiality and subjectivity.

'DREAM TWO*** CORRIDOR' is written in an almost perfectly consistent structure. Yet the final lines betray this symmetry forming a square on the page, with each line the same length.

Squares black white
black white surroun
D unrelen T jumped
and rolled through
Eyes pulsate flicke
red grew isotropic.('DREAMTWO*** Corridor')

Progressively, some letters are missing from words and words that begin at the end of one line may continue on the next one if the space runs out. There is also a conspicuous absence of hyphenation to indicate the continuation of words on another line. But what strikes us before anything else, is the shape of the poem, especially these last lines on the page.

The juxtaposition of words and spaces emphasize not only each word but each letter and this gives us a sense of the impact of structure. Several textual devices are also used to continue to accentuate this structural aspect. The empty spaces which the readers almost automatically fill in, promote a process of defamiliarisation with language as it recognizes the poem's rejection of a linear syntax. Yet, even as we anticipate the missing parts of a word as with 'surroun,' in the second line, we are continually surprised by the poem as when a capital 'D' follows 'surroun' on the next line. This kind of word fragmentation suggests the relationship between structure and unit and consequently of meaning. In the two last lines, the line break separates the word 'flickered' such that the two parts are read as words in themselves, 'flicke' and 'red': 'yes pulsate flicke / red grew isotropic.'

This breakage exposes a division between the habit of regarding language as a transparent medium and the awareness of language as a system of signs whose arrangement and placement all fix or unfix meaning. The female poet has used it here to fix meaning which is representative of a feminist linguistic agenda. The poem suggests a notion of subjectivity in its visual emphasis of the repeated word 'ALONE': this appears boldly capitalized twice in the poem:

> desolation not tech
> nicoloured carnival
> black white T.V.O.K
> no two three one fa
> ncy dress not givin
> g prizes for elepha
> feet slap and echoe
> s tunnel wet sounds
> plash ALONE drips i
> n front who behind
> find no go or one t
> wo tidy shadowy orn
> eat figure ALONE co
> ncrete in this white and black
> corridor.
> ('DREAM TWO*** CORRIDOR').

It is as if the ALONE 'i' which dangles at the end of the poem's fifteenth line, typifies the solitary and delineated speaking subject already lacking the authority suggested by the capital form 'ALONE'. This would seem to imply that the female poet is still a subject and is subjected to the overriding patriarchal artistic culture. But this idea is off-set towards the end of the poem when the conspicuous ALONE now appears in conjunction with 'CO'—, seemingly implying that it is infused with others:

> eat figure ALONE co
> ncrete in this whit
> e and black

corridor.
('DREAM TWO*** CORRIDOR')

The assumption here is that the female experimental poet is alone in forging a new poetical aesthetics and yet has already asserted and found a place in the company of artists of all sorts: blacks, whites, those more firmly established (as seen in the word 'concrete') and those still experimenting, suggested by the lines:

  i
n front who behind
find no go or one t
wo tidy shadowy orn.
('DREAM TWO*** Corridor')

The poet therefore uses the poetic form to suggest that women have already transcended the level of 'aloneness' to be able to mix with others in the centre of discourse where their voices can be heard. The form of the poem is so manipulated that every line carries no more than nineteen syllables. Since 'co' happens to be the nineteenth syllable of its line, it has to be broken from 'concrete' and it is this breakage which allows the prefix 'co' to connote with words like 'cooperate' signifying working together.

In Monk's 'Molecular Power Progressives' irregularly placed lines stream down the page, almost marching like the litany of 'boys' who have achieved 'STATUS' that the poem describes. Conformity to male hegemonic myths of power defines this status, since these boys are both 'CULT HUGGERS and BOOT CRUSHERS'. This is in conformity with their being

  Leather boys strategically studded
  Soldier boys swallowing uniformity
  City boys pinstriped and tied
  Law boys robed and wigged
  Holy boys cassocked and collared.

('Molecular Power Progressives')

In it, we see masculine figures who progressively and powerfully occupy the field of patriarchal culture, as well as the field of the articulated text. However, through the use of space, we are alerted to the unarticulated or erased social spaces positioned among the masculine references. In traditional poetry, space between words is simply often a background before or on which speech performs. Nevertheless, in this poem, white space is like a gap waiting to be filled with the appropriate feminist references. In this way, feminist language becomes a continuum of speech in which every woman can fill in the remaining gaps to tell a specific her- story as opposed to the general history. The poem ends in a way which exposes a bias against the unitary view of the world that empowers the masculine:

FIngers Waggers Thumb Screwers
RanK
MEN
TALITY.

The breaking of the word mentality into MEN and TALITY and the double meaning of rank: position of authority and something rotten and smelly, calls attention to the innovation that feminist experimental poetics has introduced into language. The insinuation here is that the power dynamics in patriarchal culture which puts men at the top-ranks of every field is rotten and smelly.

Yet in another poem entitled 'WHERE?,' Monk underscores this notion with greater emphasis. This poem recalls the Romantic tradition of the lyric speaker, in which a man speaks to men. The poem also seems to question the placement of the lyric 'I' which is often structured as masculine by romantic discourses. It is perhaps for this reason that the 'I' is implied but omitted and so the poem begins with a verb:

Went to the mountains

>   everyone
>   on a tidal washy waving
>   crest of
>   high up there!
>   ('WHERE')

The scenario of the poem is not only reminiscent of but is actually labelled 'Romantic' discourse and after this labelling the 'I' appears in duplicate, pushing the syntactical sense of lines forward and backward at once:

ROMANTICISM
and
SUBLIME
head shakings of
I
and
    I
don't know what
or not happened next.
    ('WHERE')

The conjunction 'and' which appears between the two 'I's seems to divide the poem into two halves: the first half positions the 'I' in a lyric discourse while the lower half reads like a parody of romanticism in which the Romantic 'I' is suddenly brought down to the mundane:

> except
>   we roly-polied back
>   down again to
>   DROWN
>   in a tidal washy wave
>   of celluloid soap
>   (All of a sud).

('WHERE')

The final line in brackets puns on the double meaning of the phrase: Did the transformation of the sublimity of the 'I' into mundanity take place suddenly, or does it leave the 'I' all smeared and smudged with celluloid soap? Here therefore the all-important subject and his claim to pre-poetic experience is dethroned. Above all, everything is made mundane and brought right down to the level of women's laundry detergents.

Conclusion

Through language, women poets are thus able to effect a dethronement of the phallogocentric patriarchal voice. In this dethronement of the lofty sublime of the poetic voice, the poet is exploring the ways by which the public world of art and poetry can be mediated by the private experience of being an individual. There is, therefore, a breakdown of the barrier between art and life which coalesces with the breakdown of the relationship between the public and private spheres of life and experience. This continues to validate the feminist slogan that 'the personal is political'. This final association of the poetic self with images of female work and life experiences, grounds the poetic voice in social conditions. Language is therefore used here to disentangle the masculinist assumption about the expressive self from a tradition of poetic authority and to re-assert the position of a feminist poetics. Helen Cixous (1981) in *The Laugh of the Medusa,* proposes a distinct female language based on the female body and a primeval female linguistic space free of symbolic order, sex roles, and 'Otherness'. She argues that women's language arising from the female body will encompass enormously rich resources and will relieve users from the laws of rational discourse; it will be a language of languages. Whether or not the poets in this study have succeeded in this linguistic revolution remains an open, rhetorical question. One thing, however, is evident: the

American and British poets examined in this study have all used the art of poetry to validate their personal and private experiences as legitimate topics for public expression. They have used appropriate diction to integrate the private and public spheres. They regard poetry to be an aspect of political feminism; and as poets, they base their revolution in the artistic medium sometimes radically transforming language and its representation on the page. Their vocabulary, literalness, and sometimes brevity of form are radical and shocking, perhaps even threatening. The feminist poets that this study has examined have, through the medium of their poetry, succeeded in creating a form that articulates their ardent beliefs.

Bibliography

Anon., (1992). *Mons*. Middlesex: North and South.

Bâ, M., (1968). *So Long a Letter*. London: Heinemann.

Cixious, H., (1981). The Laugh of the Medusa. In: *French Feminisms*. New York: Shocken, pp. 339-349.

Culler, J., (1973). *Structuralist Poetics: Structuralism, Linguistics, and the Study of Literature*. New York: Cornell University Press.

D'Almeida, I., (1994). *Francophone African Women: Destroying the Emptiness of Silence*. Gainesville: Florida University Press.

Elias, N., (1994). *The Civilizing Process: A History of Manners*. Oxford: Basil Blackwell.

Farrison, W. E., (1989). Clottel, William Jefferson and Sally Hemings. *College Language Association (CLA) Journal XIV*, pp.147-174.

Kaplan, C., (1975). *Salt and Bitter and Good: Three Centuries of English and American Women Poets*. New York: Paddington.

Millet, K., (1970). *Sexual Politics*. New York: Columbia University Press.

Monk, G., (1987). *The Sway of Precious De anguage, Experience, Identity in Women's Writing*. London: Pandora Press.

Montefiore, J., (2004). *Feminism and Poetry: Language, Experience, Identity in Women's Writing.* Michigan: University of Michigan Press.

Ostriker, A., (1986). *Stealing the Language: The Emergence of Women's Poetry in America.* New York: Beacon Press.

Ostriker, A., (2000). *Dancing at the Devil's Party: Essays on Poetry, Politics and the Erotic.* Michigan: Michigan University Press.

O'Sullivan, M., (1993). *In the House of the Shaman.* London: Reality Street Edition.

Rich, A., (1978). *The Dream of a Common Language. Poems 1974-1977.* New York: WW Norton.

Rich, A., (1993). When We Dead Awaken: Writing as Revision. In: *Adrienne Rich's Poetry and Prose.* New York: WW Norton.

Weintraub, J., (1997). The Theory and Politics of Public/Private Distinction. In: *Public and Private in Thought and Practice: Perspectives on a Grand Dichotomy.* Chicago: The University of Chicago Press, pp. 1-42.

Chapter Three

Transgressing Otherness through Marvellous Realism and Negotiating Self/Space in Maryse Condé's *I, Tituba, Black Witch of Salem*

Eunice Fonyuy Fondze-Fombele

Introduction

Identity politics has been at the centre of debates in postcolonial discourse since the *Négritude*, nationalist and *créolité* movements. The main thrust of these debates is to posit possible ways of understanding how marginalized groups may assert their own subjectivity and agency. This tendency is what Peter Barry describes as 'campaign for and by groups disadvantaged by some aspect of their identity, such as their gender, their race, or their sexual orientation' (Barry 1995: 146). In the same direction, bell hooks in 'Postmodern Blackness,' has tackled the issue of critical identity for oppressed groups and the imperative of self-empowerment, or liberation for marginalised individuals and groups. She insists on the assumption of voice and explains that 'Part of our struggle for radical black subjectivity is the quest to find ways to construct self and identity that are oppositional and liberatory' (hooks 2000: 133). The quest to find ways of constructing self and assumption of voice that mostly informed discourses on the movements of *Négritude*, *créolité* and nationalism projected a masculinised voice. The hopeful aim of *Négritude*, for example, was an affirmation of Black identity, encouraging, as Marie-Denise Shelton maintains, 'the black race...to stand upright' (Shelton 1994: 427), but it failed to create a space for female writers. Similarly, for black people in Africa and the Caribbean, *Négritude* offered the potential to shape a new understanding of self-determination, as long as that self-determination included enforcing a masculinised version of the individual. Furthermore, postcolonial major Caribbean male writers such as Kamau Brathwaite, Derek Walcott, George Lamming, and James Marlon have, for the most part, projected in their writings a male-centred voice of the black diasporic struggles towards identity construction. This tendency has provoked and produced gender-neutral discussions of the problems of identity politics. For example, Paul Gilroy's major discourse on the Black Atlantic plays a great role in reinforcing the black diasporic male voice as its emphasis is also geared towards the black male migration tendencies to metropolitan areas. Thus, the problem of the silenced voice of the Caribbean woman is a complex predicament that still demands follow-up. Maryse Condé and many of her female contemporary Caribbean writers like Edwidge Danticat, Jamaica Kincaid, Mayra Santos-Febres and Elizabeth Nunez have in their writings sought to transcend the masculine-centred literary representations of the black diaspora with their inscriptions of 'feminine subjectivity and sense of collective agency' (Fraile-Marcos 2014: 185). However, as demonstrated in this essay, Condé's distinctive artistic value in *I, Tituba, Black Witch of Salem,* lies in the process of her artistic recovery and re-inscription of the historically silenced female slave voice by using the marvellous in realism. The marvellous in realism becomes a potent narrative tool that helps Condé and her characters, members of the denigrated race and gender, to transgress and transcend hegemonic othering of them and their history.

This chapter reinforces Michael Dash's postulations about the essential difference between Marvellous Realism and *Négritude* in 'Marvellous Realism: The Way out of Négritude' (Ashcroft, Griffiths and Tiffin 2011: 150-151). Dash argues that if there is one sound idea that the ideology of negritude puts forward, it is certainly the notion of the double alienation of the black man – that is the belief that the problem is more than political and economic, that there was a psychological and spiritual reconstruction that should also take place (Dash 2011: 150). But as Dash further explains, it was difficult for the *négritudinists* 'to provide a solution to the problem of spiritual regeneration for the simple reason that they themselves held as true an attitude to the past as being totally un-creative' (Dash 2011: 150). In their reiteration of the injustice of the past, Dash maintains, 'they did more than emphasize the fact of spiritual loss to the extent that any notions of survival or emergence of a Third World personality were totally neglected' (Dash 2011: 150). This means that the desperate protests against the ironies of history left out of account a significant and positive part of the history of Black people. The very idea of history in the Caribbean for many prominent Caribbean writers constitutes a contested site. In Derek Walcott's opinion, history does not exist for the Caribbean people because it is to them as a myth, not a cultural construction. He foregrounds the negation of history of the Caribbean in his essay 'The Muse of History' and in his poem 'The Sea is History'. He argues that there is nothing commemorative or honourable about the violence, agonies, humiliations, violations and dehumanisation that branded Caribbean history. To him, 'History is the nightmare from which I am trying to awake' (Walcott 1974: 1). In 'The Sea is History' he contemplates the negation of this history thus, 'Where are your monuments, your battles, martyrs? Where is your tribal memory? Sirs, / In that grey vault' (Walcott 1974: 364). Walcott's contemplations on history in the Caribbean diverges fundamentally from Edward Kamau Brathwaite's perspective. Brathwaite characterises Caribbean history as fragmentary and dispersed. The problem to him is 'how to study the fragments/whole' of the Caribbean historical reality whose bedrocks are plantation slavery, colonial domination and cultural pluralism (Brathwaite 1976: 199). Thus, according to Brathwaite, although the sea was partial and intolerant in its disposition to the histories of the transatlantic slavery, that situation is not synonymous with the absence of history. Similarly, Edouard Glissant affirms and validates the existence of Caribbean history. He suggests that the history exists except that it is fractured and dispersed, constituting itself as the site of history characterized by ruptures and that began with a brutal dislocation, the slave trade' (Glissant 1996: 61).

This contestable nature of Caribbean history arises from the act of othering where blacks were and are excluded from all the arenas of representation. White hegemony assumed authority of voice and control of the word where the means of interpretation and communication was seized and put under control. Condé's radical interrogation of this othering phenomenon conveys the momentous and constructive part of the history of Black people and particularly that of black women. Her singularity as a Caribbean female writer lies in her use of the marvellous realist mode to transgress hegemony's otherness in *I, Tituba, Black Witch of Salem*. The novel is then one of those texts that do not only claim the black female voice in the politics of identity construction, but creates a counter-culture of the imagination through the marvellous realist mode. This task ties with Wilson Harris' conviction that, 'the imagination of the folk involved a crucial inner re-creative response to the violation of slavery and indenture and conquest' (Harris 1973: 12).

Condé's position as a contemporary writer, who adopts the positive imaginative reconstruction of history and reality, developed in the consciousness of the black woman through the marvellous realist mode, is the motivating factor behind this chapter. With this motivation, the following questions arise: How does Condé tap the consciousness of the dominated culture, past and present? How does she use the marvellous realist mode to transcend otherness? Of what importance can such an inner corrective on history be to Condé, a contemporary female writer? The aim of this essay, therefore, is to demonstrate that through Marvellous Realism, Condé in *I, Tituba, Black Witch of Salem*, transgresses and transcends hegemonic othering of the black female in history. It should be noted that the term transgression exists in the Caribbean imaginary in highly contradictory ways. I want to view transgression in the light of disrupting hegemonic constructs. To push this argument through, it is necessary first of all to conceptualize the Marvellous Realist mode and its transgressive variant in the art of imagination.

The Marvellous Realist Mode and its Transgressive Variant

The Marvellous in Realism breeds ambiguities because of a certain type of ingenuousness, mysticism, magic and empiricism that is implied in the term Marvellous. Several scholars like Liam Connell, Brenda Cooper and Timothy Brennan have noted that the adoption of the marvellous and/or the magical in realism in order to create postcolonial discourse can rely too heavily on the writer's assumption of a Western perspective. That is, a European viewpoint that assumes that magic and the irrational belong to indigenous and non-European cultures, whereas rationality and a true sense of reality belong to a European perspective. Also, Maggie Ann Bowers in *Magic(al) Realism: The New Critical Idiom* has maintained that since the 1980s, the terms 'magic realism', 'magical realism' and 'marvellous realism' have become both highly fashionable and highly derided (Bowers 2004: 1). These scholars emphasize the ambiguous nature of the terms 'magic realism', 'magical realism' and 'marvellous realism'.

In *Ordinary Enchantments: Magical realism and the remystification of Narrative,* Wemdy B. Feris stresses the causality and/or difference though subtle, between magic realism and marvellous realism. She states that 'Essential here for the development of magical realism in general is the idea of the marvellous growing within the richness of reality' (Feris 2004: 34). To her, magical realism combines realism and the fantastic, what Tzevtan Tordorov has described as the hesitation of characters and readers when presented with questions about reality and once the hesitation is decided, the fantastic ends (Feris 2004: 33). But the marvellous as she maintains, seems to grow organically within the ordinary while blurring the distinction between the magical, the fantastic and the marvellous. I, therefore, see the Marvellous from Feris' perspective and from the perspective of Jacques Stephen Alexis' postulations in 'Of the Marvellous Realism of the Haitians' (in Ashcroft, Griffiths and Tiffin 2011). Alexis helps situate the concept in the cultural context of Caribbean literature. According to him, the marvellous is seen as something ontologically necessary to the regional population's vision of everyday reality. Alexis maintains that 'it is because they recognize that their people express their whole consciousness of reality by the use of the Marvellous, that Haitian writers and artists have become aware of the formal problem of its use' (Ashcroft, Griffiths and Tiffin 2011: 147). This means that the term becomes the faithful picture of the conditions of rural life which the Haitian story-teller executes. The marvellous, according to Alexis, expresses the society's beauties and its ugliness, and struggles, the drama of the oppressors and the oppressed which the story-teller brings to their stage and 'the imagery in which a people wraps it experience, reflects its conception of the world and of life, its faith, its hope, its confidence in man, in a great justice, and the explanation which it finds for the forces antagonistic to progress' (Ashcroft, Griffiths and Tiffin 2011: 148). The Marvellous Realism of the Haitians is thus an integral part of Social Realism with its inherent transgressive and subversive qualities adopted as the narrative mode in *I, Tituba, Black Witch of Salem*.

Transgressive and subversive qualities are suggested in the very conception of the term. The oxymoron 'marvellous realism' reveals that the categories of the marvellous and the real are brought into enquiry by their juxtaposition. If in marvellous realism as Alexis has postulated, the marvellous is presented as a part of ordinary reality, then the distinction between what is marvellous and what is real is transcended. Bowers sees two levels of transcendence emerging out of this type of narrative mode. On the one hand, she thinks that marvellous realism is subversive because it alternates between the real and the magical while functioning with the same narrative voice. That is to say it remains identifiable as magic and real and unlike in a realist narrative, the magical and the real are given the same serious treatment. Therefore, the extent to which one should accept the real as the version of events or the magical as the version of events is continuously undermined by the existence of the narrative mode's version in the text. On the other hand, Bowers thinks that the term in question is transgressive since it crosses the borders between the marvellous and real to create a further category—the marvellous or magical real. It is this transgressive feature of the marvellous realist mode that has led many postcolonial, feminist and cross-cultural writers to embrace it as a means of expressing their ideas. This form of narrative mode sees the categories defining the difference between the magical and real being dismantled in the cultural ethics of Condé's text, an ethics that transgresses otherness. The marvellous in realism in Condé's narrative is seen in this essay to express a sort of cultural conflict between the hegemonic white ruling class and those of Condé's race and gender, who have been othered and silenced by grand-narratives of history. It should be noted here that the dominant culture remains dominant by denying others the authority to govern and the power to challenge the truths that they propose – hence otherness. The consequence of otherness projects a lack that is seen from two different angles, the lack of the political power to govern oneself and the lack of the power to define the world around the 'othered'. Therefore, when the marvellous realist mode is employed to narrate identity problems from the position of the 'other' it brings into view the transgressive power that provides a means to attack the assumptions of the dominant culture.

I choose to examine this trangressive variant through Condé's marginal character, Tituba, the narrator/'focaliser' (Genette) and 'reflector' character (Stanzel), demonstrating how she assumes the voice. Then, I demonstrate Condé's creative regenerative force that produces a hybrid space as a means of reproducing Tituba's birth, life and death and the narrating spiritual being. It is this transgressive power in the narration of identity that is the focus of the next subsection.

Negotiating Self/Space in Narration: Transgressing Otherness

The transgressive variant of otherness propelled by the marvellous realist narrative mode in Condé's narrative is immediately observed in the title of *I, Tituba, Black Witch of Salem*. Tituba assumes an active voice and resists the fact that she has been silenced and relegated to the margins. She does this by countering the historical footnote that reduces her to a belittling, superficial allusion: 'Tituba, a slave originating from the West Indies and probably practising 'hoodoo' (Condé 1992: 149). Condé's narrative is seen from the perspective of what Shlomith Rimmon-Kenan in explaining narrative levels and voices in *Narrative Fiction* calls the interchangeability of narrative levels (Rimmon-Kenan 2005: 97). Condé's novel reverses narrative hierarchy, transforming hegemony's narrated object into a narrating agent. Tituba then takes control of her subjectivity in a slave societal setting, through a strong, constitutive and self-affirming 'I', speaking her life in her own voice from the womb to the realm of the dead. By self-affirming her identity and subjectivity as *I, Tituba, black and witch of Salem* (my emphasis), she transgresses all the racist and misogynist misconstructions that have defined her, her gender and her race in colonial and postcolonial history.

Speaking in the first person, Tituba 'owns' her story, as she presents not only a self-reflexive mode, but projects a two-fold authorship perspective. Renée Larrier explains the significance of first person narration, which leads to a sort of dual or two-fold authorship. For Larrier, the two-fold authorship shared by the writer and the narrator empowers both women. They move together towards subjectivity, empowering them, thus conferring authority on them and their communities (Larrier 2000: 2). Tituba's voice is therefore Condé's as she confirms in the novel's prefatory remark, 'Tituba and I lived for a year on the closest of terms. During our endless conversations she told me things she had confided to nobody else' (Condé 1992: iv). However, Condé researched this forgotten historical figure Tituba, and then infused Tituba's voice with her own historically complex and imaginative voice as creator of a transgressive narrative.

Also, the use of the first person creates credibility for the character as well as presenting an intimate picture of her life and the challenges she faces. Condé has allowed her character to address the reader. This personal link between the reader and the narrator allows the narrator to assume her own space, which is then acknowledged and upheld by the reader. From the beginning of Condé's novel, one feels a personal connection to Tituba as she self-reflexively explains her arrival into the world. She narrates, 'Abena, my mother, was raped by an English sailor on the deck of *Christ the King* one day in the year 16 while the ship was sailing for Barbados. I was born from this act of aggression. From this act of hatred and contempt' (Condé 1992: 1).

Violently conceived, Tituba learns early that pain goes with the colour of her skin as well as her gender. Tituba finds herself in a society where she is oppressed to a non-existing state. Her encounter with Susanna Endicott and her white women friends is revealing:

It was not so much the conversation that amazed and revolted me as their way of going about it. You would think I wasn't standing there at the threshold of the room. They were talking about me and yet ignoring me. They were striking me off the map of human beings. I was nonbeing. Invisible. More invisible than the unseen, who at least have powers that everyone fears. Tituba only existed insofar as these women let her exist. It was atrocious. Tituba became ugly, coarse, and inferior because they willed her so. (Condé 1992: 24)

Tituba counters and transgresses this relegation to the margins by revealing through the strong narrative voice that she only became ugly, coarse and inferior because the white women willed her so. The transgressive variant of the marvellous realist mode reveals not only the hypocrisy of white women, but their fear for Tituba. Tituba grows resilient and refuses to remain on the margins of a society that shuns her. She does this by transcending otherness through the transgressive marvellous realist narrative mode that she uses to narrate her story.

The transgressive variant of the marvellous realist narrative mode is observed in what Rimmon-Kenan terms the 'discrepancy between the story order and text order' (Rimmon-Kenen 2005: 45) and what Gerard Genette terms 'anachronies' that produce analepsis and prolepsis (Genette 1980: 35). The complete narrative time from the beginning to the end, the 172 pages before the epilogue, is analeptic – 'second level narrative' in Genette's sense of the term. This means that what Genette calls 'first level narrative' is the 5 paged Epilogue that ends the narrative and it begins with these words, 'And that is the story of my life. Such a bitter, bitter story' (Condé 1992: 174). The marvellous realist mode and its transgressive variant is observed strongly in this first narrative, the epilogue. In the epilogue, Tituba operates from the realm of the dead as a spiritual narrating self and a spiritual experiencing self. She focalises on her activities from the spiritual realm that continue to impact on her society. It is from this sphere that she narrates her story as a homodiegetic narrator and intradiegetic character in Genette's definition.

Marvellous realism's dynamism in Tituba's narrating of her *diegesis* (Genette) is observed through her marvellous actions. She autodiegetically talks of a song about Tituba, 'I hear it from one end of the Island to the other, from North Point to Silver Sands, from Bridgetown to Bottom Bay. It runs along the ridge of the hills. It is poised on the tip of the heliconia (Condé 1992: 174). Tituba's presentation of the song denotes her state of being to her community. She is looked upon from the land of the spirits as Legendary Tituba because of the wonders she does for her people and the community. She narrates it as follows:

The other day I heard a boy four or five years old humming it [song]. In delight, I dropped three ripe mangoes at his feet and he remained rooted to the spot, staring up at the tree that had given him such a present out of season. (Condé 1992: 74)

Alexis has noted that, 'The art and literature of several people of negro origin . . . have frequently given the example of possible dynamic integration of the marvellous in realism' (Ashcroft, Griffiths and Tiffin 2011: 147). From the realm of the dead, Tituba transgresses otherness by piecing up the fragments of her life story and filling the historical void and partial cultural vacuum. She also reassures her race with dreams of liberty as she observes:

For now that I have gone over to the invisible world I continue to heal and cure, but primarily I have dedicated myself to another task ... hardening men's hearts to fight. I am nourishing them with dreams of liberty. Of victory. I have been behind every revolt. Every insurrection. Every act of disobedience. (Condé 1992: 174)

Condé in her narrative transgresses the otherness of White hegemony by tapping from this consciousness and grafting a complex culture of survival which happens to be hers and Tituba's response to oppression. Dash has observed that the third world writer's investigation of the past should move beyond the documented privations of slavery and colonisation to a more speculative vision of history in which the consciousness of the dominated cultures would predominate (Ashcroft, Griffiths and Tiffin 2011: 152).

Condé the writer and Tituba the spiritual narrator/focaliser/reflector use memory and imagination as inner re-creative forces that provide them a means to radically transgress otherness. Dash has noted that the only thing the enslaved people could possess and which could not be tampered with was their imagination (Dash 2011: 151). As a spiritual narrating self and experiencing self, Tituba insists in the epilogue that, 'I do not belong to the civilization of the Bible and Bigotry. My people will keep my memory in their hearts and have no need for the written word. It's in their heads. In their hearts and in their heads' (Condé 1992: 176). The emphasis Tituba gives to memory is the consciousness that Condé exhibits as she in her imagination reorders reality to reach 'beyond the tangible and concrete to acquire a new re-creative sensibility which could aid in the harsh battle for survival' (Dash 2011: 151). Condé accounts for the inner resources that her ancestors could have developed to combat their tragic environment and therefore, she engages in a conception of the past which would transgress the myths of historylessness or non-achievement. Condé allows Tituba and her spirit companions to adopt descendants in the land of the living whom they train from the spiritual realm. Tituba's relationship with Samantha is telling, 'Now she follows me fervently. I tell her the secrets I'm allowed to share, the hidden power of herbs and the language of animals. I teach her to look for invisible shapes in the world, the crisscross of communications, and the signs and symbols' (Condé 1992: 177). Imagination for Condé then becomes what Harris has described as the imagination of the folk involved in a crucial inner re-creative response to the violation of slavery and conquest (Harris 1973: 12). This inner re-creative response is observed in Tituba's inner satisfaction in the land of the dead. She states her convictions in the following words, 'Yes, I'm happy now. I can understand the past, read the present, and look into the future. Now I know why there is so much suffering and why the eyes of our people are brimming with water and salt. But I know, too, that there will be an end to all this' (Condé 1992: 176). Tituba's convictions indicate the importance of engaging in an inner corrective of history for a contemporary writer like Condé. In the same way, Tituba circumvents the ironies of history, Condé, a contemporary writer avoids the negativity of protest by allowing her writing to emerge into 'a literature of renascence' (Dash 2011: 151). This means that Condé's narrative by virtue of its marvellous realist transgressive variant begets a literary aesthetic and reality that reveals an emergence of a third world personality from the privations of history. Wilson Harris has commented on the possibility of a contemporary third world writer to beget a literary renaissance. He has maintained that, 'I believe the possibility exists for us to become involved in perspectives of renascence which can bring into play a figurative meaning beyond an apparently real world or prison of history – I believe a philosophy of history may well lie buried in the arts of imagination' (Harris 1973: 8). Such a vision of the imaginative reconstruction of reality developed in the consciousness of a black, female and slave woman by a contemporary female black writer, is a rewarding enterprise. Condé's narrative mode is seen to offer a way of discussing alternative approaches to reality to that of Western philosophy on history.

The narrative process reveals the means by which Tituba resolves (or attempts to resolve) the problem and finds a space for herself. The fictional nature of the novel becomes important for this analysis as it enables the author to sidestep social constraints through the marvellous realist mode and represent Tituba's agency through what Jean Franco in the Mexican context has described as, '...to trace those moments when dissident subjects appear in the social text and when struggle for interpretive power erupts' (Franco 2002: xii). I see the path that Tituba takes in order to affirm her identity or to find her voice as her moment of deconstruction and reconstruction in the social text. The epilogue as discussed above helps the reader to realise that the anachronic second narrative, which happens to be the 179 paged narrative of Tituba's life from conception to her death is narrated by Tituba as the adult narrating spiritual self. In retrospect, the narrating spiritual self, focalises not only on her experiences from conception to death, but also tells of a strong matrilineal line that encourages and strengthens her. Tituba is born and she grows up on the fringes of slave society in Barbados. It is during her formative years with Mama Yaya in Barbados that she learns the African art of healing, ancestor reverence, spiritual connection between the living and the dead and the spiritual wonderment of sexual love. Tituba ironically becomes the target of the Salem witch hunt because she dedicates herself to the ways of her ancestors and uses the virtues of healing powers to help women of the family that owns her. It is these healing powers that are misinterpreted by the dominant ideology as 'witchery', with all the negative connotations accorded that term by dominant ideology.

Also, witness the contrast that exists between Tituba's definition of the term witch and Puritan religion's views and reaction to this term. According to Tituba, the adult spiritual narrating self, young Tituba first hears the term witch from John Indian when he tries to court her, 'Tituba, you know what they say about you, they say you're a witch! . . . I want to prove to everyone that it's not true and take you openly as my woman' (Condé 1992: 18). According to the Puritans, a witch is Satan's deputy (Condé 1992: 71) and any slave 'accused of dealings with Satan' (Condé 1992: 27) is burned in the square as an example to deter any 'dregs of hell' (Condé 1992: 36) from practicing witchery. The problem that is raised here is that Tituba's narrative voice reveals that, 'Before setting foot inside this house I didn't know who Satan was!' (Condé 1992: 27). A contrast is observed in Tituba's definition of the term witch and the Puritan prayer content of. Tituba explains:

> I noticed that when he said the word, it was marked with disapproval. Why should that be? Why? Isn't the ability to communicate with the invisible world, to keep constant links with the dead, to care for others and heal, a superior gift of nature that inspires respect, admiration, and gratitude? Consequently, shouldn't a witch (if that's what the person who has this gift is to be called) be cherished and revered rather than feared? (Condé 1992: 17)

Tituba is rather intrigued by the strange content of Puritan prayers, 'How the world was created on the seventh day? How our father Adam was turned out of the earthly paradise through the fault of our mother eve?' (Condé 1992: 18). Tituba's narration of issues related to the term witch help reveal the hypocrisy that characterised Puritan New England. Tituba's encounter with Endicott further reveals that her voice that is expressed in the slave society through the marvellous in realism – what Alexis calls a reflection of its conception of the world and of life – is misinterpreted by the hegemonic white culture as evil.

From the perspective of the dominant white society, Mama Yaya's teachings incorporated by Tituba for the survival of her community are 'dealings with Satan' (Condé 1992: 27). Endicott's question to Tituba is revealing, 'Weren't you brought up by a certain Nago witch called Mama Yaya?' But Tituba's answer to her question transgresses the hegemonic authoritative but limited interpretation of her way of life, 'Witch, Witch? She took care of people and cured them' (Condé 1992: 26). Since Mama Yaya's teachings, according to the dominant culture are satanic, Endicott forces John Indian, Tituba's lover, to have her recite the 'I believe in God the father almighty, maker of Heaven and Earth . . .' (Condé 1992: 25). But Tituba's narrative voice counters these claims, 'these words meant nothing to me. They had nothing in common with what Mama Yaya taught me' (Condé 1992: 26). Her counter perspective is concurred by the Indian critic Kum Kum Sangari who proposes that the magical realist attack on dominant culture and its authoritative version of the truth actually provides a new and more 'comprehensive mode of referentiality' (Sangari 1987: 163). By this, she means that it provides a new way of understanding categories without having to rely on absolute truth or fixed definitions. Endicott's version ceases from being an absolute version and Tituba's culture transgresses this limiting definition of her way of life to demonstrate that slaves use their spiritual powers to safe, serve and heal their people.

Even so, the difference between Tituba's counter perspective and hegemonic Puritan's limiting ideologies about satanic dealings is also seen in their respective ways of perceiving and living life. The deconstructive nature of the marvellous realist mode observed in Condé's narrative is seen from the fact that while white hegemonic Puritans create and see Satan everywhere and in everything around them, Tituba hears of Satan's existence only when she starts living within the Puritan environment. When Tituba, the focaliser/character sees the Puritan Minister, Samuel Parris for the first time, her reflection on his looks, behaviour and what he says as a Minister is revealing of the negativity in his inner being. According to Tituba's description, Minister Parris is, 'Tall, dressed in black from head to foot, with chalky white skin. ... Greenish, cold eyes, scheming and wily, creating evil because they saw it everywhere' (Condé 1992: 34). The image that these descriptive words project is that of Satan himself as Tituba further concurs that '[I]t was as if I had come face-to-face with a snake or some other evil, wicked reptile. I was immediately convinced that this Satan we heard so much about must stare in the same way at people he wishes to lead astray' (Condé 1992: 34). The horror is not only felt in the way Parris is described, but also in his cold and penetrating voice, what Tituba describes as 'the ruthless violence of his cutting words, spoken in a monotone' (Condé 1992: 36) as he addresses Tituba and John Indian, 'On your knees, dregs of hell! I am your new Master' (Condé 1992: 36). Parris's hypocrisy as a Puritan minister is revealed through his voice and what he says. He condemns the slaves to otherness as follows, 'I know that the color of your skin is the sign of your damnation, but as long as you are under my roof you will behave as Christians' (Condé 1992: 41). His unruly behaviour as a minister of the church is also revealed in the content of his prayers. Tituba's narrative voice reveals that, 'I couldn't make much out of his speech, except for the oft-heard words sin, evil, Satan, and demon' (Condé 1992: 41).

Moreover, the extent to which the Puritans create evil around them is seen also in their encounter with forces of nature and their reactions to them. These relations of disconnection and fear contrast with Tituba's relationship of understanding, cooperation, connection and negotiation with the natural and spiritual forces. The rats and cats that scamper away because they have been disturbed by the arrival of Minister Parris, his family and his slaves create a revealing effect on the Puritan descendants. The conversation between Abigail; Good wife Parris and Tituba is telling. Abigail asks 'Aunt, it was the devil, wasn't it?' But, as the narrator witnesses, 'Elizabeth Parris's face convulsed. 'Be quiet!' (Condé 1992: 44). Her reaction signifies a demonstration of fear of the Satan that she identifies even in cats and rats that are scampering for safety. Tituba is the only person with a different reasoning there and her own reaction reveals a different understanding of the cosmic. She enquires, 'What will you think up next? It was only an animal that was disturbed by our arrival. Why do you keep talking about the devil? The invisible world around us only torments us if we provoke it' (Condé 1992: 44). But Abigail hisses back, 'Liar... Poor ignorant Negress. The devil torments us all. We are all his victims. We shall all be damned' (Condé 1992: 44). The irony that is embedded in Abigail's statement is quite informing. One can note that Puritans are the victims of Satan because they see Satan everywhere. Tituba on her part is in control of herself and is in a cordial relationship of connection with the forces of nature and the spiritual realm. The narrative transgresses otherness by identifying hegemonic behaviour with what Todorov has described as the fantastic - the hesitation of characters and readers when presented with questions about reality – and once the hesitation is decided, the fantastic ends (Todorov 1975: 33). Tituba's deconstruction of the fantastic projected by the Puritans is a transgression of otherness because the complete narrative is projected from the perspective of the transgressive variant in the marvellous realism. According to Tzevtan Todorov, marvellous realism is different from the fantastic in its function as a transgressive narrative mode because the marvellous elements in realism are understood to constitute in part the reality of the protagonist and are not themselves questionable (Todorov 1975: 33). This means that the marvellous does not only constitute part of reality but it projects a subversive resistance that dismantles and questions the very assumptions of dominant culture and the influential ideas of the Enlightenment.

Furthermore, the relationship of connection between Tituba and the cosmic forces around her is not only seen in her relationship with the spirit beings of her family who act as her consultants, consolers and confidants. It is also demonstrated through the marvellous narrative mode that reveals Tituba's creative hybrid space. Tituba finds home 'on the edge of the River Ormond where nobody ever went because the soil was marshy and not suitable for growing sugarcane' (Condé 1992: 10-11). This deserted island, away from the plantation represents her Eden as she narrates, 'these were the happiest moments of my life' (Condé 1992: 11). Her garden then acts as a place of becoming, a womb, a place of creating life as she focalises on her activities:

I attempted bold hybrids, crossbreeding the *passiflorinde* with the *prune taureau,* the poisonous *pomme cythere,* with the *surrette,* and the *azalea des azalées* with the *persulfereuse.* I devised drugs and portions whose power I strengthened with incantations. (Condé 1992: 11)

Tituba grows and nurtures life, connecting and pulling together the diverse and various ingredients into a coherent narrative. As a gardener, her crossbreeding deconstructs and transgresses the rhetoric of purity and virginity in colonial discourse. She presents a type of hybridity and sophistication that flouts even the structuralist dialectic of colonialism. Tituba herself being a product of crossbreeding, she acts out the creation of hybridity as she plants, sows and adds the spiritual dimension in order to heal. Tituba then exerts her agency in reclaiming her hybridity by refashioning the violence of colonial encounter on her own nonviolent terms by becoming the creator and not the created.

Lastly, situating the novel three centuries prior to its publication, Condé offers a consciously anachronistic response to the elision of women of colour in both first world feminist and third world homogenising cultural national movements. Tituba, a powerful sexual being, accepts and embraces her sexuality and does not allow the strong sexual attraction she feels for men to dilute her active solidarity with women, black as well as white. As she recurrently meditates on her relationship – as a black woman – to feminism, her voice resonates a suppressed black feminist tradition, one that women of African descent are presently reconstituting in theory, fiction, criticism, history, ecology and culture. The result is that Condé refuses not only to rigidly anchor this historical novel to the social issues of Tituba's time, but she also refuses to confine the historical novel within the ideological limits of the era when it unfolds.

Conclusion

I have tried to demonstrate that through the transgressive variant, Condé has conjured an intricate tale that enables Tituba to project her voice through an alternate means of communication – the marvellous realist mode. I have argued that, through this mode, Condé offers her character, Tituba, the possibility of filling the void of history with a presence and an active and constitutive voice. Through the narrative process, Condé and Tituba transgress all the racist and misogynist misconceptions that have othered them, their gender and their race. Condé has not only freed the subject Tituba, a black, and female, slave and witch, but she has also allowed her story of freedom to transgress various episodes of historical memory. I have presented a strong sense of solidarity between Tituba (the narrator/focaliser and reflector/character) and Condé, the writer. Condé's historical novel, furnishes Tituba with a social consciousness as contemporary as the motivating impulse behind the novel. This motivating impulse is Condé's drive to retrieve fragments of an intentionally ignored history and reshape them into a coherent, meaningful story. Condé's novel is therefore a revisionist story taking historical aspects and re-presenting them from a different perspective. I have concluded that Condé's imagination sees beyond the tragedy of circumstances to an investigation of the complex process of survival and construction of the self/space where Condé does not only recuperate the lost history and lost identities, but uses the lost history to negotiate the present, the self/space and opens the future to new directions.

Bibliography

Alexis, J. S., (2011). Of the Marvellous Realism of the Haitians. In *The Post-Colonial Studies Reader*. London and New York: Routledge, pp. 104-149.

Ashcroft, B., Griffiths, G. & Tiffin, H., (2011). *The Post-Colonial Studies Reader*. London and New York: Routledge.

Barry, P., (1995). *Beginning Theory: An Introduction to Literary and Cultural Theory*. Manchester: Manchester University Press.

Bowers, M. A., (2004). *Magic (al) Realism: The New Critical Idiom*.

London and New York: Routledge.

Braithwaite, E. K., (1976). Caribbean Man in Space and Time. In *Carijesta Forum: An Anthology of 20 Caribbean Voices*. Kingston, Jamaica: *Carifesta* pp. 199-208.

Brennan, T., (1989). *Salman Rushdie and the Third World: Myths of the Nation*. Houndmills, Basingstoke: Macmillan.

Condé, M., (1992). *I, Tituba, Black Witch of Salem*. Charlottesville: University Press of Virginia.

Connell, L., (1998). Discarding Magic Realism: Modernism, Anthropology, and Critical Practice. *ARIEL: A Review of International English Literature* , 29(2), pp. 95-110.

Cooper, B., (1998). *Magical Realism in West African Fiction: Seeing with Third Eye*. London and New York: Routledge.

Dash, M. J., (2011). Marvellous Realism: The Way Out of Negritude. In *The Post-Colonial Studies Reader*. London and New York: Routledge, pp. 150-151.

Faris, W. B., (2004). *Ordinary Enchantments. Magical Realism and the Remystification of Narrative*. Nashville: Vanderbilt University Press.

Fraile-Marcos, A. M., (2014). M/Othering Black Female Subjectivity across the Black Atlantic in the Novels of Maryse Condé, Edwidge *Danticat* and Elizabeth Nunez. In *Diasporic women's writing of the Black Atlantic: (En) gendering literature and performance.* pp.183-201.

Franco, J., (2002). *The Decline and Fall of the Lettered City*. Cambridge: Harvard University Press.

Genette, G., (1980). *Narrative Discourse*. Oxford: Blackwell.

Gilroy, P., (1993). *The Black Atlantic: Modernity and Double Consciousness*. Harvard: Harvard University Press.

Glissant, E., (1996). *Caribbean Discourse*. Trans. Dash, J.M. Charlottesville, Virginia: Virginia University Press.

Harris, W., (1973). *Tradition, The Writer and Society*. London: New Beacon.

hooks, b., (1998). Postmodern Blackness. In: *contemporary Literary Criticism: Literary and Cultural Studies*. New York: Longman, pp.

130-135.

Larrier, R. B., (2000). *Francophone Women Writers of Africa and the Caribbean*. Florida: University Press of Florida.

Orlando, V. K., (1996). *Beyond Postcolonial Discourse: New Problematics of Feminine Identity in Contemporary Francophone Literature*. Michigan: Ann Arbor.

Rimmon-Kenan, S., (2005). *Narrative Fiction: Contemporary Poetics*. London and New York: Routledge.

Sangari, K. K., (1987). The Politics of the Possible. *Cultural Critique*, Volume 7, pp. 157-186.

Shelton, M.-D., (1994). A New Cry: From the 1960s to the 1980s. In *A History of Literature in the Caribbean: Hispanic and Francophone Regions*. Philadelphia: John Benjamin Publishing Com, pp. 428-433.

Stanzel, F. K., (1971). *Narrative Situations in the Novel*. Bloomington: Indiana University Press.

Todorov, T., (1975). *The Fantastic: A Structural Approach to a Literary Genre*. New York: Cornell University Press.

Walcott, D., (1974). The Muse of History: An -Essay. *In Massa Dead? Black Moods in the Caribbean*. New York: Anchor Books, 1-27.

Walcott, D., (1986). *The Sea is History, Collected Poems: 1948 - 1984*. New York: Noonday Press.

Chapter Four

Signature and the Self-Other Dialectic in the Poetry of Robert Graves

Peter Foinjong Awoh

Introduction

This chapter focuses on Robert Graves's signature and its impact on the dialectical relationship between the self and the other. It aims at discussing the significance of signature, vis-à-vis the construction of self and social identities in Graves's poetry. To achieve this objective, an attempt will be made, among other things, to identify the poet's attitude towards his name and to foreground the various dimensions of the self-other dialectic that impacts on individual and social responsibility in Graves's poetry.

The desire to investigate the issues at stake in this chapter was prompted by the impact that the self-other dialectic has had, and continues to have, on the building of self and social identities. Incidentally, Graves's poetry is replete with such complexities as evidenced by his poetic personae who are caught between either acceptance or denial of the self or the other. Thus, the central argument in this chapter revolves around the contention that signature is pivotal in shaping individual, social and textual borders in Graves's poetry. Theoretically, the chapter subscribes to Jacques Derrida's concept of signature in textual analysis. Nonetheless, psychoanalytic theories will be explored from time to time to assess the self-other dialectic.

Before delving into analysis, it is important to explain and contextualise the main concepts ('signature' and the 'self-other dialectic') within the framework of this chapter. To begin with, signature is used as a theoretical concept based on Derrida's views, which were inspired by the act of emblazoning in a coat of arms. According to Robert Scholes, Nancy Comley and Gregory Ulmer in *Textbook: An Introduction to Literary Language,* signature, from Derrida's perspective is the experiment of investigating 'the identity not of our person but of our name.' The above writers further postulate that:

> By calling his experiment 'signature', Derrida reminds us of an ancient belief in the similarity or correspondence between the world outside and the interior life of a person that is the link between the macro and micro worlds. The link joining one's biological existence to one's cultural experience is language, with one's proper name bridging the dimension of reality. The letters of the proper name constitute a 'key' in which one's life is played out. (Scholes, Comley and Ulmer 1995: 240)

In the above light, like designers who use pun to emblazon identity in the 'abyss' (centre) of a coat-of-arms, writers translate their identities into their artistic works by punning with their names. Thus, in order to investigate how Graves's signature reveals the poet's self in some selected poems, I will explore some of the models of signature analysis that Derrida proposed. Scholes, Comely and Ulmer point out that these models include: The Register of Style which refers to 'the inimitable idiom of an artist's work' that a familiar reader can recognise without the proper name. Besides, there is the Register of Emblazoning -- the 'heraldic' placement of a name in the depths of a text, a situation in which the writer's name functions as 'the seed out of which the text has grown by a process of metaphorical or intertextual development' (Scholes, Comley and Ulmer 1995: 256-257).

With regard to the self-other binary, irrespective of what the notion means elsewhere (in postcolonialism for example), in this chapter, it will be used interchangeably with the term split personality. Therefore, arguments in this perspective are guided by Derrida's concept of invention which is couched in self and signature invention. In the philosopher's words, the other is: 'The invention that invents *us*. For the other is always another origin of the world and *we are to be invented*. ... The coming of invention cannot make itself foreign to the repetition and memory. For the other is not the new. But its coming extends beyond this past present that once was able to construct' (Gerhard 2010: *xxxv*). The above excerpt presupposes that the self and the other are not mutually exclusive but rather liaised in a more or less dialectical relationship. Consequently, the term 'dialectic' is applied from a Hegelian perspective to mean that 'apparent contradictions (... thesis and antithesis) are seen to be part of a higher truth (synthesis)' (The *Oxford Dictionary of English*). For the purpose of convenience, the chapter is subdivided into three parts as evidenced by the following analyses.

Signature and Social Frontiers: Intertextual Perspectives

The act of naming pre-dates written history. Nowadays, naming is an indispensable legal component of human culture worldwide. Besides legal requirements, a name goes beyond the limits of mere personal identification (signature) and becomes an embodiment of family and communal values. The importance of names has always preoccupied writers in different generations. William Shakespeare's *Romeo and Julliet* and Oscar Wilde's *The Importance of Being Earnest* are replete with name related issues. They will provide textual bases for the re-interpretation of Graves's name-poems – 'My Name and I', 'Name' and 'Song: John True Love'.

Inasmuch as the above poems ascertain the intertextual dimension of Graves's poetry, they equally reveal the poet's anxieties and aspirations vis-à-vis self and social spheres. His signature subtly reveals the conflicting relationship between a name and its bearer on one hand and with the society on the other hand. Graves projects such conflict in the poem entitled 'My Name and I', where he assesses the need of identifying with his name, imposed on him by his family and the society. While acknowledging the possibility of total rejection (of self), Graves maintains that the name is not a 'true ambassador' of the self; it is simply a social construct. To him, bearing a name is a mere legal exercise. As he puts it, 'The impartial law enrolled a name / for my especial use'. But, though he has exclusive rights to the name, Graves does not care whether he 'puffed it into fame/or sank it in abuse' (Graves 2003: 432). While the law subjects everybody to identify with a name, in the family cycles, a name is believed to relate a person to his /her ancestors. As a result, Graves maintains that:

> Robert was what my parents guessed
> When first they peered at me,
> And Graves an honourable bequest
> With Georgian silver and the rest,
> From my male ancestry. (Graves 2003: 433)

The poet seems to question the importance expected to be attached to something which his parents merely 'guessed' could be his name. From a psychological view, Graves is right to say his parents guessed. In *The Study of Names: A Guide to the Principles and Topics*. Frank Nuessel corroborates that:

> Most names are carefully considered so that exactly the right name is bestowed. In the case of personal names, the surname is generally a predetermined part of an individual's name. The so-called Christian or given name (a first or middle name), however, is chosen by the parents through various procedures. In this regard... a variety of influences that operate in the naming of a child...include such social influences as the religion and race of the parents. There are a number of conventions that function in the naming of a child. (Nuessel 1992: 4)

The conventions implied here are the same that guided Graves's parent to bestow their family name on their son. Therefore, the fear of identifying with a name 'forced' on him, is a microcosm of the fear he has for the world of his parents, a patriarchal world that plunged humanity into a horrendous manslaughter. Moreover, by referring to the name, Graves, as 'an honourable bequest/With Georgian silver and the rest', the speaker automatically links the poet to Georgianism, a movement that exhibited strong affinities with pastoral English landscapes. Furthermore, those who bestowed the name on Graves attached strings to it; they expect from the bearer a pattern of behaviour which the latter thinks, infringes into the freedoms of his inner self:

They taught me:

'You are Robert Graves
(Which you must learn to spell)
But see that Robert Graves behaves,
Exemplarily well'. (Graves 2003: 433)

Attempts at forcing a behavioural pattern on Graves, which is concordant with family dignity is a wasted effort because Graves's 'other' will not identify with the human shape that bears the name. The conflict between the selves comes into focus as Graves argues that 'my I was always I, / Illegal and unknown, / With nothing to arrest it by' (Graves 2003: 433). The fact that Graves's 'I' is 'illegal' and 'unknown' with nothing to arrest it brings to mind Freud's idea of the id, the insatiable uncivilized force behind human desires. If the other is likened to the id, then the name and the self, its bearer, are the equivalence of the superego. The name to which the body is attached in 'My Name and I is not totally denounced. Graves admits:

I cannot well repudiate
This noun, this natal star,
This gentlemanly self, this mate
So kindly forced on me by fate,
Time and the registrar. (Graves 2003: 433)

Expressions such a 'natal star', 'gentlemanly self', 'mate' and 'kindly forced' reveal the poet's mild tone, which, in turn, implies recognition of the name as part of his being. Though the name is forced on Graves by 'fate', 'time' and 'the registrar', he undermines the act of forcing by stating that it is 'kindly forced'.

The speaker's resolve not to 'repudiate' his name provides the basis to read the poem from a Bloomian critical point of view as a clinammen of Juliet's speech and Romeo's asides in Shakespeare's *Romeo and Juliet*. From an inter-textual dimension, the above examples go beyond the frontiers of Graves's poetics. In 'Meditation upon Priority', Harold Bloom underscores the importance of *Clinamen* - The poetic misreading or misprision which means a 'swerve' of the atoms so as to make change possible in the universe. A poet, he maintains, swerves from his precursor by reading the former's text as if to execute a clinamen in relation to it. This implies that the precursor text did not take the necessary swerve that the present one has taken. In Shakespeare's text, Juliet urges Romeo to repudiate his name thus:

O Romeo Romeo! Wherefor art thou Romeo?
Deny thy father and refuse thy name
…Tis but thy name that is my enemy
Thou art thyself and though not a Montague
…O, be some other name!
What's in a name?
…Romeo, doff thy name and for thy name which is no part of thee
Take all myself. (Shakespeare 1936: Act II.2)

Juliet's words ascertain the relationship between a name and its bearer. Like Graves's poem, her lament indicates that a name carries with it the whole history of one's ancestry. Consequently, the bearer is caught in the self-other polemic. This justifies why Romeo regrets his inability to reinvent himself and laments the verity of bearing such a name:

> By a name
> I know not how to tell thee who I am.
> My name dear saint is hateful to myself
> Because it is an enemy to thee.
> Had I it written I would tear the word. (Shakespeare 1936: Act II.2)

Unlike the speaker in Graves's poem, who detests his name, yet is ready to bear it, Shakespeare's hero is overwhelmed by a wistful desire to denounce his. In this light, Graves, though probably rewriting Shakespeare, provides a swerve through his persona's resolute strife for a harmonious relationship with his name which he refers to as his 'natal star'.

The metaphoric allusion discernible in the 'natal star' throws more light on the importance of the name. It illuminates the bearer in the same way that the star described in Matthew 2: 9-10 shone and led the wise men from the East to Bethlehem where the new-born Jesus lay. Apart from the biblical connotation, the star is an archetypal image of hope. Thus, by referring to the name as a natal star, the poet suggests that there is hope in a name. Astrologically, the star under which a person is born is believed to exercise some influence on the person's behaviour. Therefore, the comparison of his name to his star of birth implies that the name controls his behaviour. It can equally be said that the poet's compromise falls in line with what Tim Valentine, Tim Brennen and Serge Brdart term the name letter effect. They hold that:

> The mere ownership of a name (the most unique attribute of the self,...) enhances the attractiveness of the letters included in that name..., the name letter effect is due to the fact that ...first and family names are typically the very first items that children can read and write. This achievement in valued abilities like reading and writing would be accompanied by such an intense positive mastery effect that letters associated with this experience keep an enhanced attractiveness

throughout life. (Valentine, Brennen and Brdart 1996: 8-9)

Conscious that a name influences one's way of life, Graves concedes that his name and the self that bears it function only as an 'ambassador,' whose role is merely to 'fetch me home my beer and bread (Graves 2003: 433). Through the image of ambassador, Graves points out the limits of the name and the self in relation to other. The other is like a state, whose policies are carried out by the ambassador - the self. 'Beer' and 'bread' symbolize desires of thirst and hunger respectively, which in Freudian thinking are satisfied by the ego. Towards the end of the poem, Graves dissociates himself from the exemplary behaviour attached to a name and from the self that bears it in these words:

> Yet, understand, I am not he
> Either in mind or in limb
> My name will take less thought for me
> In words of men I cannot see. (Graves 2003: 433)

This declaration does not only highlight the conflict between the self and the other, or the superiority of the other to the self. It is also a complete rejection of the societal constraints that limit the free functioning of man. Graves, by rejecting the imposition of some ways of life on him because of his name, shares the view of his contemporary, A.E. Housman, expressed in the poem 'The Laws of God, the Laws of Man'. Housman challenges God and man to make laws for themselves and not for him because his ways are not the same as theirs. This implies that the desire to identify with the other or the weird, is in connection with the quest for absolute freedom. The body cannot enjoy such freedom because it is scrutinized by various ethical and moral codes. Although Graves ends up accepting his name in 'My Name and I', in the poem 'Name', he cautions parents to be careful when choosing a name for the offspring at birth:

> Be warned by one who loves you

> Never to name your fist born
> Until you know the father
> And: is it girl or boy
>
> ...
>
> Just before delivery
> Prepare for a soft wisper
> As it reveals its name. (Graves 2003: 711)

Graves's opinion on naming expressed in the above poem is concordant with Nuessel's idea that 'Most names are carefully considered so that exactly the right name is bestowed. In the case of personal names, the surname is generally a predetermined part of an individual's name. The so-called Christian or given name (a first or middle name), however, is chosen by the parents through various procedures' (Nuessel 1992: 4).

In another poem entitled 'Song: John True Love,' Graves further concedes that though names reflect their bearers, there are always exceptions:

> The surnames our parents had
>   Are seldom a close fit
> There's Matthew Good who's truly bad
>   And Dicky Dull's a wit
>
> There's colonel Staid who's far from staid
>   ...And there's Parson Bold who's much afraid
> Of bulglars in the night. (Graves 2003: 830)

In the light of the above situation, the speaker confesses that though he is called John Truelove, all maidens should be careful not to put all trust in him because 'I shall keep true to none of you/Unless the worst befall' (Graves 2003: 830). The speaker's words translate the poet's signature in the social sphere. It is worth noting that Graves's matrimonial life was rocked by a series of infidelity scandals. Moreover, he kept a good number of 'maidens'-concubines-whom he called muses.

Graves's 'The Undead' also manifests his transgression of intertextual frontiers. In the poem, he advocates recognition and identification with the other. Through words of advice to a young man, the speaker calls on the young man to always anticipate meeting his alter ego:

> For one day as you choose an unfamiliar side-street
> Keeping both eyes open, alert, not apprehensive,
> You shall suddenly (this is a promise) come to a brief halt:
> For striding towards you, on the same sidewalk will appear
> A young man with a halo of life around his head,
> Will catch you reassuringly by both hands. (Graves 2003: 557)

The action of the young man (the other), who strides towards the child and catches him reassuringly with both hands is reminiscent to that which prevails in Nathaniel Hawthorn's *Young Goodman Brown*. In the forest, young Goodman Brown encounters his alter ego in the image of an elderly man 'apparently in the same rank of life as Goodman Brown and bearing a considerable resemblance with him' (Hawthorne 1995: 732). As young Goodman Brown approaches, the man arises and walks 'onward, side by side with him' (Hawthorne 1995: 731). At the end of Graves's poem, the poet urges the child to accept the companionship of his other, just as Young Goodman Brown does in Hawthorn's story. He tells the child to 'Nod (his) accent, go with him, and do not even return to pack' (Graves 2003: 558). Through the image of the halo, Graves suggests that the alter ego is pure and free from the restraints of its human other. This accounts for Graves's advice to the child to be self-conscious so as to be able to recognize his other self and subsequently identify with it. Literally, a halo is a 'circle of light round the sun or moon, caused by refraction'. Thus, the young man with a halo round the head is, therefore, a refracted image of the child.

The Self-Other Dialectic as a Mytho-Poetic Paradigm of Signature

Graves is not a pioneer writer to grapple with the complex issue of the self and the other. However, his preoccupation with the self is not unconnected to the mytho-poetic dimension of his poetry. Thus, it falls within the framework of signature in the register of style. To approach his poems from this angle, one needs to understand the idea behind the poet's perception of the above dialectic. While clarifying the idea of the self in *The White Goddess: A Historical Grammar of Poetic Myth*, Graves alludes to an antique story of the 'God of Waxing Year' and his 'losing battle with the God of the Waning year for the love of the capricious and all powerful threefold Goddess, the mother, bride and layer-out' (Graves nd: 24). The poet, Graves explains:

> Identifies himself and his Muse with the Goddess; the rival is his blood-brother, his other self, his weird. All true poetry...celebrates some incident or scene in this ancient story and the three main characters are so much a part of our radical inheritance that they donot only assert themselves in poetry but recur on occasions of emotional stress in the form of dreams, paranoiac visions and delusion. The weird, or rival often appears in the nightmare as tall, lean, dark faced bed-side spectre, or prince of the air who tries to drag the dreamer out of the window so that he looks back and sees his body still lying rigid in bed, but he takes other countless Malevolent or diabolic or serpent-like forms. (Graves nd: 24)

Graves's explanation foreshadows the rivalry between the selves and justifies the existence of hallucinatory and phantasmagoric atmospheres that pervade some of his poems. Nonetheless, the poet's attitude towards the idea of the selves is equally compromising. Therefore, the transgression of individual frontiers becomes problematic to the personae who are caught in the self-other dialectic in some of Graves's poems. They see the other as free from societal restrictions unlike the body, which is subjected to the scrutiny of society or superego. Yet, the poet believes that for a proper harmonious life, one has to come to terms with the selves.

In the poem 'The Reader Over my Shoulder,' the conflict between the selves is expressed through the speaker's angry words addressed to the other. The speaker, probably the poet, detests the professed authority of the other. Confusion between the selves is detectable in stanza two as the other wrongly claims the role of representing or acting on behalf of the self:

> All the saying of things against myself
> And for myself I have well done myself
> What now old enemy shall you do
> But quote and underline, trusting yourself
> Against me as ambassador of myself
> In damn confusion of myself and you. (Graves 2003: 314)

The preponderant use of pronouns such as 'I', 'me' and 'myself', related to the first person singular illustrates the persona's preference for the self at the detriment of the 'human shape'. The persona's position is strengthened by the reference to the other as 'you', 'yourself' and 'old enemy'. Implied in the term 'old enemy', is the recognition of long term rivalry between the self and the other. Equally, there is a problem of authenticity as the two selves dispute over representation. The other, the persona claims, has forcefully and wrongfully assumed the role of 'ambassador', thus, causing confusion. Stanza three captures the persona's dissatisfaction with the long-lasting infringement into the liberties of the self and the subsequent denouncement of the other which is responsible for the acts against the self:

> For you in strutting, you in sycophancy,

Have played too long this other self of me
Doubling the part of judge and patron
With that of creaking grind-stone to my wit.
Know me, have done: I am a proud spirit
And you for ever clay. Have done! (Graves 2003: 314)

Hatred of the other stems from its pride and self-flattering since for long it has doubled as 'judge' and 'patron'. The images of 'judge' and 'patron', which describe the other, aptly suit the detested functions that the other assumes. As judge, it limits the desired freedom of the self. As patron, it claims ownership of the self, thereby hampering the wish of the self to be an ambassador of itself. Similarly, the image of a 'creaking grinding-stone' effectively re-echoes the disrupting role of the other, earlier highlighted in the opening stanza. The harsh tone of the last two lines of stanza three communicates Graves's disavowal of the other in favour of the self. The self-obliges the other to accept its superiority. It commands 'Know me, have done: I am a proud spirit / And you for ever clay. Have done' (Graves 2003: 314)! Through the use of contrast, discernible in the dichotomy between 'clay' and 'spirit', Graves reveals that he prefers the self. 'Clay' suggests inactivity and death; 'spirit' associates the self with life and immortality. This brings to mind the Christian belief that after death, 'the dust [body] returns to the ground it came from, and the spirit returns to God who gave it' (Ecclesiastes 12:7). Pride can actually be discerned in the commanding words of the self. Graves uses short statements such as 'Know me' and 'Have done!' to emphasise the urgency with which the spirit dismisses its rival, the body.

Graves's reconciliatory position clearly manifests itself in his poem 'Address to Self' in which he reiterates the need for perfect peaceful coexistence of the various opposing constituents of a living being. The poet writes:

Our loves are cloaked, our times are variable,

> We keep our rooms and meet only at table.
>
> But come dear self, agree that you and I
> Shall henceforth court each other's company
>
> And bed in peace together now and fall
> With open heart and mind, both alike bent
>
> On a just verdict, not on argument,
> And hide no private longings, each from each,
>
> And wear one livery and employ one speck.
> I worked against me with folly and neglect,
>
> Making a pact with flesh, the alien one:
> Which brought me into strange confusion
>
> For as mere flesh I spurned you, slow to see
> This was to acknowledge flesh as part of me. (Graves 2003: 823)

The persona reminds his interlocutor (his other) that for long they have lived in separate rooms. The image of the rooms emphasizes the difference between the two. Therefore, the walls of these rooms need to be brought down so that they reunite. In a suppliant tone, which reflects the poet's quest for self-discovery, the persona pleads with his other to promise that henceforth, they shall 'court each other's company' and behave as natural brothers and sisters. As if to show the openness of his 'heart and mind', the persona apologizes that he wronged his other and suffered from the latter's 'neglect'. The persona, towards the end of the poem, realizes that by 'making a pact with flesh: the alien one', he plunges himself into confusion and loses the love of his other. Nonetheless, this is justifiable, for it is to acknowledge flesh as part of the persona's whole being. The persona's excuse at the end of the poem carries persuasive undertones. It is an appeal to the weird, to accept the persona both as flesh and spirit. This appeal bears Graves's message of coexistence of the selves. Harmony is emphasized through the eight stanzas, each made up of a rhyming couplet. The progressive rhyme – aa bb cc dd ee ff gg hh – captures the poet's earnestness for self-redemption. Meantime, the repetition of 'and' and 'one' in stanza five reaffirms the poet's commitment in achieving harmony.

Graves's plea for harmony teaches the reader that knowing a person or knowing one's self entails having knowledge of the person's two selves. However, to Devindra Kohli, the conflict of the selves in the poem has a different connotation. He argues that 'the weird who haunts the poet lover as his co-walker' is not only the bringer of conflict but also the 'bringer of second sight which alone makes it possible for the poet to achieve a sense of integration with the Muse' (Kohli 1999: 77).

Thus, Graves's invention of the self in the image of the co-walker as well as through his poetic myth reinforces the poet's ability to transgress intra-personal as well as artistic frontiers. The mythopoetic dimension of Graves's signature as discussed in this section has a stylistic orientation. The next section investigates the poet's signature in relation to some thematic concerns.

What is in a Name?: 'Robert', 'Graves' and the Fame-Nature Connection

This part illustrates how the poet's name becomes the 'key' from which his life is played out in the work. Here, two thematic domains—fame and nature—that relate to his name, respectively, are considered. (N.B.—Robert means Brilliant Fame and Graves, dweller in/or near a grove).

To begin with fame, Graves's response to war in some selected poems reveal undertones of heroism which fall in line with the idea of 'puffing the name in fame' expressed in 'My name And I' In 'The Next War' such a quest is evidenced by the loyalty and truthfulness of soldiers. Thus, the speaker cautions the soldiers to act instantaneously in any eventuality of war:

> From that same hour by fate you're bound
> As champions of this stony ground
> Loyal and true in everything,
> To serve your army and your King.
> Prepared to starve and sweat and die
> Under some fierce foreign sky
> If only to keep safe those joys
> That belong to British boys
> To keep young Prussians from the soft
> Scented hay of father's loft.
> And stop young Slaves from cutting bows
> And bending spears from Welsh hedgerows. (Graves 2003: 47)

Besides the fact that soldiers are bound to be true to one another because fate has pushed them towards a common enemy, the poet expresses a high spirit of patriotism. In serving their army and their king, the soldiers are advised to be 'prepared to starve and sweat and die/ Under some fierce foreign sky' so as to preserve the dignity of fatherland. The repetitive use of 'and' in the above lines shows the assiduous nature of the soldiers, task and the importance of sacrificing one's life for one's fatherland. By emphasizing that soldiers must sacrifice themselves for the defence of King and country, Graves sounds like Rupert Brooke in the poem 'The Soldier', where the soldier declares his desire to die in a foreign land for England's sake. Graves's attitude is made more glaring by the sentimental feeling, evoked by the picture of pastoral English surroundings at the end of the poem. The 'soft scented hay of father's loft' and the 'Welsh hedgerows' revive sweet memories of England, a characteristic common with the Georgian poets.

As if in response to the fact that there is 'breath in dead men and beauty in death', a young soldier in the poem 'Big Words' expresses the desire to fight regardless of the threat of death at his tender age. He boasts:

> I've whined of coming death, but now no more
> It's weak and most ungracious, for say I
> Though still a boy if years are counted, why!
> I lived those years from roof to cellar-floor,
> And fell life grey beards touching their fourscore
> Ready so soon as the need comes to die:
> And I am satisfied. (Graves 2003: 17)

Rather than continue to complain about impending death, the persona braces himself for war because 'it's weak and most ungracious' to sit back either complaining or being afraid. In a normal situation, those expected to die are the elderly, that is, those with 'grey beards' or those who have attained an age of 'fourscore', but the speaker, still a boy, accepts his fated way by stating that he is satisfied. Through the persona's acceptance of his fate, Graves insinuates that death should be accepted, no matter how it comes. This implies that during war, fear should be overcome and fighting should be exercised. War equally serves as a springboard for the achievement of many glories, which are often elusive at peacetime. The persona acknowledges that war helps in the following achievements:

> For winning confidence in those quiet days
> Of peace, poised sickly on the precipice side
> Of Lliwedd crag by Snowdon, and in war
> Finding it firmlier with me than before;
> Winning a faith in the wisdom of God's ways
> That once I lost, finding it justified
> Even in this chaos, wining love that stays
> And warms the heart like wine at Easter-tide. (Graves 2003: 17-18)

Objectives like winning 'confidence', 'faith', 'wisdom', and true 'love', are attainable mostly when peace is at stake. The 'faith' mentioned in the poem may not necessarily refer to religious faith, it is possibly faith in one's self, which is linked to the 'confidence' that is mentioned in the first line of the above quotation. The intensity of the love experienced during war is emphasized by the qualities of wine, to which love is compared. It is sweet and heart- warming.

Like the Robert—fame connotation, the Graves—nature link cannot be minimized. Graves indulges in the writing of poetry with a romantic touch. The relationship between man and nature preoccupies Graves as it did the romantics. However, before delving into the link between Graves's poetry and nature, it is worth remarking that his poetic debut was with the Georgian movement which extended the romantic tradition of revering nature. Like the poetry of his fellow Georgians, that of Graves equally expresses a strong presence of nature. His love for nature can be viewed as signature considering that it incarnates elements of the poet's obedience to the White Goddess, who is birth, death and rejuvenation. Beyond that, the link is apparent in the meaning of the name 'Graves' which is 'dweller in/or around a grove'. Therefore, it is not coincidental that the bearer of such a name not only wrote nature poetry, but consciously withdrew from the rustles and bustles of urban life in England to the natural calmness of a pastoral habitat, Deya-Marlloca in Spain. His poems discussed below celebrate the harmony between man and nature and by extension, imply that in nature the selves find expression.

In 'Sea-side', for instance, a poem which captures the harmony between man and nature, Graves points out that nature is wild and confusing, but in this wildness and confusion man finds comfort:

> Into a gentle wildness and confusion,
> Of here and there, one and everyone,
> Of windy sandhills by an unkempt sea,
> Came two and two in search of symmetry,
> Found symmetry of two in sea and sand,

In left foot, right foot, left hand, right hand. (Graves 2003: 308)

The strength of Graves's argument lies in his apt choice of the sea as suitable area that can act as a sanctuary for 'two and two in search of symmetry'. As an archetypal symbol, the sea suggests, rebirth or regeneration. Thus, it has refreshing potentials for lovers. Moreover, the poet considers the close relationship between 'sea and sand' like the complementariness of 'left foot, right foot' and 'left hand, right hands, as a lesson for lovers. As Wordsworth urges man in 'The Tables Turned' to 'come forth into the light of things/let nature be [his] teacher', Graves too believes that the lovers can learn from nature (Wordsworth 1988: 580).

The connection with romanticism opens another avenue from which Graves's signature (Register of Style) transcends textual borders. Typical of romantic poets, the glorification of nature to Graves seems to be an obligation, which failure to perform is tantamount to punishment from the Goddess. He believes that Socrates was punished with a bad wife because he discarded nature, on the pretext that it had nothing to teach him. Graves's poem, 'The Tyranny of Books' is a lucid illustration of his affiliation with nature and the repercussions of failing to sing nature's praises. Conscious of this duty, the poet regrets that for quite some time, he has not played his role:

Spring passes, Summer's young,
Yet mute has been my tongue.
This is the seventh week
I have not sung.
And now I hear the verdant hillside speak
Chiding me for this wrong
That I have celebrated not in song
The new come colour of her forded cheek. (Graves 2003: 737)

To underscore the importance of nature, Graves bestows the

human ability of speaking on the hillside, which chides him for failure to glorify it. Moreover, he equates the hillside to a female when he uses the third person feminine pronoun 'her'. This suggests beauty and evokes the poet's association of the Goddess with nature. As the title suggests, books seem to play a tyrannical role because they absorb the poet's attention to the point where he fails in his obligation to nature. The poet admits that he has not been able to sing 'for by [his] elbow lies a pile / Of books, of stern insistent book' (Graves 2003: 737). To his dismay, these books are 'crammed full of knowledge' and the more he strives to acquire the knowledge, the more he is denied the opportunity to put his 'pen over the page to speed' (Graves 2003: 737) Confinement on books also deprives the poet of freedom. He regrets that 'outside, the rooks / Circle in air and mate and feed / But I must read and read' (Graves 2003: 738). Graves's dissatisfaction with books stems from the inelasticity of studying. He laments that books are so crammed with knowledge that 'Though it looks/ As if I'd finish in a little while /Still grows the pile' (Graves 2003: 737). In the precursor poem by William Wordsworth entitled, 'The Tables Turned', the speaker shares a similar view:

> Books! Tis dull and endless strife:
> Come hear the woodland Linnet,
> How sweet his music: On my life
> There's more of wisdom in it.
> And hark! How blithe the throstle sings!
> He too is no mean preacher:
> Come forth into the light of things.
> Let nature be your teacher. (Wordsworth 1988: 580)

The poem captures Wordsworth's scepticism for books. To Wordsworth as to Graves, concentration on books removes man from the refreshing nature thereby making him 'grow double'. For this reason, Wordsworth decried studying and advocated identification with nature because nature too teaches. Graves's swerved is evidenced by the link between his name and the theme of nature.

The above connection between the poet's names and some of his thematic concerns brings to mind some historical personalities whose names coincided with their achievements in related fields. Among others, Roback in *Destiny in Names* cites the following: General Marshall, in the US army, whose name coincides with the European rank of Chief Marshal; President Eisenhower (hewer of iron) who metaphorically hewed the Axis iron by leading the Allied forces that defeated Germany in Europe. In addition, there is also Sir Russell Brain who became one of the most eminent authorities in the nervous system, especially the brain (Scholes, Comley and Ulmer 1995: 242-44). Like the aforementioned historical figures, Graves's signature as revealed by the themes of fame and nature supersedes the realms of textual coincidences to the mystery of destiny/fate.

Conclusion

So far, the above analyses have proven that conflict exists between the selves and that though Graves professes harmony between the selves, he seemingly identifies more with his weird (?). But, it is worth remarking that the poet's confusion results from his attempt at self-discovery, a move which Alexander Pope urges man to take in the Second Epistle of 'An Essay on Man' when he says 'know then thyself…' (Pope 1987: 1138). Only self-knowledge can liberate man from the confusion, which Pope says makes man 'hangs between; in doubt to acts, or rest, / In doubt to deem himself a God, or a beast / In doubt his mind or body to prefer'. Such a situation, he notes, is what makes man the 'riddle of the world' (Pope 1987: 1138).

The poet's identification with the other has been perceived as an attempt to aspire for freedom since unlike the body, the other is free from societal conventions. The essence of portraying the split-personality is to demonstrate that man has to recognise his dual nature so as to achieve self and social harmony. The poet's conciliatory position is in line with Ralph Ellison (1964)'s assertion in *Hidden Name and Complex Fate* that we have to learn to wear our names within all the noise and confusion of the environment in which we find ourselves, make them the centre of all associations with the world. On a similar note, Graves kind of incorporates Buddhist spiritual wisdom of the self that 'One's self conquered is more than a thousand soldiers conquered in war' (*The Dhamapada*). Finally, the poet's attempt to synthesise opposites is an indication that one must, first of all, come to terms with the self before transgressing social and global frontiers.

Bibliography

Abram, M. H., (1981). *A Glossary of literary Terms*. 4 ed. New York: Holt Rinehart and Winston.

Brittan, S.,(1999). Graves and the Mythology of Desire. In: *New Perspectives on Robert Graves*. London: Associated University Press, pp. 84-93.

Caesar, A., (1993). Introduction. In: *Taking it Like a Man: Suffering, Sexuality and the War Poets: Brooke, Sassoon, Owen, Graves*. Manchester: Manchester University Press, pp. 1-43.

Cuddon, J. A., (1991). *A Dictionary of Literary Terms and Literary Theory*. Oxford: Blackwell.

Ellison, R., (1964). Hidden Name and Complex Fate. In: *Shadow and Act*. New York: Random House.

Firla, I., (2005). *Robert Grave: A Critical Biography*. [Online] Available at: www.robertgraves.org/bio/phy.http

Fraser, G., (1997). *Essays on Twentieth Century*. Leicester: Leicester University Press.

Freud, S., (1963). Repression. In: *General Psychology Theory*. New York: The Crowell-Collier Publishing Company, pp. 104-116.

Graves, R., (2003). *The Complete Poems*. London: Penguin.

Graves, R., (n.d). *The White Goddess*. London: Faber and Faber.

Hawthorne, N., (1995). Young Goodman Brown. In: *The Norton Anthology of Short Fiction*. New York: Norton, pp. 731-741.

Kohli, D., (1999). A Measure of Casualness: The Peripatetic in the Poetry of Robert Graves. In: *New Perspective on Robert Graves*. London: Associated University Press, pp. 19-35.

Murfin, R. & Ray, S. M., (1997). *The Bedford Glossary of Critical and Literary Terms*. New York: Bedford Books.

Nuessel, F., (1992). *The Study of Names: A Guide to the Principles and Topics*. Westport: Greenwood Press.

O'Prey, P., (1999). Captain Graves's Postwar Strategies. In: *New Perspectives on Robert Graves*. London: Associated University Presses, pp. 36-45.

Pope, A., (1987). An Essay on Man. In: *The Norton Anthology of English Literature*. New York: Norton, pp. 1130-1138.

Richman, R., (1988). *The Poetry or Robert Graves: The New Criterion*. [Online] Available at:
www.newcriterion.com/archive/07/oct/88/richman.htm
[Accessed 2005].

Richter, G., (2010). *Copy, Archive, Signature: A Conversation on Photography*. Stanford: Stanford University Press.

Scholes, R., Comley, N. & Ulmer, G., (1995). *Text Book: An Introduction to Literary Language*. Bedford: St Martins.

Shakespeare, W., (1936). Romeo and Julliet. In: *The Complete Works of Shakespeare*. New York: Garden City Books, pp. 315-350.

Tim, V., et al, (1991). What's in a Name? Access to Information on Peoples' Names. *European Journal of Cognitive Psychology*, pp. 147-176.

Valentine, T., Brennen, T. & Brdart, S., (1996). *The Cognitive Psychology of Proper Names: On the Importance of Being Ernest*. London and New York: Routledge.

Wilkie, B. & Hurts, J., (1988). *Literature of the Western World*. 2 ed. New York: Macmillan.

Wordsworth, W., (1988). The Tables Turned. In: *Literature of the Western World*. New York: Macmillan, p. 580.

Chapter Five

Globalization, Information Communication Technologies and African Narratives: Reading Chimamanda Ngozi Adichie's *The Thing Around Your Neck* and *Americanah*

Eunice Ngongkum

Introduction

As products of the continent's historical evolution, African cultural artefacts have frequently responded to the socio-historical changes that have informed the continent over time. The contact with the western world at different historical stages like the slave trade, colonial and post-colonial periods, has been defining in momentous ways. Artists of different ages and ideological formation have reacted to the momentum of change initiated by these encounters, critically portraying how they have impacted individuals and communities as a whole. As far as African literature, which is the template here, is concerned, Simon Gikandi states that 'it is about real and familiar worlds of culture and human experience of politics and economics…rerouted through a language and structure at odds with the history or geography books'(Gikandi 2001: 4). Gikandi's observation emphasizes the capacity of fiction to represent the complexities of situations and the ambiguity of 'reality' in which the continent and its peoples are immersed. As it were, written African literature such as Chinua Achebe's *Anthills of the Savannah*, Wole Soyinka's *The Interpreters*, Ayi Kwei Armah's *The Beautyful Ones Are Not Yet Born*, Tsitsi Dangaremgba's *Nervous Conditions* and Zakes Mda's *The Whale Caller*, among others, has often served as a medium to interrogate the intricacies and sheer size of Africa's experiences on the world stage. One of such experiences, the focus in this chapter, is globalisation, characterised by rapid technological developments and information revolution. How these digital developments intersect the African cultural imaginary is worthy of the kind of attention I give to it in this chapter.

I employ tenets of postmodernism to examine the place of globalisation, especially information communication technologies, in African fiction through the analytical prism of Chimamanda Ngozi Adichie's *The Thing Around Your Neck* (2009) and *Americanah* (2013). I argue that the way in which the novelist engages these agents of the global, in these texts, inform theme, characterisation, setting and technique. I aim to show that, in these works, international modern communication can be read both as a globalisation process and as an agent of globalisation. This resonates with Anthony Giddens's views that the 'intensification of worldwide social relations which links distant localities' would not have been possible without the influence of international communication technology (Giddens 1990: 64). Functioning through instruments like the radio, the telephone, the facsimile machine, the television, the computer, the internet and telecommunications, Adichie's works underscore how the latter have reduced physical distance and brought humanity closer, leading to complex transformations at various levels.

***

Globalisation has been defined variously through different disciplinary lenses. However, most of the definitions hinge on the idea of making small what is big. Roland Robertson argues that globalisation is that compressed world in which 'consciousness' has been intensified (Robertson 1992: 11). Viewing it from the growing consolidation of world economic activities, Eric Hobsbawm long considered the term as 'the drawing together of all parts of the world into a single world' (Hobsbawm 1974: 64). In their definitions, Robertson and Hobsbawm foreground the absence of the individual ethos in understanding globalisation. For David Held et al, it is a process or set of processes that embody 'transformation in their spatial organisations of social relations and transactions' to the extent of generating 'interaction and a network of activity' beyond regional and continental levels (Held et al 1999:16). In this regard, the world becomes a field guided by many processes with physical and ideological borders that tend to blend together. The networking of these subjectivities then ushers in the global, resonating with Martin Albrow's views that globalization entails the corporeal absence of individuals even so because societies have become 'sub-systems of a larger inclusive world society' (Albrow 1990:11). Farhang Rajaee in *Globalization on Trial: The Human Condition and the Information Civilization*, on his part, sees globalisation in terms of the interweaving of forces; 'a double movement affecting all aspects of life as well as all regions of the world for better or worse' (Rajaee 2000: 117). For these intersecting forces to be deemed inclusive, Shaw Martin opines that they must have developed 'on a global scale, towards a global outreach over a long historical period of time' (Martin 1996: 47). The global then is historical for, from Martin's view, it must have evolved in history. Modern communication technology squarely fits this paradigm, having evolved from the print, the radio, and on to today's complex and complicated facets of television, internet and the computer. Many African writers might not perceive such international technological networking as one of globalisation's processes, yet they agree that the digital model has greatly influenced the globalisation procedure as far as the African continent is concerned. Tanure Ojaide corroborates this when he states that 'the new reality of globalization affects the African writers at home and abroad… Many writers at home and abroad have websites and blogs and are on Facebook and in constant touch with readers across the globe' (Ojaide 2010: 5-6). One such writer, for whom these global practices and processes are integral to an understanding of her work, is Chimamanda Ngozi Adichie. The way her characters navigate the spaces of their global environment, particularly through digital technology, underscores how globalisation has informed and transformed the contemporary African landscape.

Marshall McLuhan, a Canadian communication theorist, had long spelt out the overarching effects of communication technologies in his *Understanding Media*. In this work, the author presents his society as a modern one nonetheless because it has become 'global village' (McLuhan's coinage). This terminology refers to a world in which 'action and reaction occur almost at the same time' thanks to modern technology. A modern society, then, is one in which actions are rapidly accomplished contrasting sharply with what McLuhan calls the 'mechanical age;' an era characterised by slow movements and delayed actions. The global village, he further argues, is one in which humanity carries out social operations in complete detachment— without palpable physical presences. In this context, an individual's capacity to solve a problem somewhere without physical displacement is the norm. In such spaces, technology facilitates the intersection between the global village and the global society thus ensuring a kind of 'presence' in all parts of the world within no space of time.

There is no gainsaying that Africa is part of the global, as Ojaide notes above, in as much as modern information and communication technology has contributed enormously to the ease with which people have become global citizens. Broadcast technology, radio, television, mobile phones and the internet have given Africans access to information and on-the-spot happenings in different parts of the globe, underlining the instrumentality of these forms in human connectivity and material flows. These developments, which affect Africans all over the world, bring them into a globalising networking that informs and transforms their cultural identities. Adichie's *The Thing Around Your Neck* and *Americanah*, examine the complex intersections between these technologies and the cultural environment especially as these enlighten themes, characterisation, space and narrative techniques.

As earlier underscored, tenets of postmodernism – that global theory that efficiently critiques the postmodern space – inform my reading of Adichie's oeuvre. Jean Baudrillard's and Suman Gupta's theoretical positions are particularly illuminating. Baudrillard views postmodernism in terms of man's interactivity with recurring communication devices. He reads the relation of humans to telecommunication as a sign that humanity has been 'wired' and is consequently 'a passive victim of the television, the computer and advertising' (Baudrillard 1995: 41). Telecommunication, for Baudrillard has, in a sense, hypnotised humanity destroying the 'real' to the extent that the former is now left only with images of the originals. Computer networks, for him, are nothing more than 'vampires' that constrain individuals to sit for hours on end watching their images and listening to their noises. Baudrillard's critical model is developed at length in *Simulacra and Simulation*. Here, his theory of how the 'real' in the post-industrial space is destroyed, thanks to digital communication technology, is laid bare. Yet his critique does not dismiss technology's centrality in making smooth or in complicating, as the case may be, the progress of the intercontinental. While Adichie might not be concerned with the downside of digital technology, her focus on how it affects her characters, in the multiple spaces they inhabit, highlights the former's role in the globalization process; a process hinged on everyone becoming a citizen of the global sphere.

In *Globalization and Literature*, Suman Gupta says that postmodernism registers the 'experience of living in a contemporary world; [an] experience of contemporary social existence' diametrically opposed to past experiences (Gupta 2009: 97). It is an experience of 'newness' likened to the postmodern that has progressed and disrupted modernism in order to assert itself. The postmodern condition characterized the 1980s with the advent of new media and telecommunications that impacted and transformed contemporary life. Gupta believes, like Baudrillard, that this situation has obliterated reality and conditioned lives to be directed by signs and images. For him the postmodern atmosphere is a reflexive one; encouraged by that subjectivity that has resulted in blended cultures and identities consequent on the seeming destruction of all boundaries.

In the works I study here, Adichie demonstrates, like Baudrillard and Gupta that ICTs have become life and life has become ICTs. For her characters in *The Thing Around Your Neck* and *Americanah*, the radio, the telephone and the internet are no respecters of boundaries. Through them, these personages easily access information at all times and in all places and are able to easily navigate the twin worlds they inhabit. The novelist's integration of digital technology in her texts reflects the progression of the global process which, as I have noted before, becomes a complex human condition progressively degenerating daily into more complexities. This, consequently, necessitates the use of more complex methods of communication and unlike the *World Bank*'s prediction, in the year 1996, that radio broadcasting will remain the dominant mass media in Africa, Adichie projects in these works how such dominance of the radio is gradually being replaced by the television and internet; a replacement that affects her characters and themes. I begin my analysis with the short story collection, *The Thing Around Your Neck*.

The above work is a collection of twelve stories especially devoted to the lives of women in contemporary Nigeria and the United States of America. The women in the United States are there for different reasons – a wife joining her husband after six years of separation, a young woman in an arranged marriage, another who wins a visa lottery and the wife and children of a wealthy business man enjoying an upper-middle class suburban existence here while the husband peregrinates between Nigeria and the USA. These women generally struggle to find their identity in unfamiliar settings as they face the challenge of reconciling their upbringing with the demands and pressures of new cultural environments. Questions of identity in an era of globalisation are thus central in the collection given that these characters inhabit a world 'with hazy geographical boundaries, a world of immigration, diaspora and hybridization,' to borrow the words of Susan Vanzanten (2009:1). How information communication technology interprets and transforms the way some of the characters navigate these spaces makes interesting reading from a postmodernist perspective. An analysis of 'The Shivering,' 'Imitation,' 'The Thing Around Your Neck,' and 'The Arranger of Marriages,' will underscore this view.

'The Shivering' centres on a twin tragedy in Nigeria, namely the death of the Nigerian First Lady in a hospital in Spain and the crash of a plane. Back home in New York, the major character, Ukamaka is desperately trying to get more information about the plane crash given that her ex-fiancé has been travelling to go to a wedding. Another Nigerian immigrant, from the third floor of Ukamaka's building, Chinedu, comes to offer comfort and support as she seeks to find out if her ex-fiancé was involved in the plane crash. Both spend time praying together and discussing, among other things, Chinedu's homosexuality, as they listen to the radio, changing frequency 'from NPR to an FM radio with loud music.' The heroine eventually learns from her mother's phone call that the ex-fiancé was not on the plane. The plot of the story revolves around gathering information about the plane crash on the same day the accident happened. Pictures of the 'wreckage' – a 'darkened hulk with whitish bits scattered around torn pieces of papers,' are given on television (Adichie 2009: 143). These are the signs and images that characterise the global space; photocopies of the real – the original plane wreckage that cannot be reached physically by these immigrant Nigerians in the United States of America. Though they are only photocopies of the original, they serve to convince the watcher that something like this actually happened. Ukamaka is worried and confused with the sad images she first receives from B.B.C. online news while a web page on her laptop internet page makes vivid the news: 'All killed in Nigeria plane crash' (Adichie 2009: 170). This further complicates her mood as she screams 'All aboard the air plane are gone!' She remains perplexed as to who these 'all aboard' are, until she receives the call from her mother. This jostling of different facets of digital technology, namely, the radio, the television, the internet and the telephone, in Ukamaka's space, underscores her transnational self which devolves from her capacity to 'forge and sustain simultaneous and multi-stranded social relations that link together [her] societies of origin and settlement [to the extent that her] daily life depends on multiple and constant interconnections across international borders,'(Schiller, Basch and Blanz-Szanton 1995: 48). Such jostling also validates the importance of these tools in long distance information processing, a key aspect of globalisation procedures.

In the story, one equally learns that Ukamaka and her ex-fiancé, Udenna are students whose fields of studies in America are guided by perceived needs in their home country. As a political science student, Udenna intends to return and better the political system of his country given that post-independence Nigeria has not fared well due to bad governance. Ukamaka, on her part, plans to invest her knowledge in a Non-Governmental Organization, otherwise, an NGO. NGOs are civil society agencies that focus on issues like poverty alleviation, human rights, environmental degradation and other issues of social, political and economic development. While such planning to devote her knowledge to any of these sectors of the economy demonstrates her patriotism, what is important to note is that these studies are carried out with the agency of the internet and other tools of the digital model. In portraying America as a place where students from various countries come to pursue knowledge, which knowledge, gained from one part of the globe becomes useful in other parts, Adichie continuously underscores the importance of technology in accessing and disseminating such knowledge.

In the title story 'The Thing Around Your Neck,' Akunna wins a visa lottery to migrate to America, amidst expectations from her family that her life and, by extension, that of her family back home will be improved. In spite of the challenges she encounters in her new space, the heroine sends home half of her salary as remittance to her family. Her mother's first letter is informative of how useful 'the money you sent was to give him a good funeral. They killed a goat and buried him in a good coffin' (Adichie 2009: 127). The 'him' in the quote is Akunna's father who died earlier by 'slumping over the steering wheel of his company's car' (Adichie 2009: 126-127). This sudden and unexpected death does leave the family in dire financial straits given the father's poor financial status. Thanks to modern methods of tele-charging money over long distances, Akunna's intervention in her family is realised. This is consonant with what Catherine Bretell refers to as 'transnational activities which include economic, social or political exchanges across borders' (Bretell 2006: 1) and are a crucial part of migrant realities. Akunna's case is all the more significant if one agrees with Thomas Faist that 'conceptually African women immigrants view remittances as a moral imperative, a duty and a mutual obligation to the family members back home' (Faist 2002: 216). Through Akunna's economic stake in the lives of her kith and kin, through remittances, the author underscores the familial trope that constitutes one of her major themes in the work.

Adichie presents desperate migrants doing everything possible to remain connected to their home base. Nkem's story in 'Imitation' is representative of one of the many diverse experiences a good number of Nigerian women have in the United States of America. Nkem, who lives a privileged life here with her children attending the best schools, has connections with her husband, friends and family in Nigeria, through the telephone. It is through the phone that she learns that her husband has an affair back home where he spends most of his time on business. It is also through the phone that she gets to know of the different changes that have taken place in her native Nigeria. The telephone collapses the twin faces of Nkem's life into one – her American and Nigerian lives and, by this, underscores the blended identities accruing from engagements with the digital as Baudrillard and Gupta highlight. Her connection with the telephone is also crucial in the development of her identity. As it were, it is after her phone call home that Nkem steps back, reviews her life, and makes the important decision of returning to Nigeria; a decision notably transforming her from object to subject in her cosmopolitan world. This resonates with B.S.A. Yeoh et al.'s view that 'transnational identities, while fluid and flexible are at the same time grounded in particular places' (Yeoh et al 2003: 3). The grounding for Nkem is Nigeria, her land of birth to which she must return to restore sanity to her marriage.

'The Arrangers of Marriage' deals with Chinasa's new life in New York as Ofodile's (Dave) wife. This is an arranged marriage by her uncle and aunt, contracted via telephone, mail and the exchange of digital pictures of the would-be couple. The heroine's relations believe that marrying a doctor from America is akin to winning the American visa lottery itself. Chinasa's expectations are dashed as soon as she arrives her new home. The flat is barely decorated and small; her doctor husband is just a resident in the local hospital and making very little money, whereas she had come to America expecting a big house with 'a smooth driveway snaking between cucumber-coloured lawns, a door leading into a hallway, walls with sedate paintings. A house like those of newlyweds in the American films' she saw on television programs back home. Technology, this time, through television, informs theme – the theme of appearance and reality. Upon their arrival, Ofodile asks Chinasa to call home to inform her family of their safe arrival. While the story focuses on how the heroine is compelled by her husband to conform to what he considers 'mainstream' culture, suffice it to say that technology plays an important part in bringing the two together, furnishing her dreams of life in America while helping to maintain a relationship with her family back home.

In these stories, the characters' engagement with ICTs— markers of internationalisation— emphasizes the postmodernist perspective of how contemporary 'social life,' to borrow Anthony Giddens' words, 'is ordered across time and space [...exposing] the complex relations between local involvements [...] and interaction across distance' (Giddens 1990: 181). The global order indicates that transformation is not only a cause of globalisation but an essential component of its being.

Americanah, coming some four years after *The Thing Around Your Neck*, pursues and reinforces the writer's engagement with the processes of globalisation, underlining how rapid expansion of cross-border transactions and networks, reinforced by way-finding technology, improved communications, media and information, among three countries, namely, America, Britain and Nigeria, diffuse and transform the migrant's identity. This expansive novel focuses on the protagonist, Ifemelu's experiences as a migrant in the United States of America. Told through the prism of her love relationship with her high school boyfriend, Obinze (who also has a not-too-palatable migrant experience in England) the novel records, among other themes, the manifold sociological processes of globalisation and their impact on the identities of Adichie's characters. In this light, the role played by improved digital technology, media and communication, remains central to the novelist's vision.

The spaces Ifemelu (who is cast as a representative figure) and Obinze inhabit, are defined by highly developed technologies that have made transportation and communication easily available, helping them, like other characters, to maintain regular contact with their home countries more than ever. Such interconnectedness invariably gives immigrants the illusion of presence in lieu of physical absence. Ifemelu, for instance, is constantly in touch with her parents and relations through emails and the cell phone. The reader is told that her parents always eagerly looked forward to receiving their daughter's international call. Her mother, for one, boasts about these phone calls and even 'takes the phone out to the verandah, to make sure the neighbours overheard: 'Ifem, how is the weather in America?"' (Adichie 2013: 151). Furthermore, when the heroine eventually creates her blog, to which I will return in greater detail, she receives numerous phone calls from the blog readers. These professional calls indicate that she has found her voice in a context that sought to silence it through racism and classism. The complicated nature of her transformation is underscored by the narrative voice in these words:

to receive phone calls, she wore her most serious pair of trousers, her most muted shade of lipstick, and she spoke sitting upright at her desk, legs crossed, her voice measured and sure. Yet a part of her always stiffened with apprehension, expecting the person on the other end to realize that she was play acting this professional, this negotiator of terms. (Adichie 2013: 225)

At another level, the impact of technology on the educational system in the United States of America, serves as contrast between Nigeria and the latter which constitute the heroine's worlds in the text. She says, to this effect, that 'SCHOOL IN AMERICA was easy, assignments sent in by e-mail, classroom air-conditioned, and professors willing to give makeup tests' (Adichie 2013: 172).

Most of the characters, in the novel, own social networking accounts in sites such as Facebook and Twitter. It is significantly through Facebook that Obinze gets to know more about Blaine, Ifemelu's black American boyfriend, and Ifemelu, too, also gets to see pictures of Obinze's family, especially his beautiful wife on the same social media. Other digital media like Youtube are hinted at when Dike, Ifemelu's cousin, is said to watch 'silly videos on Youtube' (Adichie 2013: 20) which he shows to Ifemelu. Interestingly, upon her return to Nigeria, it is thanks to information and communication technologies that the heroine turns, in order to find her feet as a returning subject. The reader is told that 'she scoured Nigerian websites, Nigerian profiles on Facebook, Nigerian blogs, and each click brought yet another story of a young person who had recently moved back home, clothed in American or British degrees, to start an investment company, a music production business, a fashion label, a fast food franchise' (Adichie 2013: 15). For example, Bartholomew, a character in the work, does not only comment on contemporary 'Nigerian politics with the fervid enthusiasm of a person who followed it from afar, who read and reread articles on the Internet,' but equally writes about his home country on his online magazine, 'Nigeria Village' (Adichie 2013: 90). The presence of the internet enables Ifemelu to keep abreast with events in her home country on such sites as 'Nigeria.com' (Adichie 2013: 110) while, another character, Laura, finds job opportunities on the internet as well as news about other nation groups. She avers, in this regard, that 'I read on the Internet that Nigerians are the most educated immigrant group in this country (USA)' (Adichie 2013: 135). In another dimension, Obinze, while in Britain, gets informed about Nigeria, through 'Pidgin English News on Wazobia FM' (Adichie 2013: 25). Mariama and Aisha both bring Nigeria to the global forum through selling its movie CDs or playing Nigerian films in their hair salons.

The love relationship between Ifemelu and Obinze, when they are separated from each other, is nurtured, severed, reignited and maintained through digital technology. Emails and phone calls constitute the major mode through which the physical distance between them is shortened. Before the advent of this medium of communication, the reader is informed that both longed for each other for longer periods writing 'infrequent letters' with Ifemelu stressing how much she benefitted from such communication in her new and unknown American space: 'Obinze, who anchored her through that summer of waiting – his steady voice over the phone, his long letters in blue airmail envelopes – and who understood, as summer was ending, the new gnawing in her stomach' (Adichie 2013: 97). However, when 'cybercafés opened, cell phones spread, and Facebook flourished, they communicated more often' (Adichie 2013: 20). While still unemployed, Ifemelu receives money from Obinze 'a little over a hundred dollars;' money that his uncle who visited from London gave him (Adichie 2013: 145) through internet money transfer. Adichie demonstrates that the flow of remittances, aided by modes of exchange operating with increasing ease and speed across borders, may not, in the current global dispensation, be a one-way flow but one that involves all components of the global sphere. Later in the novel, when a set of circumstances and Ifemelu's own actions conspire against her relationship with Obinze, technology is again central, not only in showing how this happens, but also how the romance is restored. It is over the phone that Ifemelu severs the relationship. Obinze's cries of 'Ifem, I love you' (Adichie 2013: 155) fall on the deaf ears of an Ifemelu struggling to come to terms with who she is in a strange environment. After Obinze's marriage, upon his return to Nigeria from Britain, e-mails restore their relationship. Ifemelu breaks the ice with an e-mail whose contents begin on the note '[…] I don't know how to start [...]. Sorry for my silence' (Adichie 2013: 237). This apology, coming after years of a lull in their relationship that had hitherto been kept moving by means of telecommunication, indicates not only how small the world has become in the hands of modern technology but also how such technology integrates the novel to advance its plot. It must be noted that the re-establishment of the rapport between the erstwhile lovers, and Ifemelu's decision to return to Nigeria, are all the outcome of e-mail exchanges between them. The reader is informed through Obinze's reminiscences that 'in the last e-mail from her, sent just before he got married, she had called him Obinze, apologized for her silence over the years, wished him happiness in sunny sentences, mentioned the black American she was living with. A gracious e-mail' (Adichie 2013: 25). These examples underscore the extent to which the overlap between technology and the novel does not only collapse the world into a small place for Adichie's characters but defines them in terms of a special technology culture that keeps them better informed than others.

One indication in the novel that international communication is becoming more complex, with the evolution of the modern multifaceted environment, is blogging. A blog made up of entries known as 'posts,' with the most recent entry appearing on the top of the page, are created using specific publishing software. This is an interactive forum; one in which personal experiences and opinions are foregrounded and shared with people across the globe. The success of a blog depends on the individual blogger and his or her shared reading audience. In effect, the instant reactions and building of networks with people concurrently influences bloggers and audience alike. Serena Guarracino, says, to this effect, that 'even when managed by multinationals – most blogs on platforms such as Wordpress or Blogspot – still need both individual and collective engagement to be effective' (Adichie 2013: 5). Ifemelu's eruption unto this advanced interactive space of digital know-how coincides with the end of her relationship with her white boyfriend, Curt. In a long e-mail to her fellow university friend, the Kenyan activist, Wambui, Ifemelu reminisces on the aforementioned relationship, expressing her deep dissatisfaction with the racial ethos that informed it. Wambui's reply, saying, 'This is so raw and true. More people should read this. You should start a blog' (Adichie 2013: 366), propels her into creating her own blog, even when we are told that:

> Blogs were new, unfamiliar to her. But telling Wambui was not satisfying enough; she longed for other listeners, and she longed to hear the stories of others. How many other people chose silence? How many other people had become black in America? How many had felt as though their world was wrapped in gauze? […] she signed into Wordpress and her blog was born. (Adichie 2013: 225)

The blog, titled *Raceteenth or Various Observations About American Blacks (Those formerly known as Negroes) by a Non-American Black*, is a platform for Ifemelu to comment on issues of race, identity and culture. The focus on race is to underscore its all-pervading and complex nature in a society defined by it. The blog particularly gives her a voice, instils self-confidence, even as her views on race, racism, depression and fashion, transcend political and geographical boundaries. A consideration of some of her posts, buttresses this view.

'Traveling while Black', draws from a friend's autobiography in progress, *Travelling While Black*, and examines the lot of the black person on the world stage where snubbing, violence, discrimination in widely separate parts of the world like Egypt, Germany Mexico, Brazil or Paris, France are his daily lot. In these contexts, issues of language, colour, class and disposition intersect race, rendering life complex for the person of colour. Ifemelu here critiques race for generating racial feelings, class distinction and for magnifying gender inequalities. Through this blog post, her opinion on the sensitive and ongoing question of race in the global sphere is brought to the fore. Thanks to the opportunity of sensitising people that blogs provide, her vision of things is sure to affect someone for the better. The blog entry, 'Friendly Tips for the American Non-Blacks: How to React to an American Black Talking about Blackness', defines the reality of discrimination in the American society and the frustrating conditions of American blacks. Since slavery, this minority has occupied the peripheral spaces of American society. Just like Native Americans whites who also suffered discrimination from immigrant populations from Europe, Russia and Ireland, the question seems to be, who therefore is American? Such interrogations might have given rise to Amber Ault's categorisations in *Race and Ethnicity*, where in the United States, 'whiteness' is the absence of 'having a race' and is likened to 'being human,' while the category 'Non-white' links what is 'different deviant and inferior, a group to which belong the African American, Asian American and the Native American' (Adichie 2013: 93). Such racial categorisations give meaning to the complaints of the American Black who has contributed to his society but has benefitted little from it. The blogger's posture is a critical one vis-à-vis Non-American blacks who must desist from being smog in telling American blacks 'things like 'Racism is over'; it ended with the Slave Trade; 'Blacks are racists too' or that your grandparents were of white descent' (Adichie 2013: 93). The complex intersections of race, an urgent feature of the global world, is debated in this blog entry for functional purposes which is an intrinsic quality of African literature.

'Is Obama Anything but Black?' (Adichie 2013: 337), 'Why Dark-Skinned Black Women – Both American and Non-American Love Barack Obama' (177), 'Obama Can Win Only If He Remains the Magic Negro,' (Adichie 2013: 247), 'Even the Idea of Being Ready Is Ridiculous' (Adichie 2013: 249) are a series of political posts in which

Ifemelu gives accounts of and comments on the election of Barack Obama to the presidency of the United States of America. She and her boyfriend, Blaine, are ardent admirers of Obama and happen to be fervent supporters of his candidacy. Debates on Obama's whiteness or blackness do not matter because as far as she is concerned, racial identities are not biologically bestowed but socially generated. For Ifemelu, 'it doesn't matter what anybody thinks of Obama. The real question is whether white people are ready for a black president' (Adichie 2013: 249). Such thought-provoking views, shared via blog posts, reach a larger audience on the internet platform. A new kind of participatory culture, born of the interactions between writers, audiences, users, and readers in the blogosphere, is now a reality of our global world, thanks to digital technology. Another fallout of Ifemelu's blogging, linked to technology, is the financial aspect. We are told that as the blog gains popularity, 'with thousands of unique visitors each month,' 'e-mails came from readers who wanted to support the blog' (Adichie 2013: 375), she was asked to speak at roundtables on panels, on public radio and community radio [...]. She had become her own blog' (Adichie 2013: 330). Through blogging, in America, Ifemelu makes it to the top financially while critiquing the status quo and providing an alternative view of the situation to her readers.

Upon her return to Nigeria, she joins The Nigerpolitan Club a group of young returnees whose weekly meetings Ifemelu views as efforts to turn Nigeria into the west. She lambasts their reasoning in imagining that societal ills have disappeared – the same ills that initially set them on the migrant trail. Her interactions with this group reveal their hankering back to life in the west, represented by their longing for 'a descent vegetarian place,' 'low fast soya milk,' 'Good customer service,' 'NPR fast internet,' 'an active civil service' and good hair salons (Adichie 2013: 407-409), to name a few. Her distressing experience with the returnees moves her to begin blogging again. The blog, titled *The Small Redemptions of Lagos* (Adichie 2013: 418), carries posts on fashion shows, Nigerpolitan mannerisms, politics and culture, practically idealising the latter, and aims at educating the west about the African continent. One of such entries on the latter titled, 'Young Women in Lagos with Unknown Sources of Wealth' (Adichie 2013: 521), inspired by her friend, Ranyinudo's, experience earns her the latter's ire and underscores the fact in the Nigerian space, 'it is not possible for the blogger to claim only 'to observe,' as Ifemelu had previously asserted,' (Guarracino 2014: 20).

Blogging, a defining characteristic of the current global arena, is used in this novel as a metaphor to debunk stereotype knowledge about Africa by white Americans and the western world that see the continent in essentialist terms. Ifemelu encounters characters who think the continent is an exotic space to be visited on vacation trips. Others see it as the crucible of poverty. One of the characters says 'it is an orphanage. We've never been to Africa. I would love to do something with my charity in Africa.' Many of these stereotypes are interrogated and debunked through blogging. Furthermore, Ifemelu's critical discussions of relevant issues of the global world, transform her immensely, as she finds her voice and overcomes a dominant and racist culture keen on denying her that voice. Blogging thus is a metaphor for empowerment as well as a political, social and economic force. At another level, it fulfils the novelist's desire for the narrative to function as 'social commentary;' saying what has to be said, 'in ways that are different from what one is supposed to say in literary fiction' (2014). The different blog posts on race, politics and culture bear eloquent testimony to this. Adichie's use of blogging reinforces her other themes while also informing the structure of her text.

Conclusion

This chapter has examined how information and communication technologies intersect the African cultural imaginary through an analysis of Adichie's *The Thing Around Your Neck* and *Americanah*.

Engagements with digital technology by the characters in the texts assist the rapidly expanding reach to make for a global village, namely an increasingly integrated world. These works show how technology plays a major role in immigrant lives, involved as it is, in bearing testimony to the varying sociological processes undergirding their identities. The works, do not only reflect on the growing transnational character of the current global arena but point to how the latter informs the affective and personal lives of migrants who must, willy-nilly, simultaneously inhabit two or more societies and cultures, while having to collapse them into one.

Bibliography

Adichie, C. N., (2009). *The Thing Around Your Neck*. Lagos: Onikan.
Adichie, C. N., (2013). *Americanah*. London: Fourth Estate.
Albrow, M., (1996). *The Global Age: State and Society Beyond Modernity*. Cambridge: Polity.
Ault, A., (n.d). *Perspectives: Race and Ethnicity*. [Online] Available at: www.courselinks.com [Accessed 30 January 2017].
Bank, W., (2000). *Can Africa Claim the 21st Century*, Washington DC: Facebook.
Bank, W., (2011). *Migration and Remittances*, Washington DC: Facebook.
Baudrillard, J., (1997). *Simulacra and Simulations*. Ann Arbor: University of Michigan Press.
Brettell, C., (2006). *Constructing Borders/Crossing Boundaries: Race, Ethnicity and Immigration*. London: Pantheon.
Giddens, A., (1990). *The Consequence of Modernity*. Cambridge: Polity.
Gikandi, S., (2001). Chinua Achebe and the Invention of African Culture. *Research in African Literatures*, 32(3), pp. 3-8.
Guarracino, S., (2014). Writing 'So Raw and true': Blogging in Chimamanda Ngozi Adichie's Americanah. *Between*, IV(8), pp. 1-26.
Gupta, S., (2009). *Globalization and Literature*. Cambridge: Polity.

Held, D., McGrew, A. & Perraton, J., (1999). *Global Transformation: Politics, Economics and Culture.* Cambridge: Polity.

Hobsbawm, E., (1975). *The Age of Capital 1848-1875.* London: Routledge and Kegan Paul.

Martin, S., (1996). *Civil Society and Media.* London: Pinter.

McLuhan, M., (1962). *Understanding Media: The Extension of Man.* Dandan : Routledge.

McLuhan, M., (1989). *The Global Village: Transformation in the World Life and Media in the 21st Century.* Oxford: Oxford University Press.

Ojaide, T., (2010). The Dreamer's Distant Love: Contemporary African Literature, Globalization, and the Quest for Peace. *Sino-US English Teaching,* 7(10), pp. 1-13.

Rajaee, F., (2000). *Globalisation on Trial: The Human Condition and Information Civilisation.* Teheran: Kumerian Press.

Robertson, R., (1992). *Globalization: Social Theory and Global Culture.* London: SAGE.

Schiller, N. G., Basch, L. & Blanc, C. S., (1995). From Immigrant to Transmigrant: Theorizing Transnational Migration. *Anthropological Quarterly,* 68(1), pp. 48-63.

Vanzanten, S., (2009). Heavy Laden. A Collection of Stories from Nigerian Writer Chimamanda Ngozi Adichie. *Books and Culture,* 15(4), p. 30.

Yeoh, B. S. A., Lai, K. P. Y., Charney, M. W. & Tong, C. K., (2003). Approaching Transnationalism. In: *Approaching Transnationalism: Studies on Transnational Societies, Multicultural Contacts and Imaginings of Home.* Boston: Kluwer Academic , pp. 1-12.

Section II:
Linguistic Shift and Accommodation

Chapter Six

Towards a Policy of Linguistic Freedom in Cameroon

Blasius Agha-ah Chiatoh

Introduction

Although multilingualism is generally acknowledged as a resource (Ruiz 1984; Alexander 2003) within research circles, in the broader society and particularly within political ranks, it is often perceived as a problem, indeed, a curse. The actuality of multilingualism reveals that whenever national linguistic options have been made, this has involved conditioning citizens' attitudes towards languages in the nation. In adjusting to the realities of accommodating some languages at the expense of others, citizens have, in turn, been engaged in positioning themselves within the politics of identification and freedom of expression in matters of national interest. Contact between languages as well as uneven distribution of functions to these languages invariably leads to situations of language conflict as forms of protestation against language-based and language-related injustices. Linguistic domination through discrimination and outright exemption of some languages from controlling domains carries with it important political underpinnings and so is resisted by minority language groups. In these contexts, the politics of language becomes a terrain for the reconfiguration of the linguistic landscape with the perpetration of socio-economic and political inequalities and injustices as its underlying motivation. At the core of these deprivations lies the desire to redefine individual and/or group identities within the nation as citizens come to be recognised and valued based on whether or not they acknowledge and so are committed towards the promotion of the values incarnated by preferred official linguistic choices.

At reunification in 1961, Cameroon's adoption of official bilingualism based on English and French was widely recognised as a worthy experiment, which if successful, could be easily exported to other parts of the continent (Chumbow 1990). Yet despite its failure at various levels, the model continues to enjoy government acclamation and promotion. In fact, it is still regarded as a source of national pride and so celebrated with pump and pageantry every year (Nanfah 2006; Chiatoh 2012). Continuous pursuance of this policy has weakened government enthusiasm and commitment towards promoting national languages as these have been systematically relegated to the background, thereby, depriving their speakers of their linguistic and cultural rights. Recently, however, the situation has evolved significantly with constitutional recognition of the value of national languages as an integral part of national cultures. But, a critical look at the changes reveals that change is more apparent than real. Like many other developments in the country, policy changes present themselves simply as widow-dressing rather than a genuine commitment to improve on the communicational and educational conditions of the national population particularly the disadvantaged rural masses.

The problem in question

Despite Cameroon's rich linguistic diversity, the country has, after more than five decades, failed to adopt a language policy that appropriately addresses the crucial question of written communication and education in national languages. In fact, no consideration has been made to assigning official status to and furthering written use in any of the 286 languages (Lewis, Simons, & Fennig 2016), not even the most widely spoken ones such as Pidgin English, Beti-fang, Fulfulde, Mungaka and Duala although they have fully attained the status of vehicular languages (Biloa & Echu 2008) for very vast sections of the national polity. By systematically underestimating the value of national languages in the nation-building process, government has opted for the organised exclusion of vast sections of the society, thus raising important questions about their linguistic human rights. This has significantly reduced the degree of attachment Cameroonians have towards their languages as they are generally regarded as only fit for the kitchen. The problem also exists at the level of the official languages where despite the *de jure* equality of English and French, the latter is accorded *de facto* supremacy over the former, thus creating the impression, in purely Orwellian terms, that 'although both languages are equal in status, one is more equal than the other'.

Observably, the politics of language in Cameroon inherently violates citizens' linguistic rights and so generates fundamental questions of national identification and citizenship. Also, it has created a fertile environment for language conflict. We see this conflict at two main levels - the horizontal and vertical levels. Horizontally, the problem manifests itself in the uneasy relationship between the official languages (English and French) as constitutionally equal languages while vertically, it has to do with the relationship between official and national languages. These two major differentiation levels signal the depth and breadth of political polarisation in the country, a situation that has had serious implications on the linguistic and citizenship rights of a vast majority of the national population. On the whole, the problem is that after more than five decades of political independence, Cameroon is yet to comprehend the necessity and urgency of liberating itself from the yoke of linguistic slavery imposed by colonial and postcolonial language policies and practices. In a nutshell, so long as we continue to pursue a foreign language-based policy, we shall remain culturally colonised and so our independence shall never be compete.

On the question of linguistic freedom

The concept of linguistic freedom can be viewed from different yet closely interrelated perspectives. It can be regarded as a right and a resource in the process of nation-building (Ruiz, 1984). This perspective brings forth the fact that rights cannot be fully guaranteed and duly enhanced without taking into consideration the languages of the citizens in a nation. A more extended view of language as a resource is presented by Alexander (2003) who identifies five key sources of the relevance of the language factor. According to him, the relevance of language in counter-hegemonic currents involves the relationship between language and the economy, language and democracy, language and identity, language and education and language and intellectualisation. In this present study, these factors mutually-reinforce one another and constitute the basis for the whole question of linguistic liberation. Consequently, linguistic freedom is only possible when language planning adequately addresses the different facets of individual and collective development. The rights-based approach to language is also re-echoed by Skutnabb-Kangas (2000: xii) who sees linguistic rights as a necessary but not sufficient prerequisite for the maintenance of linguistic diversity. She views the violation of linguistic rights especially in education as contributing to the reduction of linguistic and cultural diversity on our planet. With respect to minority settings, she holds that 'access to linguistic human rights means, in the case of minorities, access to at least two languages, the mother tongue and an official language' (2000: 7).

Kingei'i (2001: 37) regards linguistic freedom especially in postcolonial Africa as closely associated with empowerment. To him, two factors essentially affect the use of African languages in formal education, namely, 1) the language situation obtaining in a given country and 2) the country's colonial history. He sees the demerits of adopting colonial languages to reside in this kind of policy doing very little to 'realise the ideal of empowering the indigenous languages with a view to having one of them replace the former colonial language in formal education. Admittedly, the pursuance of English-French bilingualism means disregard for Cameroon's linguistic diversity and a dismissal of the requirement for local language empowerment.

Another vital dimension of linguistic freedom concerns the right by any community to preserve its languages and, by consequence its culture. In this respect, Batibo (2005: 2) thinks that, languages like human beings, have rights and that the death of a language necessarily implies cultural dislocation or deprivation of a certain cultural identity to which community members have a right. Accordingly, the promotion of minority language endangerment through hegemonic practices is both a violation of linguistic rights and a disenfranchisement process since government has the onus to ensure that 'people have the freedom to express themselves in whatever language they want'. However, it is useful to emphasise that the people's linguistic choices must not be induced by policies and practices that impose prestige and instrumental advantages on some languages considered official because these have the potential to shape and alter the natural preferences of the people. Choices that are induced are certainly not natural – they simply constitute an extended dimension of the rights and freedoms deprivation process.

Equally critical in the theorisation of linguistic freedom is the connection between language and power and then language and nationalism. At the heart of this relationship is the question of ideology understood here as a 'coherent system of symbols which, within a more or less sophisticated conception of history, links the cognitive and evaluative perception of one's social condition – especially its prospects for the future – to a programme of collective action for the maintenance, alteration or transformation of society' (Bouza Sastre 2000: 22). Viewed from this angle, language planning becomes irrelevant if it fails to relate to issues of history and political identity. Drawing from Tollefson (1991: viii), he questions:

> How possible is it [...] to characterise the language planning decisions in any state or institution without appeal to the historical and political identity of that system, and moreover, to the identities of the

forces struggling within it? There is no sense in which language planning can be undertaken, or its effects evaluated, within some social vacuum.

Accordingly, the ecology of language planning as a concept that guarantees linguistic freedom must reflect the historical and identification concerns of the state or nation.

Tracing the path to linguistic freedom

Cameroon's path to linguistic freedom has been extremely long and tedious. This journey can be presented under three historical periods, namely, post-reunification years, the 1980s and 1990s and then the years after 2000.

Post-reunification years (1961-1972)
When Southern Cameroons (West Cameroon) voted to reunite with La République du Cameroun (East Cameroon) in the 1961 UN-organised plebiscite, this actually meant taking the language policy debate in the new nation to a different level. Prior to reunification, Southern Cameroons operated an English-oriented language policy constructed around British colonial policy of *Indirect Rule* that allowed the promotion of national languages in early primary education. On its part, La République du Cameroun implemented a French-oriented policy based on the French colonial policy of *Assimilation* that was very hostile towards national language promotion. With these contrasting policy orientations and faced with the imperative of achieving political oneness, reunification architects opted for an official language policy based on English and French. While the official language policy may have succeeded in satisfying the needs of political convenience, by eliminating potential linguistic barriers on the path to national unity consolidation, it no doubt had a serious negative effect on the protection of linguistic freedoms. For Southern Cameroons, it symbolised the loss of a good old tradition – a shift from over four decades of national language promotion (linguistic freedom) to the adoption of an English-only (linguistic

slavery) education system in its own territory. For La République, this meant the maintenance of the status quo – that is, the continuation of an exoglossic (French) language policy.

Apparently, instead of drawing from Southern Cameroons' rich experience to adopt a rights-based language policy, reunification instead elected to pursue a policy of linguistic colonisation based on the French assimilation practice of foreign official language. Clearly, the choice of English-French bilingualism implied total disregard for rights and freedoms built around national languages and cultures. From thence until the coming of the Summer Institute of Linguistics (SIL) into the country in 1969, national languages were completely pushed to the periphery of society. Although the coming of SIL re-ignited interest in these languages, its activities were restricted to evangelisation and so did not produce the required nation-wide impact. With the 1972 referendum that dismantled the federal system and instituted a unitary state, official bilingualism was strengthened thus reinforcing the peripheral status of national languages. The unitary system meant that henceforth policy would be dictated from the administrative base – Yaoundé, a base that was visibly committed to furthering mainly French-oriented policies.

The 1980s and 1990s

If the post-reunification years laid the foundation for the violation of linguistic human rights in Cameroon, the 1980s and 1990s brought in a glimmer of hope with respect to national language promotion. This period witnessed a remarkable change in linguistic attitude particularly as regards scientific research more generally and mother tongue education experiments in particular. These developments started in the late 1970s with the forceful return of Cameroonian linguists from foreign universities. Encouraged by SIL and UNESCO, they soon initiated at the University of Yaounde, the Operational Research Programme for Language Education in Cameroon (PROPELCA) in 1978. PROPELCA offered the scientific framework for policy advocacy on the one hand and then mother tongue education experimentation on the other. It started off timidly in 1981 with two languages (Ewondo and Lamnso) and was gradually expanded in the years that followed. In 1987, PROPELCA lost its university support and was adopted by the National Association of Cameroonian Language Committees (NACALCO) created in 1989. NACALCO's mission was to assist local communities in promoting their languages. Convinced of the benefits of mother tongue education, the organisation made PROPELCA an integral component of its Cameroon Language Education (CLED) programme. Through the CLED framework, NACALCO was able to expand the PROPELCA experiment to 20 languages.

At the advocacy level, NACALCO made a tremendous impact on the national scene that crystallised in the formal endorsement of the PROPELCA experiment by the General Forum on Education in 1995. However, the Forum, although very positive towards the programme, fell short of making an official declaration authorising its implementation in schools. Among the major outcomes of the Forum was the constitutional revision in 1996 that provided, in Part One, Article 1 (3) for the promotion of national languages with a follow up, in 1998, being Law N° 98/004 of 14 April 1998 on guidelines for organising education in Cameroon that provided among other things for the promotion of national languages in education.

The years after 2000

The years following 2000 saw tremendous progress at both experimentation (PROPELCA) and policy levels. At experimentation level, the PROPELCA programme was expanded from 20 to 40 languages within the framework of the PROPELCA Generalisation – 2 Project. With a focus on supervision, materials production and training, the project enhanced the facilitation of mother tongue education and literacy activities. By 2003, experimentation was effectively carried out in 40 languages with over 30 000 children receiving instruction in their mother tongues in the first two years of schooling. Despite the achievements registered, the programme suffered financial difficulties from 2003 and since then its impact has continued to wane. The situation has been so serious that today, only a few communities still manage to practice informal teaching of the mother tongue. Waning in PROPELCA activities has been mitigated in some areas by the introduction of new experimental programmes such as the Kom Experimental Education Pilot Project (KEPP). But the weakness with initiatives such as KEPP is that they constitute a kind of vicious cycle where we are eternally re-experimenting programmes whose results and impact are no longer in doubt. In fact, a critical analysis reveals that the difference between such initiatives and PROPELCA is only in nomenclature and the faces behind them.

At policy level, this period, notably the years 2002 to 2004, witnessed some landmark developments in the area of mother tongue education legislation. During the period, three important pieces of legislation were enacted. The first is Decree N° 2002/004 of 4 January 2002 reorganising the Ministry of National Education that created provincial (regional) pedagogic inspectorates for mother tongues in the Ministry of Secondary Education. Although only partially implemented, this decree creates the framework for further debates in the area of national language promotion in the country. Another text is Law N° 2004/018 of July 2004 on decentralisation that empowers local councils to implement programmes for the eradication of illiteracy and management of education, section 3 of which provides for the promotion of national languages. This law is accompanied by Law N° 2004/019 of July 2004 empowering regions to undertake education and literacy and to support among other things, the realisation of the linguistic map of Cameroon, the promotion of national languages, participating in editing national languages and the promotion of the audio-visual press in national languages. By involving councils and regions in the task of national language promotion, these decentralisation laws create an ideal platform for local ownership of national language promotion, but in typical Cameroonian style, they have remained dead letters.

As a follow up to the above legislation, in 2008, a Department of National Languages and Cultures was created in the Higher Teacher Training College (ENS) of the University of Yaoundé 1, with the mission to train mother tongue teachers for secondary schools. Accompanying this initiative was the selection of pilot schools for experimental teaching of the mother tongue at the level of each region. Also noteworthy are on-going efforts to finalise the education in national languages project known in French as *Ecole et Langue en Afrique* (ELAN) that should officially open the way for national languages into the primary school classroom. But interestingly, ELAN is already suffering from a lot of criticism from research circles. One of the criticisms levied against the initiative is that it is simply a French transplant from Paris tailored to suit African governments (Mba 2013: 19). One thus wonders whether *ELAN* can ever effectively respond to Cameroon's development needs.

Pitfalls of official bilingualism as the framework for linguistic freedom

If linguistic freedom means empowering every citizen to operate in the language(s) of their choice as a prerequisite in the achievement of maximal self-fulfilment and well-being, then the Cameroonian reality reveals a very grim picture of language policy management. Despite its long struggle for linguistic liberation, the country continues to privilege official bilingualism at all levels. In fact, in formal and informal communication circles, the domination of English and/or French is clearly visible. On the streets, in offices, in churches and even at home, they are the languages that dominate. Similarly, schools, administration and the economy function exclusively in these languages without the slightest indication of a possible improvement even in the remotest future. But above all, English-French bilingualism presents itself as a playing ground for the practice of linguistic apartheid where users of un-favoured languages are systematically downgraded and pushed to the borders of society. And talking about linguistic apartheid, two levels of its practice are readily observable – the horizontal and vertical levels.

Horizontally, linguistic apartheid is observed in inequalities that characterise the treatment of English and French as *de jure* equal languages. Despite their constitutional equality, there is a deliberate endeavour to safeguard the superiority of French over English. Even if the motivation for this unequal treatment lies more in politics than in language itself, the situation is so serious that it has generated a lot of interest among researchers, politicians and the ordinary people. These discriminatory practices have created deep political and social fissures between Anglophones and Franchophones with each community valuing its official language as the primary marker of its identity and survival (Chiatoh 2015: 1). Cameroon's military, public companies, the economy particularly through the use of the franc, just to name but these, function exclusively in French. In the administration, Anglophones are treated as a minority group on the same basis as tribes and ethnic groups and so accorded limited access to high profile positions. Non-respect for English is also observed through the imposition, on Anglophones, of the Teaching of English as a Foreign Language (TOEFL) test, a test designed for Francophones who study English as a foreign language. One sees in this behaviour an implicit attempt to diminish the status of the Anglophone in Cameroon. With English reduced to the backyard and with their destinies so closely connected to its disadvantaged position, Anglophones, today, view themselves simply as victims of the official bilingualism policy.

At the vertical level, linguistic discrimination exists in the relationship between official and national languages. While official languages are accorded status in public space, local languages still play a marginal role if any at all. In fact, although current legislation provides for the promotion of national languages, it falls short of making such promotion a major development priority. This explains why primary and secondary schools still run only experimental mother tongue programmes while just few higher institutions of learning are interested in promoting these languages. Practically speaking, therefore, what we observe is that these languages are systematically exempted from important domains. With this treatment, they are only still relevant in the kitchen. One thus understands why in urban settings, speaking these languages is generally considered as 'causing rain to fall' (Chia 2008: 120; Chiatoh 2014: 379).

Towards a policy of linguistic freedom in Cameroon: Identity multilingualism

From both policy and cultural identity perspectives, a country endowed with many languages such as Cameroon should not suffer from cultural poverty. Cultural poverty as used here pertains to the inability of a country to cultivate a spirit of national identification and belonging. On this premise, therefore, cultural poverty is seen as a strong indication of cultural (mental) colonisation. By this we mean that a country that enjoys cultural freedom should be able to communicate with its citizens in more than one language, with at least one of these languages being an indigenous mother tongue. In this respect, cultural colonisation involves manipulating of the minds of the colonised with the belief that nations that adopt the colonial culture would no longer resist colonial occupation and exploitation (Shakih 2011: 112). Effectively, it is this colonial mind-set that a policy of linguistic freedom should seek to transform if our independence and sovereignty must survive.

Understandably, cultural or mental decolonisation provides the ideal basis for securing linguistic freedom in colonial and postcolonial settings in general and in Cameroon in particular. But Cameroon is unique in many respects including linguistic behaviour. In Africa, it is the sole country that is officially bilingual. Also, it is one of the very few countries in Francophone Africa alongside Gabon, Benin and Côte d'Ivoire that do not have a national language with official status. Given the centrality of linguistic freedom in national development and considering that a vast majority of Cameroonians operate mainly in their mother tongues or in a language of their immediate environment, the striking question that arises at this juncture is: *What can be done to chart a way forward for a policy that guarantees linguistic freedom in Cameroon?* In other words, what is the model for a policy of linguistic freedom for Cameroon?

Given the country's multilingual situation, an ideal model for linguistic freedom in Cameroon should be constructed around identity multilingualism that is rooted in indigenous languages while at the same time embracing the foreign official languages. Such a model should recognise a hierarchy of three categories of languages as follows:

1. Indigenous mother tongues (IMT): Each Cameroonian shall be literate in their indigenous mother tongue as the basis of their cultural identity.
2. National official languages (NOL): Some Cameroonian languages shall be raised to the status of official languages in order to give the country its unique national identity.
3. Foreign official languages (FOL): English and French shall continue to play official functions both as the languages that historically define the relationship between Anglophone and Francophone Cameroons and as languages of international business.

As a form of linguistic equation, therefore, we shall have:

$$IMT+NOL+FOL = Identity\ Multilingualism$$

Our multilingual model shall be one built on the local identity of each citizen as the basis of cultural rootedness. Within this linguistic hierarchy, indigenous mother tongues shall occupy a place of choice followed by national official languages and then English and French in that order. What this postulation suggests is a new interpretation of the concept of *bilingualism* in the Cameroonian context. Henceforth, within a bilingualism framework, the basic level for defining a Cameroonian bilingual shall be their ability to speak and write an indigenous mother tongue and then a national official language. As for English and French, they shall maintain their function of defining Anglophone and Francophone historical identity. On the grounds of this argument, Cameroon shall no longer be recognised as a bilingual country but rather as a multilingual country where an average citizen shall have spoken and written mastery of at least four languages – an indigenous mother tongue, a national official language and then English and French where the indigenous mother tongue and the national official languages serve the purposes of cultural decolonisation by enabling the citizens to acquire an identity that is uniquely Cameroonian.

What the above means to the Cameroonian language planner is that cultural decolonisation must create room for a situation of linguistic pluralism by allowing for the presence of both national and official languages in the public sphere. But to do this, there is need to distinguish between three language management options, which, according to Chiatoh (2006: 148) are: *acceptance*, *toleration or accommodation* and *rejection*. *Linguistic acceptance* involves the recognition of equitable promotion of languages in the nation without any bias as to ethnic ties and/or numerical status. It confers privileged status to the languages that have been selected for promotion in public spaces. *Toleration* or *accommodation* involves admitting and promoting languages in restricted domains with a view to safeguarding the hegemony of a more preferred language(s). It thus means linguistic concessions that impose marginal status on a language(s) while maintaining preferred power relationships. On its part, *rejection* simply implies outright non-recognition of language as a development resource in the nation.

In Cameroon, these three options are actively in application although in varying degrees. *Acceptance* is observed through French *de facto* domination over the other languages. It is the preferred language of government business at both local and international levels. *Toleration* or *accommodation* is seen through the unequal relationship between English and French. Despite its constitutional equality, English is barely tolerated as evidenced in its marginal use in government business. As for *rejection*, it is observed via the refusal, since reunification, to promote national languages on the pretext that these constitute a threat to national unity. But it is worthy to note that rejection can also take the form of deliberate escape routes that make the implementation of legislation practically impossible. In Cameroon, escape routes exist in the form of lack of specification in the articulation of policy goals and in the practice of texts of application. Vague policy goals give room for multiple interpretations thus slowing down implementation. Similarly, texts of application encourage feet-dragging because, although they are a precondition to implementation, their elaboration always takes so many long years to become a reality.

On the whole, we must realise, therefore, that while some languages must be accepted and accorded official status, others especially the extremely minority ones, can only be accommodated. The essential thing here is to recognise, once and for all, that English-French bilingualism that makes it impossible, regionally and nationally, for citizens of the same country to speak to and understand one another in its indigenous languages is not only abnormal but a serious source of national deprivation, indeed, a source of national shame. A decolonised policy for Cameroon should ensure that the country speaks to its citizens in many of its tongues and also that these different tongues must melt into a harmonious chorus of unity.

Language planning considerations

As a policy of cultural (mental) decolonisation, identity multilingualism entails making some critical language planning choices. It means, for instance, admitting that the foreign languages (English and French), although crucial in the historical definition of our identity can no longer suffice in the definition of a new national identity. Of course, this admission has significant implications in the manner in which national languages are perceived and treated. In concrete terms, this depends on some key language planning options, namely, an indigenised language policy, revitalisation of national language and officialisation of national languages.

An indigenised language policy

Indigenised language policy, here, is understood to mean the adoption of a language planning model that valorises indigenous languages as the fundamental markers of individual and collective human rights. An indigenised policy draws from the understanding that any language planning initiative that fails to guarantee indigenous linguistic rights is essentially flawed and consequently irrelevant in the nation-building project. It is thus a policy that gives greater value to national languages by systematically relocating them from the peripheries to the centre. Valuing national languages in this way is recognition that in modern day Cameroon foreign languages alone are no longer sufficient in the definition and appreciation of individual and collective identity and dignity. An indigenised language policy in Cameroon will thus manifest itself through harmonious co-existence between languages inherited from colonisation on the one hand and then indigenous languages on the other.

Above all, an indigenised policy recognises that the key weapons of our enslavement are language, education and religion (Sekhar 2012: 112) and that of all these, language is the most crucial since it is on language that the success of the other factors depends. It is admission that African thought is imprisoned in colonial languages and as a result only accessible to a very minority few. More importantly, it is acknowledgement that it is only through African languages that this thought can be liberated and rendered accessible to the vast majority of the population. An indigenised language policy is, therefore, a policy of indigenous language empowerment in a context hitherto controlled entirely by colonial languages.

Revitalisation of national languages

An important corollary of policy indigenisation is national language revitalisation. As a vital component of corpus planning, revitalisation seeks to transform policy into practice by ensuring the written development of national languages. It is driven by the fact that most of our languages are not yet written and that those that are written have not been attributed important functions because of misleading assumptions. But even more important is the need for government to re-appropriate the revitalisation process. Suffice it to note here that so far, language development has been conducted primarily by foreign bodies such as SIL-Cameroon and churches and to a limited extent by national organisations such as the National Association of Cameroonian Language Committees (NACALCO) and the Cameroon Association for Bible Translation and Literacy (CABTAL), themselves essentially dependent on foreign financial assistance. This scenario has created the impression that national languages have no value within public circles and so should not be learnt or should not serve as instruments of learning. Government re-appropriation of the revitalisation process should help reverse this trend by leading public authorities to recognise that it is their responsibility to safeguard and uphold the languages of the nation. The advantage of government responsibility in this regard is both of a moral and an ideological nature. Morally, it falls in line with the requirement to respect and protect the languages of the nation, thereby, guaranteeing the linguistic rights and freedoms of the population. Ideologically, it enables government to take into its own hands the responsibility of advancing the decolonisation project by ensuring the survival and empowerment of its indigenous languages with the underlying principle being that only a national government can truly secure the freedom of its people.

Officialisation of national languages

Attributing official status to national languages is another vital aspect of cultural decolonisation. As a component of status planning, officialisation requires that some of the languages of the nation be raised to official status on the same basis as the foreign languages. In this respect, Zamyatin (2013: 127) provides a useful functional classification of how the official language operates. According to him, the official language operates as: 1) the working language of state authorities and organisations, 2) the language of communication of authorities with citizens and other public communications and 3) state institutions provide public services in the official language. Knowing the destructive role that politics has and is capable of playing in language planning matters, it is advisable that the task of selecting languages for official status be left in the hands of language experts. One of the ways out is to consider languages that are already serving as languages of wider communication (LWC) such as Cameroon Pidgin English, Ewondo, Fulfulde, Mungaka and Duala. To do this, it must, henceforth, become clear that learning and all other official functions can be effectively assumed by any language if government is committed. Given the present apathy that exists towards national languages, this calls for serious education and sensitisation campaigns to bring such a project to fruition.

Conclusion

More than five decades after reunification, Cameroon is still painstakingly searching for a language policy that meets its national development requirements. Its choice of official bilingualism has proven to be more of a problem than a solution to the nation-building effort. Through its biased practices, it has constituted the main foundation for the polarisation of the country. As the country grapples with its internal identity conflicts as part of efforts to achieve emergence by 2035, it is necessary to revisit its language planning option with a view to liberating its citizens from linguistic and cultural slavery through the adoption a policy that empowers citizens to reaffirm their identities based on their indigenous values. A priori, this requires realising that English-French official is culturally alienating and so no longer appropriate at this stage in our history. Henceforth, therefore, we must be guided by the urgency for cultural decolonisation through an indigenised policy that guarantees the linguistic rights and freedoms of even the smallest communities in the country.

Bibliography

Alexander, N., (2003). The African Renaissance and the use of African Languages in Tertiary Education, PRAESA Occasional Papers, 13

Batibo, H. M., (2005). *Language Decline and Death in Africa: Causes, Consequences and Challenges.* Frankfurt-Clevedon: Multilingual Matters

Biloa, E. & Echu, G., (2008). Cameroon: Official Bilingualism in a Multilingual State In *Language and National Identity in Africa.* Oxford: Oxford University Press, pp.199-213.

Bouza Sastre, A., (2000). Language Planning and Political Ideology: A Cross-comparison between Catalonia, Valencia and the Balearic Islands on the re-introduction of Catalan. MA Dissertation, Southampton: University of Southampton

Chia, E.N., (2006). Rescuing Endangered Cameroonian Languages for National Development. In *African Linguistics and the Development of African Communities.* Dakar: CODESRIA, pp. 120-128.

Chiatoh, B.A., (2006). Language, Cultural Identity and the National Question in Cameroon. In *Language, literature and identity.* Göttingen: CuvillierVerlag, pp.144-151.

Chiatoh, B.A., (2012). Official bilingualism and the construction of a Cameroonian national identity. In *Fifty years of official language bilingualism in Cameroon (1961-2011): situation, stakes and perspectives.* Paris: L'Harmattan, pp.65-86.

Chiatoh, B.A., (2014). The Cameroonian experience in mother tongue education planning: The community response framework.

Current Issues in Language Planning (CILP), 15 (4), pp. 376-392

Chiatoh, B.A. (2015). The politics of language and nationalism in Cameroon. In *Recreating Centers and the Politics of Nationalism: Readings Across Cultures*. Saarbrucken: Lambert Academic Publishing, pp.197-225.

Chumbow, B.S., (1990). Language and language policy in Cameroon. In An *African experiment in nation building: The bilingual Cameroon republic since reunification*. Boulder, CO: West-View Press, pp. 281-311.

Kinge'i C.K., (2001). Pitfalls in Kenya's postcolonial language policy: Ambivalence and choice and development. *Per Lingua*, 17 (1) pp. 36-47

Lewis, M. P., Simons, G. F. & Fennig, C. D., (2016). *Ethnologue: Languages of the world* (19th ed.). Dallas, Texas: SIL International.

Mba, G., (2013). An overview of language policy and planning in Cameroon. In *Language policy in Africa: Perspectives for Cameroon*. Kansas City: Miraclaire Academic Publications, pp.12-31.

Nanfah, G. (2006). Exoglossic language policy and national unity in Africa: The Cameroonian model. In *Language, literature and identity*. Göttingen: Cuvillier Verlag, pp.129-143.

Ruiz, R. (1984). Orientations in language planning. *Journal of the National Association for Bilingual Education*, 8, pp. 15-34

Sekhar, G. R. (2012). Colonialism and its impact on English language, *Asian Journal of Multidimensional Research*, 1 (4), pp. 2278-4853

Shakih, M. K. (2011). The position of language in development of colonization, *Journal of Languages and Cultures (JLC)*, 2 (7), pp. 117-123.

Skutnabb-Kangas, T. (2000). *Linguistic genocide in education – or worldwide diversity and human rights?* Mahwah: Lawrence Erlbaum

Zamyatin, M. (2000). Human rights, autonomy and national sovereignty, *Ethical Perspective*, 7 (1), pp. 24-36.

Chapter Seven

Justice Across Linguistic Frontiers: Preserving Second Official Language Rights in Cameroon Law Courts

Kiwoh Terence Nsai

Introduction

Cameroon is a medium-sized country situated in the Central/West African region with a population of approximately 26.5 million people (*www.Worldometer.info* 2020). It shares boundaries with Nigeria to the west, Chad to the North East, the Central African Republic to the East, and the Congo Republic, Gabon and Equatorial Guinea to the South. The polity has a lot of linguistic viability. It has over two hundred indigenous languages. This figure conflicts with others and no scholar has been able to pinpoint the exact number of indigenous languages in Cameroon (Chia 1983, SIL 2002, Biloa 2006, Eberhard et al 2020). These languages are used in intra-tribal communication. For intertribal communication, a number of lingua franca serve the purpose, with Pidgin English, Fulfulde, Wandala and Beti-Fang, being the most noticeable (Kouega 2001). English and French are used as the official languages of Cameroon. This official status is enshrined in the country's Constitution, particularly in Article 3 of the 1996 version, which states: 'The official languages of the Republic of Cameroon shall be English and French, with both languages having the same status. The State shall guarantee the promotion of [official] bilingualism throughout the country'. These two languages therefore enjoy the protection of the State and have no rivals as far as their existence in Cameroon is concerned. Before continuing, it is important to understand how the two languages came to be part of Cameroon's linguistic heritage.

English was introduced in the territory that is known today as Cameroon before its colonisation. Traders and explorers who visited the coast of the polity introduced it. Subsequently, with the arrival of the German colonialists, schools and religious bodies already used English as their official medium of communication. It is on record that Douala chiefs wrote a letter to Her Majesty the Queen of England in English requesting for annexation (Mveng 1985). Even during the German colonial period, English was allowed to be used as a medium of instruction until 1910 (Anchimbe 2005). Despite the later ban by the Germans, the language was still used by Christian denominational groups in Cameroon. The defeat of the Germans in the First World War resulted in English being established as an official language in the part of Cameroon that was mandated to Britain. Here, the language was used alongside indigenous languages in schools and local governance. Besides instituting the English language in their part of Cameroon, the British also introduced a judicial system that was based on the principles of the British Common Law. Consequently, British Southern Cameroon became accustomed to the British way of life and justice. This situation persisted from the Mandate and Trusteeship periods to the independence of the territory by joining the already independent *La République du Cameroun* on October 1st, 1961. After reunification, West Cameroon, as the British part of the country was called, conserved the English language and the judicial system it inherited from Britain. Consequently, legal matters were tried in higher courts using the English language and the British Common Law as a legal base. This continued until 2005 when attempts were made to harmonise the legal systems in Cameroon, beginning with the Criminal Procedure Code. However, citizens of former Southern Cameroons in the Francophone part of the country did not enjoy the right of being tried following the Common Law system.

The French language, for its part, began to be used in Cameroon only after the First World War. After the partition of Kamerun, schools abandoned by the Germans were reopened by the French who had received 4/5 of the territory. Besides, the old linguistic order (Pidgin English, English, indigenous languages and German) was outlawed and replaced with French (Stumpf 1979). The French used a variety of strategies to impose their language on the indigenous people. These strategies included high taxes for those who were not willing to learn, flogging, forced labour and the use of stars and other signs to indicate that a learner was not doing well in French (Kiwoh 2010). Candidates who were doing well in the language were described as *civilisés(civilised)* or *evolués (advanced)*. The administration, schools, judiciary and all spheres of public life were 'frenchified'. The French Civil Law Code was used to try all cases that were brought before the authorities.

Reuniting the West and East Cameroons made Cameroon peculiar in many domains. It made Cameroonians to have two official languages: the first and second official languages[1]. Further, the polity had a unique judicial system. This is because two types of judicial systems co-exist in the country. These judicial systems reflect its bi-cultural nature, with an Anglo-Saxon Common Law judicial tradition in the former British Southern Cameroons and a Civil Law tradition in the former *la République du Cameroun or* East Cameroon. From reunification until very recent times, only English-speaking magistrates worked in former British Southern Cameroons and vice versa. This implies that Cameroonians crossing linguistic borders to the other side where justice is rendered in the second official language tradition, must have their rights protected using diverse strategies in law courts. It was done within the framework of protecting what is known in linguistics as *Language rights, Linguistic rights or linguistic human rights*.

According to Paultson (1997) the three terms, mentioned above, are inter-related. However, they can function at different realms. Language rights cover the right of languages to exist and to be

---

[1] A Cameroonian who originates from the former Southern Cameroons has as first official language, English and as second official language, French and vice versa for one who originates from the French speaking part.

protected from dying or becoming extinct. These types of rights are usually community-bound. On the other hand, linguistic rights and linguistic human rights are those that pertain to the users of a given language.

The Constitution of the Republic of Cameroon guarantees the use of English and French as official languages within a multilingual society. It allows these languages to be taught in schools, used in all official public interactions and in diplomacy. This status protects the two languages from being extinct, a right which other languages in the same polity do not enjoy. The co-existence of the two languages begs for a pertinent question: How are the linguistic human rights of users of the two language cultures protected when they cross linguistic borders to the second official language environment within an official English-French bilingual setting like Cameroon?

Linguistic human rights here are viewed from the perspective of De Varennes (2001: 6) who argues that these rights 'are derivable from general individual human rights, namely, the principles of non-discrimination and freedom of expression'. Phillipson (1992: 97) for his part contends that linguistic human rights involve 'the right to develop and promote their own languages, including their own literary language, and to use them for administrative, judicial, cultural and other purposes'. This, therefore, means that any Cameroonian, who speaks English or French, has certain rights by dint of the language they use.

The governing class in Cameroon recognises this, and tries to protect these rights by providing a number of laws, particularly in the domain of justice because some Cameroonians seek it across the official language divide. The domain of justice is chosen because of its sensitive nature. It is worth noting that incomprehension due to linguistic barriers in a domain which as sensitive as this, could lead to miscarriages in the way justice is administered. Through observation, interviews and a review of empirical literature, an exploration is carried out on the various strategies that have been put in place to protect linguistic rights or linguistic human rights of users across the official language divide in Cameroon. Furthermore, an appraisal of the effectiveness of these strategies is done by comparing what obtains in Cameroon to international principles and practices. Analyses begin with the strategies put in place by the legislature to protect linguistic rights across the official language divide in Cameroon and how these work to protect (or not), the linguistic rights of migrants.

Strategies Used to Protect Linguistic Rights in the Cameroon Justice System in a Second official language environment

The Constitution of the Republic of Cameroon provides a number of articles to protect the rights of its citizens in all domains. Apart from the Constitution, a number of other legal instruments have been adopted by the legislative body. The *International Covenant on Civil and Political Rights,* for instance, adopted by the United Nations General Assembly and to which Cameroon is a signatory, states as follows:

In the determination of any criminal charge against him, everyone shall be entitled to the following minimum guarantees, in full equality.
(a) To be informed promptly and in detail in a language which he understands of the nature and cause of the charge against him; [...]
(f) To have the free assistance of an interpreter if he cannot understand or speak the language used in court (United Nations General Assembly Resolution 2200A (XXI) of 16th December 1966).

From the above, the right to understand what is brought against an accused person in the language that they master is fundamental. Furthermore, the Cameroon *Criminal Procedure Code* or Law N° 2005/007 of 27th July, 2005 seems to have been inspired by this recommendation from the United Nations. It lays out principles that relate to the protection of the linguistic rights of every suspect. This is evidenced in Section 90 (3) of the above-cited law which states as follows:

> When all or part of a written report is devoted to the recording of statements from or to the confrontation of persons, the said persons shall, after the *reading and, where necessary, interpretation of statements*, initial each sheet of the report and all erasures, alterations and interlineations therein. *The interpreter shall also initial each sheet of the report and all erasures, alterations and interlineations therein*.... [My emphasis].

Other instances abound. Section 183 (1) of the Cameroon *Criminal Procedure Code* further states that:

> a) Where a witness does not speak one of the official languages which the Registrar and Examining Magistrate understand, the latter shall call on the services of the interpreter.
> b) The interpreter shall not be less than twenty-one (21) years of age.
> c) The registrar, witness and the parties shall not perform the functions of an interpreter.
> d) The interpreter shall take an oath to give a true interpretation of the statement of any person who speaks in a different language or dialect. The fact of having taken an oath shall be mentioned in the record of the proceedings.

In addition, Section 354 of the same Code emphasizes that:

> (1) Where an accused person speaks a language other than one of the official languages understood by the members of the court, or where it is necessary to translate a document produced in court, the Presiding Magistrate shall of his own motion appoint an interpreter of not less than twenty-one (21) years of age, who shall take oath to interpret faithfully, the testimonies of persons speaking in different languages or faithfully translate the document in question.

These are some instances alongside an armada of other

international conventions that protect the official linguistic rights of persons having issues in Cameroon law courts outside their first official language judicial environment. However, the question that arises is: Are the provisions of the various relevant legal instruments respected? The following section attempts answers to this question.

Happenings in Law Courts and Peripheral Structures

By peripheral structures here, we mean those structures that perform auxiliary services related to implementing the law. These include the police and gendarmerie stations. In Cameroon, the judicial police is in charge of all initial investigations, the execution of arrest warrants and other justice related instructions. Judicial police officers are drawn from the National Police Force and the National Gendarmerie. These individuals undergo training to function as such. In addition, whether trained or not, every head of a police or gendarmerie post becomes an ex-officio judicial police officer (Section 181 of the Cameroon Criminal Procedure Code).

The implementation of the provisions in section B above begins with preliminary investigations. However, the problem lies with the fact that some of these individuals are not competent in the two official languages. As a consequence, a French speaker may head a brigade or police post in a locality where only English is spoken and vice versa. The off shoot of this is incomprehension between litigants and the investigator in a criminal matter. A case in point was found in Nkor-Noni Sub-Division of the North West Region. The Brigade Commander at the time was transferred from Moloundou in the East Region to the Brigade in question. In the following interview, he admitted to have never had contact with the English, his second official language, from primary school till his recruitment into the gendarmerie in 1987[2].

---

[2] *Adjudant Chef Major* Raymond Mbede was interviewed on the 28th of March 2010 at the premises of the Kumbo Court of First Instance where he had brought in suspects for arraignment in court.

Depuis que je travaille à Nkor-Noni, j'accomplie ex officio le rôle d'un officier de police judiciaire. Par conséquent, je dois mener toutes les enquêtes et traduire les suspects devant le Procureur de la République. Mais je rencontre un problème délicat : celui de la communication. Pour moi c'est la première fois que je travaille dans la zone anglophone et je ne suis pas bon en anglais. En fait je suis nul en anglais.

[From the day I started working in Nkor-Noni, I play the role of a judicial police officer by virtue of my position. Consequently, I have to carry out all investigations and present suspects to the State Counsel. But I face a very delicate problem, communication. It's my first time of working in an English-speaking area and I'm not good in English. In fact, I' m blank in English] (my translation).

As the commander of the Gendarmerie Territorial Brigade, he is responsible for judicial investigations in a locality where most people barely understand English (their first official languagelet alone French(their second official language)which the language spoken by their lone judicial police officer.

In another case between the State of Cameroon and Neba Chrysanthus against Mr Nforbah and co. at the Yaoundé *Centre Administratif* courthouse, it was reported that the case had dragged on for over sixteen months because the defendants could not understand French (their second official language) and the court was still looking for an interpreter. Finally, Mr Nforbah, the accused, and co-defendants had to accept to be tried in French, a language they barely understood. Here is an extract of the proceedings as recorded on the 2nd of October 2009:

State Counsel : [...] Madame le juge, dame Mankah Pascaline est coupable au même titre que son ami Nforbah. Je voudrais poser cette question au témoin : Quelle est votre position vis-à-vis monsieur Nforbah ? (No answer from the accused). Je vais vous lire un extrait du procès-verbal de l'officier de police judicaire : « mademoiselle Mankah Pascaline a été arrêtée chez Mr Nforbah le 13 juin 2008.

Celle-ci, après interrogation, a déclaré qu'elle était venue chez Nforbah pour prendre le sac de voyage de celui-ci, qui se déplaçait pour Douala avec l'enfant kidnappé ». Madame le juge, je reformule ma question à mademoiselle Mankah : quel est votre rapport avec Nforbah ? (No answer)

Lawyer : Madame le juge, vous pouvez voir que le témoin ne comprend pas ce que Mr le Procureur de la République expose.

Judge : Donc nous n'avons pas toujours d'interprète ? Est-ce qu'il y a quelqu'un dans la salle qui peut interpréter pour la demoiselle ?

Pupil Lawyer in crowd: I can interpret my lord.

Judge: Oui, pouvez-vous venir à la barre? (Pupil lawyer moves towards the bench)

State Counsel: Madame le juge, comme je disais, il y a un moment, dame Mankah Pascaline est coupable au même titre que son ami. Je répète ma question au témoin : quelle est votre position vis-à-vis l'accusé ?

Pupil lawyer: Who is the accused, Mr Nforbah, to you?

Mankah Pascaline: He is my boyfriend and we have been together for five weeks.

State Counsel: J'ai compris ce qu'elle dit. Je continue. Elle a été arrêtée chez l'accusé le 13 juin 2008 et elle a déclaré qu'elle était venue prendre le sac de voyage de celui-ci qui se déplaçait déjà pour Douala avec l'enfant. C'est le rapport de l'interrogation qui le dit...

Pupil Lawyer: You were arrested on the 13th of June 2008 at Mr Nforbah's house and you said to the police during investigation that you had come to take Mr Nforba's bag who was on his way to Douala with the kidnapped child.

Mankah Pascaline: I did not say so. I said that Mr Nforbah told me that he was going to Douala and that if I need something from his house, I should go and see his sister in the house. So I went there to get a travelling bag, since I had to travel to Bamenda to see my mother for us to talk about the visit that Nforbah had to pay to my parents.

State Counsel: Mais ce n'est pas ce que le procès-verbal nous dit.

Donc vous refusez ce que vous avez déclaré à la police. Pour quoi avez-vous signé le PV après lecture?

Pupil Lawyer: But what you say is not what you told the police. Are you refusing what you said to the police? Why did you sign the report after it was read to you?

Mankah Pascaline: I signed it because the gendarmes were beating me. They did not read anything to me; they only asked me to sign the paper and when I refused they started beating me. So, I signed it for them to stop beating me.

Judge: Mademoiselle, ce que vous dites là est très grave. Vous êtes sûr de vos propos ?

Pupil Lawyer: Are you sure of what you are saying?

Mankah Pascaline: Yes

Judge: Où sont les agents de police judicaires concernés ?

State Counsel : Madame le juge, vous voyez comme moi. Ils ne sont pas là […].

Cases like these abound as confirmed by *Maitre* NZODE Yves[3] of the Achet Law Firm in Yaoundé:

The Criminal Procedure Code of the Republic of Cameroon states it clearly: the accused or the suspect has linguistic rights that have to be respected within the framework of the law. But just go to the police stations and gendarmerie posts and see what is happening there. Don't dare, especially, to talk about your rights: you run the risk of regretting it. These judicial police officers seem to forget that there is a process to follow during interrogations. This happens especially, without any prejudice, with French-speaking judicial police officers. They feel very threatened when an accused speaks English. In fact, they seem to know nothing about the Criminal Procedure Code.

As discussed in the next section, the situation in some areas, however, shows the need to respect the linguistic rights of citizens in

---

[3] At the time of interview, *Maitre* Nzode Yves was a Barrister of the Achet Law Firm in Yaoundé. He was interviewed at the Yaoundé *Centre Admistratif* Court house.

line with the law. In Buea, for example, interpreters are hired by the court to interpret in case one of the parties does not understand the official language being used. Magistrate Manghe Eleonor[4] testified to this in an interview in which she was asked to comment on the strategies used by those who try to protect linguistic rights in law courts.

Strategies Used to Mitigate Second Official Language Difficulties in Law Courts and Peripheral Structures

Upon reunification in 1961, the government of the Federal Republic of Cameroon adopted a strategy to deploy only judicial staff that understands the official language of the locality where they are supposed to work. This strategy worked until the late 1980s when judicial police officers were indiscriminately posted to work all over the country. This was justified by migratory tendencies which led to linguistic interaction across the official language divide. This situation created a number of linguistic huddles that were not catered for by the authorities. Particular court houses and individuals adopted various strategies to handle these problems. Most court houses decided to leave suspects to their own devices. This is sufficiently evidenced by the above cited case between the State of Cameroon and Neba Chrysanthus against Mr Nforbah and co, which dragged on for sixteen months for lack of an interpreter. On the advice of his legal adviser, Mr Nforbah accepted to be tried in French since he understood a bit of it. His lawyer, *Maitre* Nzode Yves, confirms:

So many suspects suffer a lot from linguistic incomprehension with the police and the examining magistrates. Look at the example of this case, (C/R Mr Nforba against Neba Chrysanthu cited above); it dragged on for almost two years because the examining magistrate was still looking for an interpreter. At the end, we decided that the

---

[4] Magistrate Manghe Eleonor at the time of interview was a pupil magistrate in Buea South West Region of Cameroon. She was interviewed on 11th August 2010 in Buea.

case should be examined without an interpreter since the accused, Mr Nforbah, could understand some little French but not his witnesses (interviewed on 2nd October 2009 in Yaoundé).

Other judicial police officers attempted providing translation and interpretation services to suspects. For instance, *Adjudant-Chef* Mbede Raymond admits:

> Très souvent je faisais recours à un collègue pour les interrogations préliminaires, mais depuis qu'il a été muté ailleurs, je me débrouille comme je peux. Souvent je fais un rapport que le procureur n'admet pas parce que l'accusé a tout nié. [...] Tu vois un travail que tu as effectué avec beaucoup de dévouement en gaspillant les différentes ressources réduit à zéro. Vraiment c'est une frustration totale. Je crois sincèrement que pour que la justice soit efficace et le problème linguistique résolu, il faut vraiment une formation bilingue pour tout le monde qui fonctionne comme officier de police judiciaire au Cameroun. Si non, les innocents vont toujours se retrouver dans des situations difficiles et les coupables seront libérés à cause de petites nuances sémantiques. [...] Bon, en guise de solution pour l'instant, je fais recours à un professeur de lycée de la place. Il faut savoir que ses services ne sont pas gratuits (interviewed on 28th March 2010 in Kumbo-Bui Division).

[Very often I solicited the help of an English-speaking colleague for preliminary interrogation, but since he was transferred, I manage the way I can. Often I write reports that are rejected by the State Counsel because the accused person rejected them. [...] You see work that you have painstakingly done, spending various resources, reduced to nothing. In fact, it is really frustrating. I sincerely think that for justice to be effective and the linguistic problem solved, there is a need for bilingual training for persons who play the role of judicial police officers in Cameroon. If not, innocent citizens will face difficult situations and the guilty ones will get away because of some semantic inconsistencies. [...] Well, as a temporary measure, I make use of a bilingual secondary school teacher. You should understand that his services are not for free (my translation)].

Moreover, Manghe Eleanor Asu reveals the strategy used by her own service:

There is a particular case in Buea and I prefer not to disclose its references and those concerned due to professional reasons and the fact that it is going on. The complainant comes from a French-speaking region of Cameroon and does not understand any English. Therefore, each time the case is supposed to be heard, the Presiding Magistrate searches for an appropriate interpreter well in advance so as not to disturb the smooth-functioning of the case. However, cases that need French-English interpretation are not very common in Buea, but there is a constant need of French-English translation of documents. Unfortunately, courts in Cameroon don't have translators and their rates are so expensive that we find difficulties in paying for (interviewed on the 11th of August 2010, in Buea).

Many court officials and their auxiliaries resort to interpretation so as to bridge the comprehension gap between English and French speaking Cameroonians before the law. The law allows for that to be done. However, very few judicial authorities follow the laid-down rules. Any kind of person could be called up to serve as an interpreter. In the case of the State of Cameroon and Neba Chrysanthus against Nforbah, an individual is pulled from the audience to serve as an interpreter. In the Nkor-Noni in the Sub-Division of Bui Division, the judicial police officer uses a fellow colleague and a schoolteacher as interpreters. This is further confirmed by Mrs Chindo Emilia[5], former Director of the Bamenda Regional Linguistic Centre, in the following words: 'By dint of understanding or speaking the second official language, many officials think we in the Bamenda Linguistic Centre can serve as interpreters and translators. I am regularly called to court to serve as an interpreter; a domain that I am not well versed with'.

This strategy is good, but it has its flaws as misinterpretation can

---

[5] Mrs Chindo Emilia at the time of interview was Head of the Bamenda Regional Linguistic Centre. She was interviewed in her office on the 14th of December 2009.

send an innocent person to prison or free a hardened criminal. Examples abound in the world. In the United Arab Emirates, a court overturned a ten-year-jail sentence that was given to a Ugandan woman charged with the murder of her HIV-positive husband because of interpretation lapses (*Gulf News,* November 2006). Again, in Libya, five nurses and a doctor were almost executed following a death sentence from a Libyan court due to a translation error. The word 'recombinant' which means, a specific strain of the HIV was interpreted as 'genetically modified' (*CNN,* February 2006). In Cameroon, no case of poor interpretation has been reported in the judiciary. This does not mean that the interpretations are expertly done. However, if serious investigations are carried out such lapses may be identified.

Conclusion

In an officially bilingual country like Cameroon, where there are two official languages in use, there are bound to be situations where there is a need to interpret across the two official language cultures. In order to give a fair trial to everyone, all actors involved in court matters, namely, judicial police officers, magistrates, plaintiffs and defendants should be able to understand one another. To avoid linguistic problems, state-certified court translators and interpreters could be trained in the Advanced School of Translators and Interpreters (ASTI) and posted to various judicial jurisdictions. These people should function under oath. This will go a long way to shorten the duration of court matters because the search for interpreters will be eliminated from the justice delivery chain. It will also help in cutting cost as these civil servants will be paid from government coffers, not by various judicial jurisdictions. This will not be peculiar to Cameroon. The United States of America, a polity which is predominantly English-speaking, has adopted this system. Spolsky (2010) reports that the United States Supreme Court has provided certification for interpretation of some minority languages that exist in the country. These include Chinese, Navajo, Haitian Creole and Spanish. These interpreters are trained, tested and finally certified by the Chief Justice before they can enter into function. The same obtains in Japan where the law requires that only Japanese may be spoken during any investigation and public trial. However, in the year 2000 a count showed that 34 000 police officers and 5 300 civilian interpreters were trained in English, Spanish, and Chinese, among others, and hired by the Japanese government to work in various judicial services (Taki 2005). Cameroon can emulate these examples as this will help save time, cut cost and render the justice system not only effective but credible.

Finally, there is need for a constant retraining of judicial officers in developments in the law. Some police and gendarmerie officers still think that allowing a suspect to speak in the second official language of their choice is a privilege and not a right(C/R Case between Neba Chrysanthus and Nforbah above). This line of thought originates from the colonial epoch where the police functioned more as a repressive force than as a protector of individual freedoms and liberties. If these measures are implemented, they will go a long way to respect the rights of all second official language users in various court houses in Cameroon.

Bibliography

Anchimbe, E., (2005). Anglophonism and Francophonism: The Stakes
of (official) Language Identity in Cameroon. *ALIZES: Revue Angliciste de la Reunion,* 25(26), pp. 7-26.
Biloa, E., (2006). *Le Français en Contact avec L'Anglais au Cameroun.* Meunchen: LINCOM EUROPA.
Chia, E., (1983). Cameroon Home Languages. In: s.l.:s.n., pp. 19-32.
De Varennes, F., (1996). *Language, Minorities and Human Rights.* Boston/London: Nijhoff Publishers.

Eberhard, D. et al (2020) *Languages of the World*. 23rd Edition. Dallas: SIL International

Kiwoh, T. N., (2010). *Official Language Bilingualism and Language Management in Cameroon*. Yaounde: PhD Thesis University of Yaounde 1.

Kouega, J. P., (2001). *Pidgin Facing Death in Cameroon*. [Online]Available at: www.terralingua.org/DiscPapers/DiscPaper17.html

Mveng, E., (1985). *Histoire du Cameroun*. Yaounde: CEPER.

Paulston, C. B., (1997). Language Policies and Language Rights. *Annual Review of Anthropology*, Volume 26, pp. 73-85.

Phillipson, R., (1992). *Linguistic Imperialism*. Oxford: Oxford University Press.

SIL, (2002). *Cameroon Annual Report*. Yaounde: s.n.

Spolsky, B., (2010). *Language Management*. Cambridge: Cambridge University Press.

Statistics, N. I. o., (2014). *Annuaire Statistique du Cameroun Chapitre 4*. Yaounde: NIS.

Stumpf, R., (1979). La Politique Linguistique au Cameroun de 1884 à 1960: Comparaison entre les Coloniales Allemande, Britannique et du Rôle Joué par les Sociétés Missionnaires. In: *Europaische Hochschul-Schriften:Reichem27, Asiatische und Afrikanische Studien 4*. Bern: Peter Lang.

Taki, T., (2005). Labour Migration and the Language Barrier in Contemporary Japan: The Formation of Domestic Language Regime of a Globalising State. *International Journal of the Sociology of language*, pp. 55-81.Http//.www.worldometer.info/ Cameroon. Accessed 1st July 2020.

Chapter Eight

Voices Behind Writings on Walls: Effective Communication or Not?

Fonka Hans Mbonwuh

Introduction

Iten (2005:1) points out that both theorists and ordinary language users agree that one of the core uses of language is the exchange of information about the world. The mode of usage, however, differs depending on the people, places, contexts and other related factors. This chapter examines communication within the educational context, and specifically in Cameroon. All human communication, whether identified or unidentified can be traced to a source and the message from that source, specified or unspecified, is intended for a target. An observation on the various universities and secondary schools Campuses in Cameroon reveals an affluent of inscriptions on walls of the lecture halls. These are certainly not appropriate channels to convey information in well organised institutions. Considering the confrontational nature of some of the messages, authors prefer anonymous paths to conventional communication channels. If at all this is communication, it may as well be seen as communication that transgresses the borders of traditional communication. This is because messages on walls may or may not be given due attention since the target audience may never read them or may read but ignore them.

This chapter attempts to reveal the different concerns raised by these hidden voices behind the writings on school walls. Some of these messages convey insults, expression of difficulties in understanding a particular subject, expressions of love and sex, affirmations, advertisement of individual products and services, and rebellion against certain rules, among others. The chapter examines only messages inscribed with chalk. We chose only chalk messages because the fonts are legible enough to draw the attention of the target readers.

Usually, these messages are written in strategic areas such as in front of classrooms near the lecture board, directly at the back classrooms facing the board, along open areas like corridors and entry and exit points, amongst others. These messages which are written for different audiences and different purpose, provoke different reactions. Given that state universities in Cameroon still very much use the chalk board in the teaching and learning process, students use the leftovers to write their messages. From our observation, apart from messages announcing meetings and advertisements, hardly was anything found written in ink by students expressing the different concerns highlighted in this paper. Whether or not these writings are communication effectively will depend on what effective communication really is as examined in the next section.

Communication

The word communication is derived from the Latin word *communis*, which means common. When one communicates, one is out to establish communality with another person (Overton 2007).With the help of verbal or non-verbal symbols, a message can be sent through a channel to a receiver. Communication is a complicated process that demands putting together information from many sources, and expressing thoughts with clarity and relevant content, according to established *conventions,* and an awareness of our *conduct* through the reactions of others to what we say and do (Sage 2006). Chaturvedi and Chaturvedi (2011: 9) define communication as 'a natural activity of all humans, which is to convey opinions, feelings, information, and ideas to others through words (written or spoken), body language or signs'. This does not give a complete definition of what communication is and by not doing so, gives credibility to Arredondo's (2007) opinion that in our workplaces, groups are frequently hampered by conflicts resulting from poor communication, misunderstandings, misinformation and growth of problems, among others. This is contrary to what communication should be because according to the received view of linguistic communication, the central function of language is to enable a speaker to reveal his or her thoughts to a hearer (Gauker 2003).

The process of communication which examines all what it takes to communicate effectively is hardly observed in some communication acts. Bennie (2009:1), on his part, views communication as the process by which information is exchanged through a number of ways including written word, spoken word, pictures and diagrams, facial expressions, behaviour with posture and non-verbal sounds. If one were to take Bennie's definition, it would mean that every utterance one makes becomes communication, whether there is feedback or not. Berge (2001: 23) adds another dimension when he views communication as 'an information process going on between at least two human communicators (not necessarily two persons as long as one can communicate with oneself) embedded in a context and a situation'. All the definitions show scholars view communication differently. I will examine the communication process in this chapter principally in relation to written communication.

Before looking at what written communication is, I will first examine the process of communication which will enable us see whether the writings on the wall respect the chain of communication. This process is examined in the light of the theory of communication by Shannon and Weaver (1949).

The Process of Communication

The process of communication begins with the desire in a speaker to express an idea, thought or feeling to a receiver. Communication basically involves the sender, the message, the communication medium and the receiver. According to Chaturvedi and Chaturvedi (2011:11), communication is intended to control/manipulate the receiver. However, effective communication does not come automatically. The failure of some people to achieve their objectives in relationships, negotiations or decision-making processes is to a greater degree due to failure in communication. There can be failure to communicate the content of the message, or the form of the message, or both. Earlier consideration of the communication process saw it as a one-way process which had to do with the flow of information from the sender to the receiver. According to this lineal view as indicated in Chaturvedi and Chaturvedi (2011: 11), the receiver passively receives the message and acts as directed or desired by the sender. In this case, it is assumed that the message has passed through the medium chosen without any form of distortion or alteration. The lineal process takes the following form:

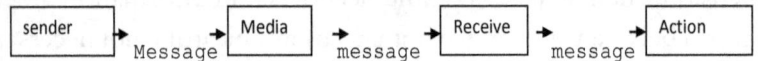

As this lineal communication system indicates, the receiver passively receives the message and acts as directed or as desired by the sender. Communication in this case can be considered as a way to control or manipulate the receiver. It is considered that messages pass through the medium chosen by the sender to reach the receiver without any distortion or change.

According to the Shannon- Weaver Model, adopted in this chapter as our analytical framework, the idea of feedback is introduced as a corrective counter to noise. This theory was published in *The Mathematical Theory of Communication* in 1949. Chaturvedi and Chaturvedi (2011) hold that in the Shannon- Weaver model, feedback was not considered as an integral component of communication because the model conceived the communication process as a linear act and feedback as a new act of communication as seen in exhibit 2.

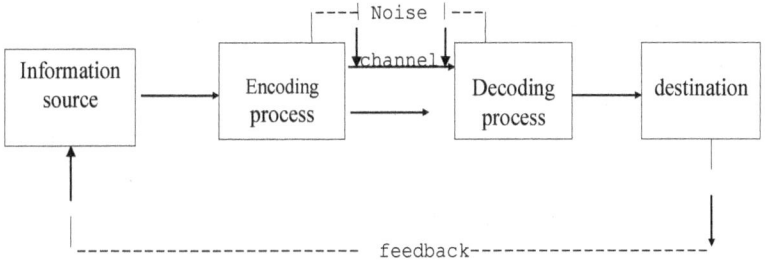

The model is based on the idea that communication occurs only when the message has been received without any form of distortion. This is considered the theoretical concept of perfect communication. The major stages that stand out in a communication model, which ever we take, are sender, message, code, channel and receiver. Noise is an external or internal intrusion that occurs in the course of communication while feedback is the necessary component which assures the sender that the message has arrived the destination. If the message does not reach the destination exactly as it left the information source, probably because of interruption, it is feedback that brings awareness to such breakdown in communication.

Feedback is, therefore, important in any communication process since the receiver is also expected to react. It should, however, be noted that the receiver can also deliberately refuse to send feedback after having received the message, making it difficult for the sender to know whether or not the message reached the destination.

For one to transmit one's mental images, ideas and feelings directly to another person, they have to believe in telepathic communication. We have to translate or encode our thought in such a way that the others can receive and interpret what we think (Hartly and Bruckmann 2002). If the writer, in the case of this chapter, is able to anticipate how others will interpret what he has written, communication can be made effective. The writer uses codes he knows his receiver can decode; else the communication process becomes fruitless as nothing will be got from it. A code in the words of Hartly and Bruckmann, (2002:17) is a coherent set of symbols plus the rules needed to structure a message. A code consists essentially of a list of words, and a set of rules for preparing the text. Rules have to do with the grammar and syntax of the language used for communication. Understanding the reason for communication will help in deciding in the subsequent sections whether writings on walls can be considered effective communication.

Reasons for Communication

Although different people communicate for different reasons, there are, however, some general reasons for communication pointed out in Bennie (2009:1). Though these reasons hinge more on business communication, I have found them relevant to this article. Amongst the reasons People communicate are:

- to pass on information
- to persuade people to buy a product or use a service
- to discuss an issue
- to recommend a course of action
- to make or answer a request
- to make or answer a complaint
- to keep a record of something that has happened or been agreed
- to explain or clarify a situation
- to give an instruction
-

Amongst other reasons already given here, Forsyth (2008: 3) adds that communication is meant to change attitudes. This is of prime importance in this chapter because students write to effect some attitudinal changes around them. In the analysis of the data for this study, it will be observed that most of the reasons enumerated here account for the different writings on school walls by students.

Written communication

Writing, as Chaturvedi and Chaturvedi (2011:113) put it, is a mode of communicating a message for a specific purpose. It reveals one's ability to think clearly and to use language effectively. Any written business document must stand up to analysis, and its only real test is whether its reader approves that it did the job it was intended to do. This means it must have a clear purpose, and that what is said, and how it is said, are understandable; indeed, that it exhibits any other characteristic that it needs to meet its specific intention (Forsyth 2008:133). Writing requires a set of skills to enable the writer writes simply, clearly, accurately and concisely. It is required that the writer recognizes the needs, expectations, fears and attitudes of the audience or receiver and reader of the written information. Unlike verbal communication where the feedback is almost always immediate, written communication is one-way, from the sender to the receiver with retarded feedback or no feedback at all. For writing to be effective, three principal points have to be observed- clarity, accuracy and brevity (Chaturvedi and Chaturvedi 2011:117). Bennie (2009:7) regards the same points in terms of precision, unclutteredness, and straight to the point. Clarity as very important in communication because how clear a message is, has an effect on what occurs after it is delivered. At best, poor communication produces confusion; at worst, it fails to get done whatever should be done. Conversely, ensuring that a message is clear and unambiguous can result in positive action (Forsyth 2008:4).

In communication, whether written or spoken, there are some salient questions that the sender needs to ask and answer before going on.

   a. Should you be writing or speaking to the person concerned?
   b. Are you addressing the right person? In other words, who is

your reader? You can waste a lot of time if you address the wrong person initially, and in the case of a written document, it could be lost or ignored in the process. Wilkie (2001:10) says if you visualize and write for that person, you will have a good chance of getting your message across.

c. Do you need a reply? If you do, and do not let the other person know, you would have failed to achieve your purpose.
d. What is your purpose in writing or speaking?

Methodology

The data used in this chapter were collected over a period of three years, from 2011-2013. The data have to do with all information written on the classroom walls of academic institutions like Universities and secondary schools. The institutions from which these data were collected include the University of Yaounde I, the University of Buea, the University of Bamenda (Higher Teacher Training College Bambili) and secondary schools- *Institut Baudelaire Bilingue* and Mario Academic Complex, all in Yaounde. This researcher collected data for this study in schools in Yaounde and employed friends in other regions who perform the same task in designated schools. This information collected is classified according to the different concerns raised in such writings as presented and analysed below. The classifications to be examined are advertisement, expression of difficult learning conditions, supplications, love and friendship, warnings and many others. No personal contacts were made because we never met any person writing on the wall in any of these institutions. However, we did some calls and found out that the products advertised were already bought or already sold. Given the large amount of data in each classification, only 32 messages are selected and analysed. All of the data is found in the appendix. Apart from the Shannon-Weaver model that is used for the analysis of data, this chapter, considering the difficulty to interpret the minds of the writers at the time they are writing their messages, we used other communication models like *The Self-regulatory (Autopoesis) Model* explained by Berge (2001).

Data Presentation and Analysis

The data here is presented and analysed based on the concerns raised in each message following a personal classification. Of the different types of concerns raised, advertisement, expression of difficult learning conditions, love and friendship, and supplications are analysed while the others – advice, warning and insults, affirmation and religion among others are just mentioned in passing.

Advertisement

Dyer (1982:1) says that:

> Even if you don't read a newspaper or watch television, and walk around the streets with your eyes down, you will find it impossible to avoid some form of publicity, even if it's only a trade display at a local store, uninvited handbills pushed through the letter box or cards displayed in the window of the corner newsagent.

What this means is that one does not choose to see or hear advertisement because one finds it almost everywhere. Advertising according to Dyer (1982: 2) means 'drawing attention to something or notifying or informing somebody of something'. Although Kelly-Holmes (2005) says that advertising is more than simply explicit advertising messages; it encompasses a whole range of texts and objects, such as toys, books, television programmes, packaging and so forth. The advertisement examined in this portion of the work considers only written messages on walls and specifically in chalk. The following are the different advertisements of personal items found on the walls:

- Two RAM bars for use in 512MB laptop for sale (*Vente de deux plaquettes de RAM pour laptop de 512MB*)
- *A bed for sale*
- A *CRT 17 screen for sale-125000* - (*Ecran CRT 17 à vendre - 125000*)
- A modern room to let - *(Chambre moderne à louer)*
- Condoms on sale here - *(Preservatif en vente ici*)

Although I have not written their numbers in this write-up, all these adverts carried the contacts of the persons selling the advertised items. Definitely not all the writings on the walls are written out of fear; some of the writers probably see the wall as an easy channel to communicate their products to potential buyers. Since they do not pay for using the walls to advertise their products, they use chalk to write boldly for potential buyers to see.

Students also use the wall to express their needs. In personal adverts, contacts are also given when expressing needs.

- I need a Nokia N72
- Need for home teacher in Spanish- *(Recherche d'un répétiteur en espagnol)*
- In need of a good labtop (90000)
- In need of a television – 20.000frs - *(Recherche d'une television 20.000)*
- In need of a gaz bottle - *(Recherche bouteille de gaz)*

This type of advertising that targets a wider public is what Kelly-Holmes (2005) calls commercial consumer advertising. Since the walls are used in commercializing products and services, buyers and sellers also use the same wall to express their wants. This does not mean these students do not know where these products are sold in the market. Those who buy through this medium are looking for cheap products which, out of desperate need to survive, someone is always ready to sell.

Expression of difficult learning conditions

This is one of the areas in which much was written. While some of these expressions are directed to lecturers, some are directed to students. In each case, there is an expected effect that can be deduced from the message. In the following cases, Ngoa-Ekelle, the area in which the University of Yaoundé I is situated, is simply personified. They are not saying that the University in itself is a problem; it is about those operating in the system who have, according to the following expressions, transformed the University into a grave where wisdom is buried.

a) Ngoa, don't send us back to the quarter - (*Ngoa, ne nous renvoie pas au quartier*)
b) Ngoa Ekelle is like a grave for youths - (*Ngoa Ekelle est comme un tombeau pour les jeunes*)
c) Ngoa has killed my genius - (*Ngoa a tué mon géni*)
d) Ngoa, you kill the genius of children - (*Ngoa tu tues le génie des enfants*).

It is not really clearly who the writings from (a) to (d) target. We can, however, presume that the target audience are, most probably, lecturers or the school administration. Fellow students may have little to do with killing genius or sending somebody back to the quarter. The following cases are directed to fellow students with the intention of preparing their minds about the difficulties that lie ahead of them all. The response given to some of these messages is an indication that the receiver has identified himself/ herself with it. However, not all messages are responded to. Such messages, like (b), (c) and (d) in this section are regarded from the perspective of the autopoesis model in which the communicators (or as they are called, the 'emitters' and 'receivers') do not communicate in order to transfer and create a message (as in the conduit and dialogue models), or even to create some information, a conveyed message, and an understanding, but simply to integrate elements from the communicative situation (the environment) which can contribute to the communicators' so-called self-regulation and self-creation (hence the term 'autopoetic') (Berge 2001:24).

On the basis of this model, the messages on (i) and (j) are not meant to communicate any information to anybody; they are simply self-expressive, which is communicating to the self and not to any second or third party.

e) Welcome to Ngoa, you will confirm it - (*Bien venue à Ngoa, vous allez confirmer*)
f) Ngoa, hell on earth - (*Ngoa, un enfer sur terre*)
g) Oh !you are not obliged to live in the hell. You can decide to leave it and you will never fill the pains. Lazy fellow- (*Oh ! tu n'es pas obligé de vivre cet enfer. Tu peux décider d'en sortir et tu ne pourras plus te pleindre. Lâche !*).
h) Ngoa is hell for you who sleeps - (*Ngoa est un enfer pour toi qui dors*)
i) Understanding is an issue, validating is another - (*Comprendre c'est bien, valider c'est autre-*)
j) I always validate during resit - (*Je valide toujours au rattrapage*)

These messages in (e) and (f) are arguably addressed to fellow students. It is clear that the receiver has identified himself/herself with the message. This is seen from the response that (g) gives to (f) when the latter classifies Ngoa-Ekelle as hell on earth. The receiver thinks the sender is willingly living in hell he/she can avoid by going away. What this response indicates is that even those messages that have not been addressed directly have equally reached the target. If the lecturers have not responded to messages meant for them, it does not mean they have not read them. The simple issue writings on walls is that no particular individual feels obliged to give a response like the students have done. It should be noted that these same messages are written on the walls of different classrooms and by different hands.

Love and Relationship

The largest amount of the data is on sex and love relationships. The walls serve as the middleman between suitors and those they admire. Some of the students are not bold enough to make advances to create relationships. In almost all the cases for those asking for love or friendship, contacts are provided. In sample 3 below, the word is simply representative, meaning a woman who is in need of sex.

1. In need of a beautiful maiden (Recherche d'une jolie copine au numero…..)
2. Ladies for your evening, feel them and desire to have sex, You will not be disappointed- (*Les filles pour vos soirées. Sen les et envie de baiser, Vous ne serez pas déçus – tel given*)
3. In need of a bitch in gestation - (Recherche d'une chienne en gestation)

In the cases below, the writers seek to justify why they have sex – for money, marks and because there is no embargo on it. The messages these voices are sending out are quite varied. In sample (5) below, the taste in every hole, is a common saying among youths, which would simply mean *no woman is bad for sex*. In (6), though the voice on the wall uses 'him' and not 'you' to speak directly to the reader, she wants the teachers who trademarks with sex to know that it is just a game of interest and affection. Though no name is mentioned here, the concerned lecturers who read this will certainly identify themselves to it. This may not be asking them to stop, but rather reminding them that they are only in a business deal that will stop when the need for the marks ends. In (7) and (8), the voice on the wall says she does not pay rent for having sex, so she is free to do prostitution since it gives money. The fact that (8) begins with 'why should I not…' indicates that it is perhaps a response to a challenge on the writer's sexual life. From the messages uttered by the unidentified voices from the walls, it is clear that in the event of an open sex market, they will freely disclose their identities, but the environment in which they are does not permit such.

4. 'sex is good for health' what do you think? (*'baiser c'est bon pour la santé' qu'en pensez vous ?*)
5. all holes have a taste – (*Tous trous á gout*)
6. I don't love him I only have sex with him because I want the marks.
7. Money has no colour that's why I prostitute to have it even though in school.
8. Why should I not have sex, do I pay rents for it?

Data samples (1) to (5) are from the University of Yaoundé 1 while sample (6) to (8) are from the University of Buea. Given that the messages in (6), (7) and (8) are just utterances, the principle of Truth Condition is used in their analysis. According to Strawson (1971:178) Truth Condition is:

> a truth implicitly acknowledged by communication-theorists themselves that in almost all the things we should count as sentences, there is a substantial central core of meaning which is explicable either in terms of truth-conditions or in terms of some related notion ...

On the basis of the above concept, this chapter argues that there is truth condition in, for example (8) above in that sex workers in Cameroon do not pay any tax for their activity. Equally, the personal pronoun 'I', gives credibility to the truth condition since the person communicating is the actor. Carston (2002:22) further argues that it seems to be impossible to specify the necessary and jointly sufficient conditions for the truth of some utterance without making reference to the context of utterance and, crucially, the speaker's intentions. The social context under which utterance (6) above is made is the school environment, and in my view, a number of intentions can be drawn from the statement:

a) I am not a prostitute, I am just forced to do so
b) Not all marks earned in the university are merited
c) Someone should help investigate the situation of sexual harassment on campuses

It should, therefore, be noted that the above conclusions have been drawn from analysis beyond the sentence, taking into consideration the social context and the intension of the speaker. The different utterances, though from different universities, can be taken to present a general situation on university campuses in Cameroon. The following section examines supplication as identified from the voices on the walls.

Supplication

From the different writings on the walls, it was also found that students also plead for certain actions to be carried out by friends and by their lecturers. According to the *Cambridge Advanced Learner Dictionary* (2008), a supplicant is 'a person who asks a god or someone who is in a position of power for something in a nervous way that shows that they do not think of themselves as very important'. The following voices indicate such a nervous unassertive position that needs rescue.

a) Please Lecturers, help us to validate. Ngoa Ekele is not our office - (*S.V.P les profs, aidez-nous à valider. Ngoa Ekelle n'est pas notre bureau*)
b) Please share with others - (*S.V.P partagez avec les autres*)
c) Let's keep our classes clean - (Gardons-nous salles propres)

From this data presented here, (a) is directed to lecturers, and the writer pleads that the former should help students pass their courses and leave. It is not clear exactly what kind of help is needed here. However, it can be interpreted in the following ways:

   i. Lecturers should teach well to enable students pass their

courses
ii. Lecturers should mark scripts well so that merit is given its place
iii. Assessments should be within reach and based on things taught in class
iv. Lecturers should give bonus marks

In (b) that is directed to fellow students, different interpretation can also be given to it.
i. Let us all copy from each other during exams so that we can all pass our exams.
ii. Share with us the different ways you are using to pass your exams.

The interpretations given here may not in any way be true because they do not come from the writers of these messages. These voices, it should be noted, use the walls because they do not want to be identified. Some of them, at the time this information was copied, might have long left the institutions because there was no date indicating when each piece of information was written.

In (c), the message is again addressed to fellow students asking them to keep their halls clean. This is from the background of very untidy lecture halls at the University of Yaoundé I. Though the University administration ensures that halls are clean, this voice recognizes that students are responsible for making them dirty.

Comments

The voices on the school walls are so varied in the issues raised. This type of communication has remained at the level of students for over years and has been effective in that products advertised, for example, are sold. This explains the reason more voices from the wall are those of advertisement. The provision of contacts, as is the case for most advertisements, creates a channel for feedback.

Some voices receive immediate feedback from those who feel that they can respond, even if they are not the target. This is the case with expression of difficult learning conditions where the response to the expression that 'Ngoa-Ekele is hell on earth' is an admonition for the writer, who is blamed for willingly living an avoidable situation. The issue here is that the person responding might not have been the target and such a response kills the seriousness of the message. It can equally be argued that since the message does not identify any particular target, any person who is urged to respond to it becomes the target.

Voices that speak love are quite many. This is understandable since the different institutions examined are made up largely of unmarried youths. There are open expressions of the desire to have relationships of diverse types – friendly, sexual and more.

Conclusion

Every word that is written on school walls is written by somebody to somebody, although a few are self-expressions that do not need any response. The targets are sometimes directly identified by the communicator while in some cases, the targets identify themselves to the various messages. The most significant innovation here is the fact that a new system of communication has been adopted wherein the speaker uses the wall to communicate and the feedback sometimes come from the wall. This, nevertheless, is a type of communication where the target decides to hear the message or not, depending on the contents of the message. This is, therefore, a very difficult kind of communication because even if feedback is expected, it may still come from a wrong sender since everyone can respond to any message. Feedbacks may equally be given to messages that are of the Self-Regulatory model which are not written for the purpose of feedback. Voices behind writings on walls is effective communication because the whole chain of communication according to the Shannon-Weaver Model, a theory adopted this chapter, is respected. However, writers who have genuine concerns should rather review their communication model because they may not have the desired feedback since even those not targeted can respond to messages, giving a false impression or unintended feedback.

Bibliography

Arredondo, L., (2007). *Communicate Effectively: 24 Lessons for Day to Day Business Success.* New York: McGraw-Hill.

Bennie, M., (2009). *A Guide to Good Business Communication.* 5 ed. Oxford: Spring Hill House.

Berge, K. L., (2001). Communication. *Concise Encyclopedia of Sociolinguistics.*

Carston, R., (2002). *Thoughts and Utterances: The Pragmatics of Explicit Communication.* Oxford: Blackwell.

Chaturvedi, P. & Chaturvedi, M., (2011). *Business Communication: Concepts, Cases and Applications.* 2 ed. Noida: Dorling Kindersley Pvt Ltd.

Dyer, G., (1982). *Advertising and Communication.* London and New York: Routledge.

Forsyth, P., (2008). *The Art of Successful Business Communication.* London: The Institution of Engineering and Technology.

Gauker, C., (2003). *Words without Meaning.* Palatino: SNP Best-set Typesetter Ltd.

Hartly, P. & Bruckmann, C., (2002). *Business Communication.* London and New York: Routledge.

Iten, C., (2005). *Linguistics Meaning, Truth Conditions and Revelance: The Case of Concessives.* New York: Palgrave Macmillan.

Kelly-Holmes, H., (2005). *Advertising as Multilingual Communication.* New York: Palgrave Macmillan.

Overton, R., (2007). *Business Communication.* Boat Harbour: Martin Books Pty Ltd.

Sage, R., (2006). *Supporting Language and Communication: A Guide for School Staff.* California: SAGE.

Shannon, C. & Weaver, W., (1949). *The Mathematical Theory Communication*. Urbana, IL: University of Illinois.

Strawson, P. F., (1971). *Logico-Linguistic Papers*. London: Methuen.

Wilkie, H., (2001). *Writing, Speaking Listening: The Essentials of Business Communication*. Oxford: How to Books Ltd.

Chapter Nine

An Emic Reading of Taxicab Inscriptions in Cameroon

Joseph Nkwain

Introduction

Language comprises a veritable dress of thought with innumerable patterns in diverse contexts and aims at expressing a wide range of feelings and experiences. These thoughts often vary depending on the users, the subject matter and are usually representative of different realities. Particularly revealing are linguistic realities in multilingual and pluriethnic communities of speech wherein, conspicuous patterns of usage are recurrent. One of such communities in which language behaviour continues to intrigue observers and researchers alike is Cameroon.

This chapter delves into an often overlooked, yet, illuminating and interesting domain of language use – taxicab captions. Taxicab captions as used here refer to the different inscriptions taxicab drivers or owners inscribe around their vehicles for public reading. The captions are therefore akin to slogans - short memorable catchwords or phrases often used in adverts, politicking, religion and other contexts to espouse particular ideologies or situations. Though the authors' intentions are not always evident at first sight, the captions tend to express their visions and life experiences. The captions constitute one of the delicate and complicated domains of language use wherein one discerns the power of language in communication. This study intends to investigate language use by this category of users, the different thematic concerns, the linguistic sources and processes employed and the functional load of the devices.

The socioeconomic and linguistic backdrop of the study

The diversity inherent in plurilingual and multiethnic Cameroon proffers a propitious environment for the investigation of a cross range of interesting linguistic, political, cultural, religious and economic phenomena. This diversity is attested in the different speech communities that make up this homogenous entity. One of such highly homogenous communities which constitutes a microcosm of this diversity is Yaounde, the administrative capital of the country. The cosmopolitan status of the town is better explicated by political, religious, administrative, educational, economic as well as social forces which continue to exert a centripetal force on citizens from the other nine regions of the country and even beyond. They all converge here for the fulfilment of their different aspirations. One of such aspirations is the betterment of status through employment which is, however, often difficult to come by. This is usually fraught by the unfortunate situation where, in principle, the level of education determines employment chances, as well as the quality of jobs proposed. As such, those with a low level of education who eventually find themselves in the town do unskilled and poorly paid jobs. The sector of taxicab driving has and continues to provide a haven for this category of job seekers. It is, however, worthy of note that despite the hitherto belief that the profession is reserved for school dropouts, the uneducated and the underprivileged in general, the present situation is characterised by the flooding of the sector by university graduates following the precarious economic atmosphere of rising unemployment. Fortunately, the harmonious co-existence of the different stakeholders involved in the sector has been explained by their understanding of the prevailing situation and above all, their propensity to peacefully reconcile their differences whenever issues of education, family background and social status arise.

At the linguistic level, evidently, the cosmopolitan nature of Yaounde insinuates a highly multilingual setting with almost all the speakers of the estimated 266 indigenous languages (Ethnologue 2005) present here. This linguistic diversity is attested in one way by the gamut of inscriptions which are encoded on taxicabs either by their drivers or owners, some of whom often take turns in driving them. As such, inscriptions abound in English, French, Pidgin English, indigenous languages, Camfranglais, Arab and even the sporadic use of a foreign language such as Spanish. These inscriptions are therefore indicative of the linguistic backgrounds of their authors who are, for the most part, the drivers. Besides, the inscriptions equally tend to be revelatory of the sociocultural, political, religious and educational backgrounds of the authors. These expressions transgress formal writing conventions and get into informal spaces where writing no longer have visible authors and messages from writings are at the reach of every taxi user.

Methodology

The method adopted for this study is mainly the qualitative method. The data set for the study constitutes a total of 150 captions culled randomly from taxicabs in Yaounde. The choice of the town is explicated by the fact that, as the administrative capital, it has been engorged by Cameroonians from all the regions of the country on different missions. It thus constitutes a propitious ground for the practice of professional taxicab driving.

The data collection procedure involved a systematic noting of the different messages as they appeared on taxicabs as well as the registration numbers of cars so as to avoid reduplication. Where similar captions recurred, they were noted once only. This was through the observation of taxicabs in parking lots, fuelling stations and as they plied the streets of Yaounde. The data included messages in all the languages in which they appeared. This was in order to reconcile the noted messages with the linguistic representation of the country. The study was carried out during the period from July 7th to August 28th 2015.

The messages culled were analysed following Halliday's (1990) Ecolinguistic Approach and the Descriptive Analytical Approach. Embedded in the former approach, the Linguistic Ecology Approach was adopted as a more specific approach. First used by Voegelin et al. (1967) and later pioneered by Haugen (1972), the approach describes diverse forms of world languages and the way language influences interrelationships between humans and organisms in their natural environments. The approach considers language behaviour in both the social and ecological contexts and even extends to the impact of specific discourses rather than languages in general. Through it, one better gleans how language use by a specific group of users is influenced by their immediate environment. The latter approach entailed a systematic classification of messages following thematic categories and the semantic shades of the messages decoded within their specific contexts. It is worthy of note that authors of the texts could not be interviewed in order to find out the exact meanings or what the texts were intended to express. This is because most of them were noted down when the vehicles were parked and empty or when they drove along. The interpretations and meanings attributed to the texts were therefore based principally on the investigator's intuition as a competent member of the speech community. Thus, the texts are open to other possible interpretations. An evaluation of their frequency of occurrence was carried out and the functional load of the messages was equally examined. The identification of the various stylistic processes and linguistic sources of the inscriptions were also attempted.

Data presentation and analyses

Following the method described above, a total of 150 captions were obtained and distributed accordingly.

Thematic distribution and semantic shades of captions

The data set for this write-up demonstrates the fact that captions could be redistributed following several thematic categories ranging from religion, naming, wisdom, vigilance, acknowledgement, love and solidarity and a mixed bag of captions. They are distributed as follows:

Table 1: *Thematic distribution and frequency of captions*

Thematic category	No. of captions	Frequency(%)
Religion	47	31.34
Naming	40	26.66
Wisdom	19	12.67
Vigilance	14	09.33
Acknowledgement	9	06
Love and solidarity	9	06
A mixed bag of captions	12	08
Total	150	100

The foregoing thematic concerns are explicated in turns:

Religion

From the above representation, for the bulk of captions (31.34%) to be religion-oriented is not surprising as it is a true reflection of this society's increased sense of spiritual recognition and awareness. This is further corroborated by the unprecedented rise in the number of religious groups and churches here (Drønen 2013). This strong spiritual awareness coupled with the zeal to win more souls better explicate the high frequency of such texts. Understandably, the religious liberalisation policies and the cropping up of Pentecostal churches around the town constitute complementary evidence.

The gospel of instant prosperity advocated by these churches is considerably impacting the spiritual lives of many users as they profess their faith through a myriad of religious expressions. These expressions exhibit the central role played by an invisible and all-powerful hand in the life of mankind and the wish that God's will be done. Thus, expressions such as the following are used with a laudatory intention: *Na God, Dieu n'oublie personne (God forgets nobody), Dieu est vivant (God is alive), God is great, Merci Seigneur (Thank you Lord), Gloire à Dieu (Glory be to God), In God we trust, The Lord is all, Le Seigneur est merveilleux (The Lord is marvellous), Dieu est le seul juge (God is the only judge), La grâce de Dieu (God's grace), On ne peut rien contre la volonté de Dieu (Nothing can be done against the will of God), Prayer is the king, Don de Dieu (God's gift), I thank my God, God is great, God only, God is faithful, Praise the Lord, Alpha & Omega, God bless the strugglers, Thy will be done, Divine favour 11, My Lord my all, Inchah Allah (By God's grace), God's time is the best, Confiance en Dieu (Confidence in God), Par la grâce de Dieu (By the grace of God), Jehovah Shamah, Nyuy yoh buni (God does not sleep), Ndah ndem (Only God),*Louer Yaweh (Praise God)*, etc.

No ticket to heaven is remindful of the religious truth that salvation is personal and cannot be bought. Besides, others express the necessity to cover one's existence under the protective canopy of the Almighty God/Allah or by the precious blood of Jesus Christ. This is evident in captions such as *Que Allah nous protège (May Allah protect us), Blood of Jesus, The Lord is my shepherd* and *I am covered by the blood of Jesus*, which are all evocative of divine protection.

Whereas some simply acknowledge the power of prayers – *Prayer is the king*, others ask for divine forgiveness for wrongdoers as encapsulated in the caption *Forgive them*. In strict religious metaphors, some taxicabs are referred to as *God's property, Chamber of God, Holy Ghost fire* and *Ambassade de Christ (Christ's embassy)*. Some authors draw profusely from popular instructive Bible verses such as *Mathew 77, Ps.*

36 and *Ps. 23*. Apart from saving space and time, this strategy effectively expresses the authors' visions with regard to their life experiences.

Through these inscriptions, the authors exhibit their resilient faith, their spiritual and religious inclination. Besides, they tend to seek divine favour and protection and this is corroborated by the conspicuous presence of tracts and notices with beguiling spiritual messages and images of popular men of God, religious symbols, etc., meant to impact readers and to show off religious security since the pastors are purported to have protective powers.

Naming

In the second position came captions inspired by naming at 26.66%. This strategy constitutes the use of different indexicals and other forms of designation with names of influential personalities, loved ones, iconic figures, names of taxicab drivers and owners. This trend is explained by users' fervour to show off, the strife for allegiance, affiliation, reverence, self-affirmation, status and identity. This consists in (self-)naming in general with users identifying themselves with nicknames which are picked up following personal or group experiences. These names are drawn from different spheres of social influence and often constitute, for the most part, the names of idols admired for one reason or the other. It is equally a case of self-identification with popular figures whose names are adopted as a mark of their appreciation. This is often the case where points of convergence are registered with regard to the degree of popularity of some public figures. This explains the inscription of names of icons such as *Eto'o, Le golden boy, Le Pichichi (Spanish football league title conferred on Samuel Eto'o Fils)* and *Drogba, le meilleur (Drogba, the best)*, both, representative of the two contending camps which, each, considers one of the stars to be either richer or more skilful than the other.

Other forms are taken up as a social identification strategy. Here, the user seeks to be identified with a particular social status despite their profession as a cab driver. As such, forms such as *Cheriff (Sheriff), La Monaco, Le Boss, Le Saint, Le Marsellais, Ami des stars (Stars' friend), Complice (Accomplice), Yes, Le blanc (Yes, The Whiteman), Passager 57 (Passenger 57), Grand katika, (Big Boss), Awilo Longumba, Petit Amigo (Young friend), Turbo, Le Doyen (The Dean), La vieille dame (Old lady), Daisy Joyce), Majolie Katrina, Raul, Rodriguez le free , Le Bakis, Azonto, Carlos Blanco, Sissoko, El Senator,* etc., modes of address suggestive or used in recognition of the role played by the personality who, in these cases, is often held in high esteem.

Apart from association with social status, other modes are revelatory of place of origin, *viz. Le Prince Mbamois (Prince of Mbam), Fils du Nde (Son of Nde), Yes, Major du Noun (Yes, Major of Noun), Bfssam frère (Bafoussam brother)*, etc. In these ways, they are readily identified as originating from the Mbam (Centre Region), Noun and Nde (West Region) respectively. As such, the users define geographical origin and can easily identify with others from the same area.

Again, other address modes tend to impinge on users' specific character traits or qualities they want to be associated with. Whereas some see in themselves an incarnation of hope – *Espoir,* many others, in an attempt to show off and benefit from the beauty of their new, brightly coloured and well decorated taxicabs, reserve them for VIPs – *VIP* (Very Important Personality). In the same vein, authors inscribe easily identifiable first names and surnames which could either be theirs or those of close ones, thus, *Solo, Fozong, Matam Assan, Mouna, etc.* The inscription *The only son* is suggestive of uniqueness or the user looks upon himself as a treasure and should be treated carefully. Whereas *Le débrouillard* (someone who struggles to survive) readily defines the status of the user as one who works hard, *Young money* is descriptive of a successful young and rich person.

Wisdom

Captions which constituted moral signposts represented 12.67% of the data. These are captions meant to warn against certain excesses, to reiterate some virtues and to moralise in general. They are better understood against the backdrop of falling moral standards in this community. These short witty expressions are characteristic of communication situations conditioned by time and space. This explicates the use of expressions which take the form of proverbs and epigrams through which users express different realities. Apart from standing out as virulent moral signposts, these expressions equally capture their visions and life experiences. Examples such as the following are in place: *Na last time be time*, probably a restatement of the argument that the end justifies the means. *Vous voulez des problèmes, mariez-vous (If you want problems, get married)* directly invokes the problematic nature of marriage. *Like what you have* and *A bird in hand* carry undertones of contentment with what one has at hand and which should be better harnessed. *J'ai peur de mes amis même toi (I'm afraid of my friends even you)* addresses forms of dishonesty on the part of drivers and partners, colleagues and even some clients. *Occupe-toi de tes affaires (Mind your business)* warns against unnecessary interference in others' affairs. *Plan B* is suggestive of the necessity of an alternative solution when planning. *Le risque c'est tenter d'échouer (Risking is attempting to fail)*, *Qui ne risque rien n'a rien, (Who does not take a risk gets nothing)* and *Get rich or die trying* all invoke the relevance of the risk factor in business. With regard to the sector in question, risks involve accidents, car-jacking, breakdown, unreliable insurance policies, etc., which often retard progress or completely foil taxicab business ventures. The risks notwithstanding, the expressions still recognise the fact that the risks are worth taking. The negative consequence of the risks is down toned in the caption *Any disappointment is a blessing*, an optimistic way of consoling victims of related mishaps, thereby, instilling in them some element of hope. Other captions allude to the element of time which is quite significant in business. *Sleep no be die* insinuates the fact that difficult situations do not always last and this is corroborated by the caption *Time will tell*. Similarly, *No time to waste* warns against the waste of precious time especially in such a business wherein time is money. *Même l'eau a soif (Even water is thirsty)* is a beautiful metaphor on Man's insatiable rush for wealth and when this wealth is used lavishly and injudiciously, in case of complaints, users respond with *Aller dire (Go to hell)* or *Let them say*, a show of resoluteness and impunity. This is probably engendered by the worldly adage that *Les beaux jours sont rares (Happy days are rare)* and so, one should seize such opportunities to relax since *Le bien est bien (All is well)*. After injudicious spending, the user regrets the situation in the caption *Money na film (Money is a movie)* – expressive of the ephemeral nature of money especially when spent lavishly.

Vigilance

Some captions evoked security concerns and represented 9.33% of the data set. They constitute a résumé of some of the most vital rules in safety and defensive driving. Vigilance and precaution are some of the watchwords in driving as the least error of inattentiveness could prove fatal. As extra measures, these users tend to remind drivers of other vehicles of the need to be more cautious. As such, this is reincarnated through precautionary captions such as *Doucement SVP (Slowly please), Prudence (Caution), Watch out, Take care, Du calme (Calm), SVP Prudence plus(Please, more caution), Molo molo SVP (Slowly please), Slow, Doucement (Slowly), Safely, 5 meters, Stop 5m, Distance de sécurité – 5m (Security distance – 5 m)* and *Lentement va surement (Slow and steady)*. Characteristic of this category of captions is a polite undertone as in the use of French SVP - *S'il vous plait (Please)* which is equally evident of the recommended politic behaviour of some of these users with their clients. The captions tend to create some sense of awareness on other drivers, thereby, warning them of impending danger in case such rules are flouted. They therefore act as effective hindrances against driving misdemeanour such as excessive and unnecessary speeding.

Acknowledgement

Captions on acknowledgement had a total of 6% and addressed issues of recognition and praise especially to benefactors and those who contributed in any way to the users' welfare. Here, users tend to appreciate both divine favour and any other forms of favour from personalities in diverse ways. Characteristically, the name of the benefactor is engraved on the taxicab. The following examples were identified: *Merci, Soso Waka (Thanks Soso Waka), Merci PCA (Thanks Chairman of Board of Directors), Merci maman (Thanks Mother), Merci Seigneur (Thank you Lord), Bless you, etc.* Through this strategy, users show off benefactors and recognise their contribution to their prevailing situation as cab owners or as drivers.

Love and solidarity

One of the specificities of taxicab inscriptions is their sentimental nature. Here, users (in)directly express warm feelings towards loved ones. Captions revelatory of sentimental attachment and solidarity equally registered 6%. They are expressive of users' emotional relations with esteemed ones and are often engendered by past or present romantic experiences. They are then engraved on taxicabs in remembrance of either the loved one or a specific experience lived. Thus, *One love, the young shall grow* prescribes love as a necessary prerequisite for the progress of the youth. Whereas some exalt and prescribe love as in *Ndolo l'amour (Love), Aimons-nous (Let's love ourselves)*, some of them are more direct, though, only the author knows the addressee. This is evident in the caption *Je vous aime (I love you)*. Other related expressions are reminiscent of romanticism and expressive of the users' personality. This is captured in forms such as: *Le chaton, Petit cœur, La merveille, Le mignon, Fraicheur, etc.*, respectively, the wish to be regarded as a kitten (with care), a lover, a marvel, handsome and unsullied; expressions which are deeply rooted in romanticism.

A mixed bag of inscriptions

This set of captions encompasses expressions which are difficult to fit squarely under the categories described above and they constituted 8% of the entire data. This is explicated by the fact that they tend to cut across a broad spectrum of ideologies and could be subjected to several interpretations. Thus, they addressed other issues, some of them really difficult to understand because of their ambiguous or latent nature. This is evident as the exact meaning and intent remain known only to the author. Since it was out of the competence of this study to seek the different meanings of such expressions from the authors, some of them could only be subjected to the different possible interpretations arrived at. In this way, captions such as *Success 2* could be illustrative of a second success story in the user's taxi business adventure. *Qui sait? (Who knows?)* is rhetorical and indicative of Man's limitation with regard to knowledge of existence and the unpredictability of the future. Fear woman is probably a direct warning against the creature 'woman' who can tend to be an incarnation of negativity. *Don't give up, Keep on trying, Le combat continue (The struggle continues)* vividly capture human nature which is characterised by the incessant struggle for survival. **Gud luck* should be the users fervent wish that luck be on their side and might be on the side of others too. Is *Family planning* denotative of its relevance in today's society or its celebration by an adept who probably benefitted from it? **For ever bright* could still be expressive of the user's wish for an ever bright future or a simple acclamation of the neat and orderly state of his taxicab. In *Champions league*, one discerns a football fan, life as competition at the highest level. Whereas *Air Swisse* is probably suggestive of the quality of service offered, *Fils de l'homme* could just be suggestive of sociability, maturity and courage, etc.

Linguistic resources

The set of captions obtained in this investigation are traced to different linguistic sources which are reminiscent of the complex sociolinguistic configuration of the speech communities inherent here (Nkwain 2010). The captions are distributed thus:

Table 2: **Linguistic resources and distribution of inscriptions**

Linguistic source	Distribution	Frequency(%)
French	65	43.34
English	53	35.33
Camfranglais	15	10
Pidgin English	06	04
Home Languages	03	02
Others	08	05.33
Total	150	100

That a majority of the inscriptions emanate from the French language (43.34%) is not surprising as this is a reflection of the use of the language in 8 of the 10 regions of the country. This therefore entails that a majority of users here are of the francophone background. Evidently, 35.33 % of English captions should come from users of the English language who constitute a minority here. Worthy of note is the fact that more captions were registered in Camfranglais (10%) as compared to those in Pidgin English (04%) which, by virtue of its number of users, should enjoy more spread and use in this community. Understandably, the use of Camfranglais and Pidgin English by this category of users is in place considering their level of literacy or the numerical strength of urban youths who are involved in the business and obviously seek to identify themselves with a more appealing and vibrant code as compared to Pidgin

English. The low use of Home language expressions (02%) is equally understandable as users seek to transmit messages to the widest possible audience. This is true of other languages such as Spanish and expressions untraceable to any Cameroonian Home languages.

Contrasted with earlier findings such as Alobwede (1998), who reveals a 15% use of Pidgin English in Yaounde as opposed to 8% for English, this discrepancy is justifiable considering that this survey targeted a very limited domain of language use. With regard to French, Tchoungui (1983), in an earlier study, reported a 93% use of French in the same city and this high frequency is equally reflected in this survey.

Stylistic dimension of captions

Users of captions effectively manipulate a plethora of stylistic devices in bringing out the envisaged message. There is abundant use of **metaphors** through which varying realities are captured. This is the case with captions such as *God's property, Chamber of God, Holy Ghost fire and Ambassade de Christ (Christ's embassy)*. Enveloped in strict religious metaphors, these captions draw a parallel between the taxicabs and divine protection or favour. Similarly, there are popular biblical allusions such as *Mathew 77, Ps. 36 and Ps. 23, etc.*, which are not only informative but are equally indicative of users' religiosity and their urge to spread the good news.

Likewise, there is a frequent use of **designation,** the process of direct or indirect naming involving forms of indexing or reference to relate to particular people, things or situations. As such, users take up names of personalities they revere and these modes of address become incarnations of praise, admiration, success and hope. Examples such as *Eto'o, Le golden boy, Le Pichichi, Awilo Longumba, Rodriguez le free, Carlos Blanco, etc.* are in place. Apart from names of revered personalities, other modes are revelatory of status, viz: *Cheriff (Sherriff), Le Boss, Le Saint, Le Marsellais, etc.* This process of designation is embedded in that of **presupposition** where there is inference or deduction of meaning from the text. As such, forms such as *Le Saint (The Saint)* and *Le Doyen (The Dean)* could respectively presuppose honesty and longevity in service.

There is an effective use of both **proverbs** and **epigrams** - witty idiomatic expressions such as *A bird in hand, Qui ne risque rien n'a rien (Who does not take a risk gets nothing), Get rich or die trying, Na last time be time, Même l'eau a soif (Even water is thirsty), Sleep no be die,* etc., through which users capture their different worlds of experience, demonstrate their artistry and contribute to the aesthetic value of language use in context.

Clippings and **abbreviations** are equally noticeable devices employed in inscriptions. There are cases with inscriptions such as *Ps. 36, Ps. 23* and *VIP (Very Important Personality), Bfssam frère (Bafoussam brother), Doucement, SVP (Slowly, please),* etc. Through these devices, fundamental aspects such as time and space are effectively compensated without jeopardizing the envisaged message.

Where the user intends to opt out, there is the use of **rhetorical questions** such as *Qui sait? (Who knows?), A qui la gloire? (To whom be the glory?), A qui le tour? (Whose turn is it?),* etc. In this way, the user provides several leeways with regard to the interpretation of the message. Besides, like other rhetorical questions, it is a clear instance of flexibility in language use as different answers could fit different situations depending on the interpretations arrived at.

Captions are deeply laden in **imagery** and **symbols** which cut across the socio-cultural landscape of the speech communities here and even beyond. The image of the woman in *Fear woman* is particularly telling of the nature of the woman as a delicate, yet, sometimes complicated and problematic being. *Le Prince Mbamois (Prince of Mbam), Yes, Major du Noun (Yes, Major of Noun)* and *VIP* are connotative of nobility and reverence. *Water* in *Même l'eau a soif (Even water is thirsty),* equally a **personification,** is indicative of the insatiable nature of humans especially with regard to material wealth. Similarly, *sleep* in *Sleep no be die* is symbolic of momentary periods of hardship which are characteristic of human existence. Through these devices, one discerns another dimension of language universals.

The personality of the woman is equally presented in strong **hyperbolic terms**. Apart from *Fear woman*, the caption *Vous voulez des problèmes, mariez-vous (If you want problems, get married)* reinforces the problematic or delicate nature of the marriage institution in general. This exaggerates the whole situation especially as not all couples go through perpetual marital crisis.

There is the **reduplication** of clipped forms which give rise to neologisms as in the case of *Faro Faro*, from informal French *faroter* (verb) and *faroteur* (noun) used to refer to a generous person. *Molo molo, SVP (Slowly, please)* is Bassa language for *slow* and used to caution road users to drive slowly.

The functional load of captions

Because of their structure and the author's style in general, taxicab inscriptions are most likely to engender problems of ambiguity and misinterpretation. Despite these shortcomings, these problems are easily resolved through a copious and meticulous use of the reader's intuition to emerge with envisaged meaning. The principal underlying motif in the use of taxicab inscriptions is the communication intent. As an information-providing device, they tend to reflect both users' experiences and life expectations. In this way, through different devices, the users shape thought through short flexible texts to capture the surrounding world of experiences.

Apart from an informative role, taxicab inscriptions equally serve an attention-getting purpose. This is often triggered by the users' advertent or inadvertent design to show off. This is equally pushed by the users' intent to be associated with a particular societal model that is highly revered. In this way, different modes of address and related forms are adopted with varying stylistic effects that provide the captions the necessary steam and verve meant to attract readers. As such, an embellished caption, no doubt, has a desirable and convincing effect.

Evidently, they paint a vivid picture of the religious, sociolinguistic, cultural and moral atmosphere at given times. Through them, current moral, religious and sociolinguistic trends are easily gleaned. For instance, a plethora of religion-oriented captions is not only an indication of the users' penchant for religiosity, but, an indication of a conscious war against rising immorality and other forms of misdemeanour. At the sociolinguistic level, there is the use of forms drawn from, and representative of the linguistic shades (English, French, Home languages, Pidgin English, Camfranglais, etc.) in the speech communities in this context. In their manipulation of these idioms, the artistry of the users is effectively measured.

Conclusion

This study investigated taxicab inscriptions with emphasis on their thematic concerns, semantic shades, linguistic sources, stylistic dimension and functional load. The study revealed that inscriptions address a wide range of issues ranging from religion, naming, acknowledgement, vigilance, love, solidarity and others. The inscriptions, their latent nature and problems of ambiguity notwithstanding, generally capture thought which constitutes users' visions and life experiences. The inscriptions are drawn mostly from the different languages used in the speech communities which constitute the area targeted for the study. The captions are realized through several stylistic devices, further portraying users' artistry and helping to keep the different languages alive. In this way, authors make use of poetic techniques, suggestive tones, word plays, simple sentences, real and fictional names, repetition, verbal imagery, etc. Besides, as fruits of the users' imagination, the inscriptions provide insights into their consciousness, expose how they react and adapt to differing socio-cultural, religious and even political forces. The captions constitute a novel communication strategy, a veritable linguistic resource with a high functional load and used to attain a wide range of communication goals.

Far from announcing novel findings, this chapter adds to earlier voices on the applicability of the Ecolinguistic Approach in investigating linguistic behaviour in complex multilingual settings wherein language behaviour continues to stun keen observers and researchers. Further research could be carried out to explore the co-relation between inscriptions and sociological variables or with emphasis on specific languages. In this way, usages such as *Gud Luck (instead of Good luck), *Aller dire (instead of Allez dire) and many other congruent captions could better be accounted for either as misprints, deliberate errors of style or errors reflective of users' (low) level of education.

Bibliography

Alobwede, C., (1998). Banning Pidgin English in Cameroon?. *English Today*, 35(3), pp. 54-60.

Anchimbe, E., (2006). *Cameroon English: Authenticity, Ecology and Evolution*. Frankfurt am Main: Peter Lang GmbH.

Dronen, T. S., (2013). *Pentecostalism, Globalisation and Islam in Northern Cameroon: Mega Churches in the Making*. Leiden: Brill.

Ethnologue., (2005). *Languages of the World*. [Online] Available at: www.ethnologue.com [Accessed 1 September 2007].

Halliday, M., (1990 [2001]). New Ways of Meaning: The Challenge to Applied Linguistics. pp. 175-202.

Haugen, E., (1972). *The Ecology of Language*. Stanford: Stanford University Press.

Nkwain, J., (2010). *Does Language Contact Necessarily Engender Conflict? The Case of Cameroonian Quadrilingualism*. [Online] Available at: www.linguistik-online.de/43_10/nkwain.html

Tchoungui, G., (1983). Focus on Official Bilingualism in Cameroon: Its Relation to Education. In: *A Sociolinguistic Profile of Urban Centers in Cameroon*. Los Angeles: Crossroads Press, pp. 93-115.

Voegelin, C. F., Voegelin, F. M. & Schutz, N. W., (1967). The

Language Situation in Arizona as Part of the Southwest Culture Area. In: *Studies in Southwestern Enthnolinguistics: Meaning and History in the Languages of the American SouthWest*. The Hague: Mouton, pp. 403-451.

Chapter Ten

Euphemism Versus Blunt Language in Linus Asong's *The Crown of Thorns*

Miriam Ayafor

Introduction

Throughout the history of human language in general and the English language in particular, people have always spoken (and written) in various ways and styles. This makes that the art of using language is not static or confined to some borders. Sometimes direct words are used to express thoughts and feelings; at other times it is concealed language that is used. Concealed language can take the form of slang, vulgarisms, acronyms, jargon, technical terminology, idioms and proverbs (Neaman and Silver 1983: viii). Neaman and Silver believe that these language forms, apart from idioms and proverbs, may be euphemistic. They add that whether the forms are euphemistic or not depends on the speaker and his/her audience, therefore blurring the epistemic borderline of the concept. They opine that this is so because a vulgarism, for example, may become a euphemism when it is less distressing to the speaker and the listener than the more orthodox term it is disguising. They pursue their argument by saying that slang is often euphemistic when it is the property of a limited group of people 'in the know'. In this case, the substitution of a slang word for a more widely known one that is unacceptable allows slang to function as euphemism. The same is true of jargon, which, because of its limited accessibility, is particularly effective as a concealment device. Acronyms are euphemistic when they cloak obscenities, when they mask the unpleasant, or when they neutralise the frightening or forbidding. Neaman and Silver (1983) postulate that the speaker who utters a word, the conditions under which the word is uttered, and the person to whom it is addressed will often determine whether that word is a euphemism or not.

The term *euphemism* is defined by the *Compact Oxford English Dictionary* (COED 2003: 375) as: 'a mild or less direct word substituted for one that is harsh or blunt when referring to something unpleasant or embarrassing'. Neaman and Silver (1983: 4) report that by the early 1580s the author, George Blunt, used the term *euphemism* in English, defining it as 'a good or favourable interpretation of a bad word'. The word describes 'a manner of speaking that leans towards indirectness in the service of pleasantness' (1983:4). Therefore, people use euphemisms to avoid unpleasantness and so as not to embarrass or shock their listeners.

Neaman and Silver (1983) do not consider idioms and proverbs as language forms that can sometimes be euphemistic like the others. If we consider dictionary definitions of these terms (idioms and proverbs), we may not agree with these authors. The 3rd edition of the *Cambridge Advanced Learner's Dictionary* (CALD 714) says that an idiom is: 'a group of words in a fixed order that have a particular meaning that is different from the meanings of each word understood on its own', and the COED confirms this definition by saying that the word means: 'a group of words whose meaning cannot be deduced from those of the individual words' (COED 2003:553). These definitions are not restricted in terms of unpleasantness or offensiveness; therefore, idioms can be unpleasant and pleasant, offensive and inoffensive. Consequently, when they are pleasant and describe something for which an unpleasant or offensive terminology exists, they can be said to be euphemistic.

The same argument can be considered to hold true for proverbs. A proverb is defined by the same dictionaries as: 'a short saying stating a general truth or piece of advice' (COED 2003:911), and 'a short sentence, etc., usually known by many people, stating something commonly experienced or giving advice' (CALD: 1143). The *HARRAP's 21st Century Dictionary* (soft copy) gives a more elaborate definition of the word: 'any of a body of well-known neatly-expressed sayings that give advice or express a supposed truth'. From these definitions, one may be tempted to say that proverbs cannot be euphemistic. However, that may be too hasty a conclusion to make. If one considers the fact that the message in a proverb may not always be easily understood by everyone and may be indeed intended to conceal meaning, to speak in a more pleasant manner, or to avoid embarrassing one's interlocutor or audience, then a proverb may be considered euphemistic. In such contexts proverbs may be similar to slangs which are defined as 'typically restricted to a particular context or group' (COED 2003: 1079) and as mentioned above from Neaman and Silver. In the course of this paper, African idiomatic expressions and proverbs will be examined in their contexts in Asong's (1995) *A Crown of Thorns* to see if they contain elements of euphemism.

The opposite of euphemism is blunt language, that is, language that does not seek to embellish, soften tone, or hide obscenities. It is not concealed language; it is 'direct'. It is language that does not care about decency. It is language that transgresses moral purity.

In reading through *A Crown of Thorns* in search for idiomatic and proverbial language, which may or may not be euphemistic, one comes across a lot of blunt language as well. *Blunt* in this paper should be understood more to be unpleasant, offensive and impolite than to be direct, unconcealed or unidiomatic. In the novel under study, therefore, both blunt and indirect language is examined.

With data collected from Asong's novel, this paper seeks to answer three research questions:

1. Are Cameroonian and by extension African idioms and proverbs euphemistic in nature? If so, can these idioms and proverbs be equated to euphemism in western cultures, or are the two (or three) concepts different?
2. How extensive is the use of blunt language as compared to idiomatic/proverbial usage in the novel?

3. What could be an explanation for blunt language usage if it is proven that this usage is very extensive? In other words, what may be the reason(s) for the writer's choice of style?

The theoretical frame which underlies this paper is politeness and face theory. Politeness and face theory is a theory that was propounded and propagated by Brown and Levinson (1978), and which has ever since been used and commented on by several conversationalists, pragmatists and sociolinguists in general. 'Face', according to this theory, is the public self-image that every adult tries to project and protect, while 'politeness' is a speaker's intention to save face for his/her listener. Being polite in speech therefore means making an attempt to save the other from any embarrassments or humiliations that one's words may cause. People use various politeness strategies to protect the face of others when addressing them.

Brown and Levinson (1978) outline four main types of politeness strategies: bald-on-record, positive politeness, negative politeness, and off-record or indirect language use.

1. Bald-on-record strategies usually do not attempt to minimize the threat to the hearer's face. Using such a strategy often will shock or embarrass the addressee, and so this strategy is most usually utilized in situations where the speaker has a close relationship with the audience, such as family or close friends.

2. Positive politeness strategies seek to minimize the threat to the hearer's positive face. They are used to make the hearer feel good about himself, his interests or possessions, and are most usually used in situations where the audience knows one another fairly well.

3. Negative politeness strategies are oriented towards the hearer's negative face and emphasize avoidance of imposition on the hearer. These strategies presume that the speaker will be imposing on the listener and there is a higher potential for awkwardness or embarrassment than in bald-on-record strategies and positive

politeness strategies.

4. Finally, there is the indirect strategy. This strategy uses indirect language and removes the speaker from the potential to be imposing. For example, a speaker using the indirect strategy could simply say, 'I am feeling hot in here', insinuating that it would be nice if the listener would get up and switch on the air conditioner without directly asking the listener to do so.

The politeness and face theory is thought to be appropriate for this paper in the sense that Linus Asong, the author of the novel used as data for this work, can be considered Speaker, while the reader of the novel Listener. The choice of words Asong uses can constitute face-threatening acts to the Listener, in the case of some of the blunt language used, or non-threatening, in the case of euphemistic usage through idioms and proverbs. The former may be considered impolite and the latter polite. With this theory in mind, we will start the examination of data for this paper with indirect language use before going on to blunt language use later.

Idioms, Proverbs and Euphemism in Linus Asong's *The Crown of Thorns*

For easy reference or follow-up in the novel, data have been displayed following the chronological order in which they appear. What is considered idiomatic, proverbial or euphemistic in the context of the novel has been selected. **Table1** displays words/expressions that conceal meaning, whether they are pleasant or not. The idioms are emboldened, while the proverbs are not.

Twenty-nine idioms and ten proverbs have been identified in *A Crown of Thorns*. Data 21 and 27 are clear euphemisms that anyone who knows the English language will not hesitate to acknowledge as such. To walk the way one was born is to walk naked, while to see one's flower is to menstruate. Concerning the latter example, Neaman and Silver (1983:57) declare that 'the monthly flowers, a somewhat romantic term for a woman's period, has been used in England since the fifteenth century. It is from the Latin *fleure*, 'to flow', but perhaps was mistakenly translated into the French *fleurs*'. As for the former, it can be equated with the English 'birthday suit' still in use in Britain, Canada and the United States and referring to the state of nudity (1983: 17).

Table 1: Indirect language in *The Crown of Thorns*

No	Data	Page	Language Form
1	Let me **see your heart**	26	idiom
2	**Hide in a farm that has just been cleared**	26	idiom
3	Talking **with water in my mouth**	28	idiom
4	Have **a hangman's blood in your veins**	30	idiom
5	The **thorn in my heart**	30	idiom
6	There is **dust in my eyes**	38	idiom
7	Let us know **in the market** like this?	44	idiom
8	This kind of **dance he is dancing** with our Chief	44	idiom
9	**Tigers have become goats!**	49	idiom
10	He had **below his belt** five shots of Gin	54	idiom
11	He had refused to **be bound by the ropes** which the Fathers had used to bind the hands of his uncle	81	idiom
12	The Goment had **put his hands between the tree and its back**	85	idiom
13	The leaves – **the mouths** of the plant	87	idiom
14	The same man who **removed the chair from under him so that he fell**	98	idiom

	into mud from which he will never climb out?		
15	If you like you can **enter a bottle**	116	idiom
16	When a hen leaves the incubator, it must be chased far out of the house if the house-keeper does not want to step on warm excrement.	116	proverb
17	The shoulder can never grow above the head	118	proverb
18	We cannot stretch our hands longer than the bones in them	121	proverb
19	If I am mistaken let my brothers **straighten my path**.	121	idiom
20	A calabash should never have anything to do with a stone.	130	proverb
21	If you think there are thorns under that your crown we shall take it from you so that you **walk the way you were born**.	132	idiom
22	The throne ... **rests on the shoulders of a giant**.	134	idiom
23	The fly followed the corpse to the grave because it had nobody to advise it.	134	proverb
24	... talking as a people who **have eyes and ears**.	134	idiom
25	We are not asking you **to lick your elbow**.	136	idiom
26	It was the Chief who first made the mistake of **catching his fish and going back to the river to wash it without killing it**.	138	idiom
27	Angelina had come to our Chief to tell him that she had just **seen her**	145	Idiom

			flower.
28	Let me **look into your heart** and into **the heart of tomorrow** and tell you.	146	idiom
29	Are you **seeing my footprints**?	147	idiom
30	Who gave the tax-collectors the right to question our Chief and even **sit on his head**?	149	idiom
31	Let us not follow a mad man into the market naked because he has taken our loincloths.	150	proverb
32	Here we are, forcing purgatives down the throat of a man who has a running stomach.	151	proverb
33	Let us call him and **wash him**, and make him see that the shoulder can never grow above the head.	151	Idiom
34	We cannot tie a juju and be the first to spit on it!	151	proverb
35	There can never be a smoke without fire	177	proverb
36	**Our tongue is in his mouth**	181	idiom
37	If you want to eat with a devil, you must use a long spoon.	188	proverb
38	We might have **slipped on a banana peeling somewhere along our road**.	211	idiom
39	If the big Goment is coming to take us from here, he will be told that it was not our fault that **he left so many dried leaves lying so close to the fire of Nkokonoko Small Monje**.	211	idiom

Now, the question to ask is whether all the other idioms and

216

proverbs listed above are free of euphemistic connotations. To answer that question, we need to examine each item in its context of use and find out if the expression hides some unpleasant word or not. We will start with the proverbs. Data 16, 17, 18, 20, 23, 31, 32, 34, 35, and 37 are proverbs.

In 16, Chief Nchindia had been confined for twenty-one months after his coronation, having no direct access to the outside world. Now, the period of his confinement is over and he wants to go to the city immediately. Ngobefuo, the village notable, tries to let him know that it was not possible for him to travel without prior information about his coming given to the village community in the city. The Chief determines to go. The elders, unable to convince the Chief of the contrary, reason out that the Chief had been in his house for too long, was bored and angry, so it was better for him to be allowed to travel and wear out his anger somewhere else. The proverb in 16 is saying, in other words, that precautions should be taken to prevent problems that are foreseeable if one does not want to face them. No element of euphemism is found in this proverb. On the contrary, the mental picture of 'step [ping] on warm excrement' is rather nasty.

In 17, the proverb is used when the leader of the Chief's tribesmen in the city describes the 'shameful burial' of Anuse, saying that it was a very good lesson for those who were still growing up, and who did not know that 'the shoulder can never grow above the head', in other words, authority (government, traditional, family) can never be challenged. Here again, no unpleasantness is being avoided.

In 18, Ngobefuo, the spokesman of the council of elders, is reminding the Chief of the atrocities that his late brother had committed against the tribe and which had caused his banishment. Therefore, now dead, his corpse could not be brought back to be buried in the land. The Chief does not see the reasons given for the refusal of a decent burial for his late brother as tangible. Ngobefuo shrugs his shoulders and speaks the proverb. The elders cannot do the impossible. They cannot go beyond their human capacity to try to convince the Chief. Euphemism is absent from this proverb.

In 20, the proverb can be equated with the English 'those who live in glass houses should not throw stones'. A calabash is a very fragile recipient and so can very easy break. Much care needs to be taken when using it. A stone near a calabash is high risk, just as is a calabash near a stone. Chief Nchindia in the city confronting his uncle Anuse and getting into a quarrel with him was making a mistake because no matter what happened, the Chief was the one to be disgraced, being the 'calabash' in this circumstance. No euphemism can be traced here.

Refusing to take advice, refusing to 'listen to the voice of wisdom' can lead someone to an early grave. Chief Nchindia is being warned by Ngobefuo through proverb 23 not to continue in his stubbornness but to take advice from the councillors in order to avoid impending death. No euphemism is seen here. On the contrary, the language is blunt.

To follow a madman into the market naked because he has taken one's clothing is tantamount to being mad oneself. In number 31, the proverb means that we should not behave as badly as our adversary or else we would be as bad as s/he is. In other words, we should not return evil for evil. The words in the indirect language are not more pleasant than those in the direct language.

The proverb in datum 32 does not seem to contain any element of euphemism. The elders have realised that the government has made their Chief suffer poverty and humiliation. He is already in pain so there is no need to inflict more pain on a man who is already hurting.

Tying one's juju and being the first to spit on it means being the first to mock at or insult one's own creation or handiwork. This can be extended to mean destroying one's own work. Achiebefuo draws the attention of Ngobefuo that they, the most responsible of the village councillors, have been doing just that, so they need to stop that absurdity. The words of proverb 34 are as harsh as those in the unveiled language.

In 35, 'no smoke without fire' talks of a cause and effect situation: one thing must happen before another can take place, just like there must be a fire before one can see smoke. The word 'fire' is euphemistic in the sense that it represents danger or great trouble. 'Fire' is the underlying trouble that brings about consequences like 'smoke', a milder event. The villagers of Nkokonoko Small Monje did not go to the market on their market day. This is unusual. It is the smoke. But this smoke has been caused by more serious and dangerous happenings – the selling of the god of the village and all other misbehaviour by the Divisional Officer (D.O.) and the missionary. In this context, the proverb can be considered euphemistic.

The villagers of Nkokonoko Small Monje are on strike. They want both the D.O. and the missionary out of their land. The D.O. wants to use caution in trying to quell down the rebellion, but the missionary thinks the D.O. is weak. He advices him to use military force. However, the D.O. knows better and tells the missionary that violence will not help in the given circumstance; it will instead create more trouble. He then concludes by saying the proverb in 37 which means that caution and tact are needed when dealing with an enemy. This proverb cannot be considered euphemistic; the devil is certainly not a pleasant person to be with.

Only one out of ten proverbs in the novel under study can be said to be euphemistic. That gives a small percentage of ten. We will turn now to idioms to see if the situation is different.

As far as the idioms on Table 1 are concerned, we will analyse only those that can be considered euphemistic, for lack of space. Thirteen out of twenty-nine idiomatic expressions in the novel are euphemistic in their contexts. Data No. 2, 6, 10, 11, 12, 14, 19, 25, 26, 30, 33, 38 and 39 can be considered euphemistic, while the rest of the idioms do not portray any mildness or intention of replacing unpleasant words with more pleasant expressions. Some of them are actually very harsh and insulting. I will briefly explain each of the euphemistic idioms so as to justify the claim that they are indeed euphemisms.

Data No. 2 means trying to cover up a crime or shame that is so obviously known already. It is a useless effort. Ngobefuo addresses Achiebefuo in the following terms:

> Akeukeuor, the god of gods of the tribe of Nkokonoko Small Monje has been cut off, stolen and sold to a white man. And all the fingers of this tribe are pointing at you.

And then he goes on to say that Achiebefuo 'cannot hide in a farm that has just been cleared'. That is why the idiom Ngobefuo uses is said to be euphemistic. In response, the accused person expresses himself also in mild terms, not understanding what is actually happening to him at that moment. He is unable to comprehend the events surrounding the theft of their god; he claims innocence of the crime. When someone has dust in his/her eyes and cotton wool in his/her ears, s/he will not be able to see and hear and so will not understand anything happening around him/her. This explains the idiom in No.6, which I consider euphemistic.

The D.O. had been drinking before the arrival of the village Elders who have come to question him about their stolen god. The D.O.'s sense of understanding and interpretation of facts is blurred by the alcohol in his stomach – the Gin 'below his belt' (No.10).

Missionaries have cunningly and tactfully occupied the lands of Takala by first converting him to their new religion and then making him the catechist of his village and its environs a week after his conversion. All disputes concerning Takala's lands died a natural death. When Takala died, his next-of-kin, Ngangabe, succeeded him. The Fathers tried to play the same trick on him as they had done on his uncle but they failed: Ngangabe refused conversion and consequent baptism, yet the Fathers wanted to make him catechist even without baptism! That is why he declares that he will not be bribed as his late uncle had been, and rendered unable to defend his lands. This is the meaning of datum 11, which is highly euphemistic.

The Government had made many unfulfilled promises to the people of Nkokonoko Small Monje. At the time of the promises, the people had believed them to the point that they changed the will of their late Chief and satisfied the wishes of Government. Unfortunately, the Elders now realise, too late, that Government had separated them from their beloved and highly respected traditional ruler to whom they were much attached -- the late Chief and also his successor. The people have now become very rebellious against Government and are ready to go to any lengths in their civil disobedience. Government will now have tough times with the people, as it 'ha[s] put its hand between the tree and its back' indeed (No.12).

We could go on and on analysing these samples but it is not necessary. The point has been made that some African idioms are euphemistic in character. Judging from the numbers in the data for this work, one could calculate the percentage of euphemistic indirect language generally. One out of 10 proverbs plus 15 out of 29 idioms gives a total of 16 out of 39. Hence one may conclude that 41% of indirect language usage is euphemistic, and that idioms are more prone to euphemism than proverbs.

To answer the first research question, we can say that some, but not all, African idiomatic and proverbial speech are euphemistic and so may be equated to western euphemism as exemplified in the English language. Consequently, perhaps the definition of the term *euphemism*, as defined in English dictionaries, should be modified to include this African additional meaning to it thus: a mild or less direct word substituted for one that is harsh or blunt when referring to something unpleasant or embarrassing, as well as an idiomatic or proverbial speech which declares unpleasant truths in a pleasant manner.

Having answered the first research question concerning euphemism in *A Crown of Thorns*, the next section of this paper examines the contrary to pleasant and inoffensive language: blunt or unpleasantly direct language.

Blunt Language in Linus Asong's *Crown of Thorns*

To start with, it is important to note that African idiomatic expressions, though consisting of indirect or concealed language, can sometimes be very offensive to those who understand the meaning of the idiom or the proverb. In this light, we can study the remaining 59% non-euphemistic data on Table 1 and, judging from the meaning of blunt language, distinguish a number of rather offensive idioms and proverbs. Numbers 3, 4, 9 and 15 could be considered such.

It is insulting to tell one's interlocutor who may not have understood what one is saying, 'I am not talking *with water in my mouth'*, especially because this statement is usually made when the speaker is rather angry. Telling someone that he has *a hangman's blood in [his] vein* is equally insulting, as well as accusing. When someone is told to his face, *'Tigers have become goats'*, s/he is openly being told in an unpleasant manner that s/he is no longer the strong person s/he used to be; s/he has become a weakling! It is not possible for a human being to ever *'enter into a bottle'* as if s/he were a fly or some other insect. This expression is used in Cameroon when the speaker is extremely impolite and wants to annoy an already angry listener even more. These are the four idioms which can be considered blunt and offensive. The percentage is 10.25.

The rest of the section on blunt language is divided into three parts. First, we have blunt language use for words denoting body parts; next, there is blunt language use coming from a particular word – excrete -- and its inflections and derivatives; then there is blunt language use coming from another word – spit – with its inflections and derivatives.

Words denoting body parts and others

It is not common to find people naming male and female genital organs as bluntly as Asong names them in the novel under study. *Penis* and *vagina* are words that are embarrassing and that are generally avoided in decent speech. Euphemisms like *manhood* and *birth canal*, respectively, could have been used instead. *Sleeping with* a woman rather than u*sing* a woman is milder. Instead of saying that former Chiefs had people who *held open the legs of stubborn women for the Chief to use*, Asong could have described the scene in another way like saying that there were people who physically forced stubborn women to go to bed with the Chief. What about cleaning themselves up after using the latrine instead of *wiping their anuses*? Table 2 gives a full list of this kind of bluntness in language use.

Table 2: Blunt language with words denoting intimate body parts from *The Crown of Thorns*

No	Data	Page
40	Do we **have boils on our buttocks** and jiggers on our feet that we cannot enter under the roof and sit on the chairs …	50
41	A virgin had been chosen to '**wash the genitals**' of the Chief on the first night of his …	64
42	We had to bring the blood of Fonkyino to **wash his pennis** last night.	65
43	He had crowned these atrocities by **licking the lips of harlots**	120
44	She had made it impossible for the Chief **to use any other woman.**	133
45	Did she think that she was the only woman to whom God had given **a vagina?**	133
46	We are too old to forget that when a man goes to **the latrine without something with which to clean his anus** he can do many wrong things.	134
47	… people who never **wipe their anuses after going to the latrine.**	135
48	You who had once had ten women under you **to wash your penis**, what does that … ?	145
49	How can we know what could have **dropped from the penis of the Chief** that night?	146

50	Here we are, forcing **purgatives down the throat** of a man who has a **running stomach.**	151
51	People who **held open the legs of stubborn women for the Chief to use.**	153
52	He **blew his nose over the edge of the table and used the back of his hand to clean it.**	207

As already discussed, some of the blunt language is expressed through idioms – a rather ironical statement since idioms are generally understood to be concealed language and not blunt. Thus data 41, 42 and 48 mean that the men and women in question are having sexual intercourse. They are not only outright unpleasant expressions; they, in fact, lower the level of the woman to a position of a servant doing some house chores when love-making is concerned. Data 44 and 51 confirm his: the Chief 'use[s]' a woman instead of loving her! 'Licking the lips' (43) is an indirect but unpleasant way of saying *kissing*. Datum 49 is equally idiomatic. When Achiebefuo asks Ngobefuo the question in 49, he is asking how anyone could know what may have happened in the night if the Chief had had sexual intercourse with his wife, suggesting that he may have made his wife pregnant with a son.

The last example on this table is not having to do with an intimate body part but was included for its extreme nastiness. The description of the act is so vividly done that the reader can clearly visualize the scene and can feel the disgust. Asong is indeed blunt in his language use in *A Crown of Thorns*.

Most obnoxious of all the bluntness in the novel is the use of the word *excrete* and two of its derivatives: *excrement* and *excreted*. Together they are used as many as eight times to describe situations that could have been expressed differently if the author had wanted to. The word *excrete* is used for the first time idiomatically to express the fact that someone was being insulted. People held a loin cloth behind the Chief while he *excreted* could have been rendered: People held a loin cloth behind the Chief while *he stooled* or while he *put himself at ease*.

Rubbing oneself with excrement simply means *disgracing oneself* in the contexts where that expression has been used in the novel. Asong could have used the word *disgrace* if he wanted to, but he chose to use the disgusting word *excrement* five times. Again, some of the examples, though blunt, are idiomatic.

Table 3: Blunt language with the word *excrete* and its inflections and derivatives

No	Data	Page
53	**To excrete** in his mouth	31
54	... people had been known to swear by Ku-ngang by **licking excrement**.	47
55	... the **lumps of excrement** which he allowed to fall from his bowels down…	104
56	When a hen leaves the incubator, it must be chased far out of the house if the house-keeper does not want to step on warm **excrement**.	116
57	The **excrement in the house was smelling** and it had reached a point where they could no longer endure it, try as they could.	134
58	You will not eat; you will not smoke, until we have washed **this excrement** from our bodies.	144
59	Why then are we **rubbing ourselves with excrement**?	148
60	And here was our Chief, **rubbing himself with excrement** on the main road.	149
61	How shall we be able to explain why we gave **the uncircumcised sons of the tribe** the right to **rub the Chief with excrement** on the main road?	150
62	... people who held the loin cloth behind the Chief **while he excreted**.	153
63	I am asking you as a people who were once free **to excrete** in their own houses.	199

Spitting in public is a disgusting habit. Yet in the novel, the number of times characters are said to have spat, either at peoples' 'faces' or on the floor near them, is too many. Each time this is said to have been done, a vivid mental picture is brought to the reader's mind and s/he can almost see the spittle. Table 4 gives examples of this unpleasant use of language, those marked with asterisks being idiomatic.

Table 4: Blunt language with the word *spit* and its inflections and derivatives

No	Cases of spitting	Page no.
64	*He must **spit** back in his face too.	25
65	*...the money you were **spitting** out in Sowa.	29
66	Ngobefuo **spat** in front of Achiebefuo.	37
67	*I also felt **the spittle** of Ngobefuo on my face.	44
68	*By this one act of betrayal they have **spat** on the faces of the tribe and on the faces of our fathers who have gone before us.	56
69	This is your **spittle**; don't let it get dry on the ground before you return	58
70	*This is **spittle** which we have **spat** on our heads.	58
71	*Your brother has **spat** on the face of the tribe. *See his **spittle**.	59
72	Ngobefuo used his **spittle** to put out his pipe which he placed under his stool, ready ...	107
73	Then Ngobefuo turned away and **spat**. When he turned again to look in the Chief's direction, the latter **spat** too. If his **spitting** had been intended as an insult, he had returned it. He then ... as if he had not really **spat** in revenge ...	127
74	..., cleared his throat and **spat** a thick glob of mucus in the shadow ...	144
75	..., cleared his throat and **spat** again, this time	144

	between his legs.	
76	Ngangabe was **spitting** as he walked. **Spitting** in front of the Chief.	148
77	*He was not wrong to **spit** on the Chief's face.	149
78	...barking a deprecating laugh and **spitting** on the floor to show his contempt.	170
79	The D.O. swallowed his **spittle** very loudly and turned to the others ...	176
80	*When the D.O. pointed to him, he **spat**: 'My father ...	177
81	He cleared his throat, brought the phlegm to his mouth, and **spat** it out carelessly.	191

I had originally set out to study euphemism in Asong's most popular novel. However, in the course of reading the book, I found a lot of the opposite of what I was searching for. To answer research question 2 which is the extent of use of blunt language as compared to idiomatic/proverbial usage in the novel, we shall use the numbering of examples in all four tables above.

There are altogether 81 examples. Four of these from Table 1 have been demonstrated to contain blunt language usage. Tables 2, 3 and 4 all contain blunt language, whether idiomatic or not (No 40-81). That makes a total of 45 (4+41) examples of blunt language as against 36 examples of euphemistic usage in *A Crown of Thorns*. We can see that the use of blunt language is very extensive; it is more than the use of euphemism: 55.55%.

The third question to answer is why Asong chooses to use so much blunt language in his novel? Why does he choose, as it were, to shock or embarrass his readers, thereby applying the 'bold-on-record' and 'negative' politeness strategies as described in the theoretical framework section of this paper, instead of using the 'positive politeness' and 'indirect strategies'? For, indeed, the reader is sometimes really shocked and embarrassed by some of the offensive expressions in the novel. The writer does not try to 'save face' for his readers or audience. One may attempt answers to this question as follows.

Linus Asong may have felt that his readers/audience have a close relationship with him, such as his family and friends have, and so felt free to express himself towards them with such bluntness. He was a much loved and well-known secondary school teacher of literature of English expression in his country when he wrote the novel, as well as being a very friendly man who spent most of his leisure time in public places, drinking beer. Open and friendly conversation with people who may have been total strangers to him in the public places was common practice with the man. Wherever he was, laughter was sure to be frequent among his listeners.

Another reason for the choice of this style may be the historical period in Cameroon in which Asong wrote the novel. The novel was first published in 1990, just before the political move for multiparty politics by the Social Democratic Front (SDF – the first opposition party in the country since the re-introduction of multiparty politics in 1990) in Bamenda, Anglophone Cameroon. Anglophones had been disgruntled for some time against the Biya regime, (hat is, the regime of the present Head of State which started in 1982 and is ongoing). Instead of the rigor and moralisation that he preached or gave as watchwords for his reign when he became the second Head of State in the country, bribery and corruption was the order of the day, coupled with high level tribalism and nepotism. Many Cameroonians, especially the English-speaking citizens who felt marginalised, maltreated and refused their share of the 'national cake' became very disgruntled and wanted a way out. When Ni John Fru Ndi, the chairperson of the SDF, who believed that going back to a multiparty system of politics would solve some of the problems of the country, formed his party and wanted a change from a single political party to a multiparty state, most Anglophones and an unbelievable number of French-speaking Cameroonians joined him. It was a period of political upheaval in Cameroon, characterised by ghost-town movements in the former Southern Cameroons and in the West and Littoral Provinces that share boundaries with her.

The setting of the story in *A Crown of Thorns* is in Anglophone Cameroon. It may therefore be deduced that the rebellion manifested by the people of Nkokonoko Small Monje against the government (Gomen) and the church (Mission) are symbolic of the rebellion against the system of government and its ills that existed in Cameroon at the time. The unhappiness of the people of Small Monje could be equated to the dissatisfaction of Cameroonians in general and the Anglophones in particular during the late 80's and early 90's. With such a state of mind, social psychologists say that people do not care about the manner in which they speak. They are not interested in refined language; they are not out to please anybody. They use insulting or rude language as a sign of disrespect of authority – this authority that they believe has not treated them well. No wonder, then, that Asong uses raw or blunt language in situations where mildness or euphemisms are possible.

A third reason for more blunt language use than euphemism may be that the latter is a foreign (Englishman's) way of portraying that he is a gentleman, that he is cultured. However, in Asong's *A Crown of Thorns*, the characters are dumping all manner of foreign culture and civilisation. They are rejecting all that is going against their age-old tradition: the new roads which have come only to destroy their farms and to take up farming space; Gomen and all that it represents; Mission and all her teachings and 'treachery' contrary to the tradition of the people. If these things which are foreign to the people of Nkokonoko Small Monje are being rejected, it would be incongruent to employ style in writing (or speaking) that is foreign to the people. The African (and therefore Cameroonian) generally does not know how to hide his/her feelings, especially in the use of language. S/He is straight-forward in speech, especially when hurting. Proverbs are used oftentimes, but these are not intended to hide meaning; rather, they are used to shed more light to what is being said, and Asong uses a good number of them in his novel.

Conclusion

This paper discussed the definitions of the terms *euphemism, idiom, proverbs* and *blunt language,* with the purpose of examining how these are used in *A Crown of Thorns,* and whether western style euphemism can be equated to African idiomatic expressions which conceal meanings and replace harsh, raw language with expressions that are softer, milder and less unpleasant. Findings show that indeed, some idioms and proverbs can be considered euphemistic and so can be equated to European euphemisms. In this light, a suggestion is made as to modify the dictionary definitions of euphemism to include African idiomatic expressions as part of euphemistic usage. Blunt and unpleasant language is found to be dominant over pleasant language in the novel under study, and some reasons are attempted as to why the novelist chose that style. Three reasons are given thus: to show closeness to his readers/audience; to express disgust and disrespect to government authority; and to demonstrate rejection to all that is foreign to the native culture of the people. It is hoped that this work would also contribute to the discussion concerning the language of literature in multi-lingual societies, especially in those societies where New Englishes exist.

Bibliography

Cambridge Advanced learners' Dictionary. , (2008). 3rd edition, Singapore: Cambridge University Press.
ASONG, L., (1995). *A Crown of Thorns.* Bamenda: Patron Publishing House.
BROWN, P. & LEVINSON, S. C., (1978). Universals in language usage: politeness phenomena. *Question and politeness.*
HARRAP'S 21st Century Dictionary. (online).
SOANES, C., (2003). *Compact Oxford English Dictionary.* (ed). 2nd edition. Oxford: Oxford University Press.

NEAMAN, S. J. & Silver, G. Ca., (1983). *A Dictionary of Euphemisms*. London: Unwin Paperbacks.

Section III:
Displacement and Recognition

Chapter Eleven

Displacement and the Quest for Self in Amos Tutuola's *The Palm-Wine Drinkard*

Henry Kah Jick

Introduction

Amos Tutuola's publication of *The Palm-Wine Drinkard* in 1952 places him as one of the pioneers of novel writing in black Africa. The importance of this time is central to discourse in black Africa, as nationalism and anti-colonial ideologies surged through the continent. Despite Tutuola's publishing done in the metropolis, his work was caught between and betwixt reception. Purist scholars and critics, Nigerians and others like Gerald Moore, Willie E Abraham and Ann Tibble thought it was ' not a novel at all but some curious dead-end in the evolution of the African novel' (Chinweizu, Jemie & Madubuike 1988: 17). Others described the novel as a 'dangerous barbarian' (Lindfors 1999: 140) because of the novel's supposed limited vocabulary of the English language which is loathing to civilised and modern tendencies that the continent was and is struggling to imbibe, others like (Larson 2001, Nyamnjoh 2015 & 2019) have celebrated the work as a culturally relevant postcolonial novel. In so doing, Lindfors, Larson, Choudry (2013), Nyamnjoh and Silue (2017) have all discussed the novel as a cultural and linguistic enterprise with the mission which is some form of 'talking back' to Britain and Europeans about the Yoruba culture. No doubt then that almost all of the critics one has mentioned, quoted this from Amos Tutuola who said in an interview with Mike Awoyinfa and quoted by Bernth Lindfors that 'so far as I don't want our culture to fade away I don't mind about English… I don't want our past to die. I don't want our culture to vanish' (in Nyamnjoh 2015: 6). Tutuola's declaration makes him a real postcolonial advocate in the mission of 'talking back' with the assignment to rescue the language and culture of the Yoruba people that colonialist demonised and silenced. Interestingly, Tutuola's statement also buttresses George Lamming's ([196], 1992) view in that the occasion for speaking can only be achieved from outside since no Nigerian and Yoruba publisher was ready to have Tutuola's novels published for the reason that his English was not very good or did not respect English grammatical regulations. However, *The Palm-Wine Drinkard* explores the relevance of Yoruba folk tradition at the cross roads as it negotiates the trajectory of blending British colonial and Yoruba cultures and 'provide[s] popular ontological insights that could contribute significantly to the reconstruction of a decolonised social science (add humanities and literary production) in Africa' (Nyamnjoh 2015: 1-2). While a postcolonial outlook of cultural readings and re-readings is relevant in contemporary conversations in Africa's literary and cultural space about Africa, The focus in this chapter is to highlight the fact that Tutuola's *The Palm-Wine Drinkard* is a narrative of travel and understanding of one's self. The chapter assesses the impact of traveling and how it helps the character(s) to understand themselves. Thus, it tentatively underscore the fact that, through folklore, Tutuola's characters transgress linguistics, cultural and geographical frontiers to understand themselves. In this case, one defends this contention, with the application of concepts in the postcolonial theory, that *The Palm-Wine Drinkard* represents Africans and Africa at the cross roads as they move towards discovering who they are and in so doing, are creating their own space that transgresses the 'authentic' traditional Yoruba space and the British colonial space.

Where Things Went Wrong

The focus in this section is to establish the fact that the environment and the mind-set of the people in Tutuola's *The Palm-*

Wine Drinkard is a problematic one even though there seem to be some kind of harmony. In fact, the harmony at the beginning of the narrative needs to be disharmonised to reset a different mind-set in this tutuolan world. The narrator/character opens the narrative thus: 'I was a palm-wine drunkard since I was a boy of ten years of age. I had no other work more than to drink palm-wine in my life. In those days we did not know other money, except COWRIES, so that everything was cheap, and my father was the richest man in our town' (Tutuola 1952: 7). The citation which opens the narrative shows that the town of the narrator/character at the age of ten was a harmonious one. His argument that things were cheap also fosters the point that harmony reigned and everyone was seemingly happy. Speaking of himself now, the narrator/character seems most privileged in this general harmony that he depicts as he is rich and his father is considered to be the richest. It means he belongs to the aristocracy of his community and therefore, deserves to be a model for others to follow.

Alas, the very opening of his introduction seems to be a misnomer to societal codes and ethics as the narrator/character seemingly proud to say, describes himself as a palm-wine consumer at the age of ten. Even though it is not clear whether he is just drinking or he gets drunk, the fact that a child of ten is already attuned to drinking alcoholic wine is in itself problematic. In every sense, the pride that is translated in the narrator/character's tone shows that being a palm-wine consumer; an alcoholic liquor from palm-trees, as an infant, is a mark of his privilege position as the son of the richest man in his town.

Based on the above, it is visible to see a setting and/or community where laziness and drunkenness abound as the very young are trained into abusive consumption of alcoholic liquor and not in the values of hard work, respect and truth. Lèfara Silue (2017) discusses the narrator/character within his *corpology* discourse as one with the *carnal body* that eats, drinks and suffers. The idea of eating and drinking just to suffer at the end makes the whole idea of pleasure that the narrator/character seems to narrate to the reader very challenging. The narrator/character in this case, describes a society that is in crisis. Silue comments to this fact that: 'The drinkard's refusal to work like the young men of his age can be seen as questioning the patriarchal aristocracy. Beyond this question, one can see symptoms of family crisis' (Silue 2017: 59403). Though Silue reacts to the issue of the programming of a patriarchal aristocracy very briefly, it seems to me that it is, in itself, at the centre of the problematic systemic structure that is constructed as a community in the novel. The first thing one notices is the absence of a woman in this period of harmony; the father of the narrator/character, the tapster and the narrator, we are not told of any mother, wife or sister at this point of this defrauded harmony that the narrator, with nostalgia, seems to narrate to the reader/audience. In this connection, it seems clear that the problem of disorder is in the hands of the ruling or leading male class that, within the context of the narrative and Africa in general is governed by unbridled appetite; reaping even from where they are not supposed to. Chinua Achebe (1975) has soundly reiterated the collapse of the African societies when he said Africa and Africans are suffering from the eat syndrome. Like the narrator/character's rich father (he does not talk of a mother), the huge appetite for food and drink ruins the community. Achille Mbembe sees the patriarchal aristocratic system in Africa as 'the grotesque and the obscene … that identify postcolonial regimes' (Mbembe 1992: 4), it is preposterous and a travesty to community growth to be established on a child of ten who has to grow up with drinking as his sole job. Much terrible is the fact that this is done with the unction of an elder to be considered a role model in this community.

While Silue is right to discuss the family in crisis because of the *carnal* body seen in the drinking prowess of the youth, I think it stretches to the community that is a waste land, where the vision of the land is on people's stomachs. The stomach-centric cult characterising the ruling and leading classes in Africa reveals a lot of contradictions between value and greed. In most of Africa, palm-wine is a revered drink, it is at the centre of Africa's communal ethos; where men sit and palm-wine is shared from the same pot. The revered nature of palm-wine also makes it the drink for all rituals in Africa and that obtains to this post-independence era. So, it is normal for there to be many hectares of palm-tree farms to meet with the ever demand for the liquor. In fact, in societies where palm-wine plays the above rules, the tapster is treated with great respect and so, to get the narrator/character a 'palm-tree farm which was nine miles square' (Tutuola 1952: 7) and a tapster only justify how attached the father is to the son. This is a great value to emulate but greed comes in when the son does nothing but drinks palm-wine. He arrogantly, without shock, tells us that he drinks 125 kegs of palm-wine a day. This is nothing more than greed and in this state of greed, it is clear that the narrator/character, the community and his family are in crisis that will normally plunge the community into a waste land.

In terms of narrative duration, the narrator/character's drinking is also much accelerated based on its brevity in the whole narrative. This shows that the harmony built on palm-wine consumption is anathema to progress, development and harmony. From the *actant schema* of the palm-wine drinking narrative, the *supporter* to the narrator/character (the *subject*) are agents that all die. Death becomes the *addresser* in the *actant schema* and his rule as an agent of action is central to the narrator/character's quest for himself. The narrator says:

> But when my palm-wine tapster completed the period of 15 years that he was tapping the palm-wine for me, then my father died suddenly, and when it was 6th month after my father had died, the tapster went to the palm-tree farm on Sunday evening to tap palm-wine for me. When he reached the farm, he climbed one of the tallest palm-trees in the farm to tap palm-wine but as he was tapping on, he fell down unexpectedly and died (Tutuola 1952: 7-8)

This very complex construction of language to explain the death of father and tapster is revealing as it shows death's role in the ending of the *carnal* self that blurs the real self. It is interesting to note that from the tapster's revelation in Deaths' Town, he does not even know how he dies and is told that 'he fell down from a palm-tree on a Sunday evening when he tapping palm-wine' and the narrator/character says he said 'that if that should be the case, he over drank on that day' (Tutuola 1952: 100), only foster the crisis which death comes as arbiter to resolve.

The fact that death visits his father and tapsters this early (we can infer that the tapster is now 25 years old) is redeeming and salvaging to the carnal patriarchal bodies that in the end put family and community into crisis. The narrator/character is prone to wine and his life is dependent on the wealth of his father and the artistry of his tapster. Besides this he is nobody, he does not exist and does not know himself. By inference, Tutuola's narrative is a critique on Africans who have refused to think about themselves and have reclined to mimicry and consumerism; consuming what does not belong to them. Such is the political and intellectual elite in Africa. Death as an *addresser* in the actant schema of the drinking narrative is, therefore, a welcomed intruder that will help the *subject* (the narrator/character) to gain his *object* (knowing himself).

Death and Travel

This study has established that death comes to disrupt a somewhat problematic harmony that the narrator/character seems to be enjoying in a community that is more of carnal and epicurean in nature. It is clear that such a community cannot be sustained as a community where work is not valorised. The death of the narrator/character's father and his tapster begins the turning point in the life since they are the support to him. It should be stated that the narrator/character fashions his life and character based on what he receives from his father and tapster. Therefore, their death begins the feeling of loss and worse still, lack and for the first time, one finds him in the process of thinking about his life. He even begins by looking for alternatives, drinking water, looking for a different tapster and struggling to keep his friends, who are fast distancing themselves away from him. Indeed, the fact that he does not find a suitable tapster to replace his former tapster is an issue to him. He says:

> When I saw that there was no palm-wine for me again, and nobody could tap it for me, then I thought within myself that old people were saying that the whole people who had died in this world, did not go to heaven directly, but they were living in one place somewhere in the world. So that I said that I would find out where my palm-wine tapster who died was. (Tutuola 1952: 9)

These words by the narrator/character are cardinal because they seem to me to be at the centre of action in the narrative and they also define the narrative. In reality, one would think that the narrator/character is speaking from one of his drunken bouts. Otherwise, it is troubling for a real human to decide to go and look for a dead person. However, this only enforces the magical realism that dominates the narrative; a characteristic of the folk tale. Stephanie Newell submits that Tutuola 'employed non-realist narrative techniques, or did not engage with the terms of realism at all' (Newell 2006: 184). However, this anti-realist outlook of the narrative, besides being fundamentally African and Yoruba, is a way of speaking and could be seen as the beginning of the narrator/character to come to the realisation of himself and is in the process of thinking; the quote above makes us see the narrator/character in the process of wanting to define himself.

It is this process of thinking that Silue sees as the split body when he writes that: 'The split body must be read as a transformed body. It is a body which the writer submits to a series of manipulations, transformation and interpretation' (Silue 2017: 59404) and here there is transformation as the narrator/character starts thinking and therefore the transformation process from naivety to understanding begins. Therefore, movement in the narrative begins as a psychological and mental process as the narrator/character begins to shift and split in terms of thought and body and realise by his decision to physically move; an adventure that in realist world is very absurd and supposedly irresponsible and unrealistic.

The transformation of the narrator/character also reveals the element of bonding in terms of relationships. One wonders why it is the death of his tapster that touches him much more than the death of his father. The obvious conclusion is that in his carnal body, the narrator/character is closer to the person that gives him palm-wine than he, who has invested for him, to have palm-wine. Therefore, in the narrator/character's mind set, what matters is the drink in its quality and not who pays for the drink. The events around his father's death are most accelerated and narrated from and zero focalised angle of narrating. This only reveals that the bonding between father and son is not strong and possibly artificial. This is nearer the Freudian oedipal discourse. Though there seem to be no conflict or disagreement with the father and the son, the father's blurring the son's identity, is problematic in that the independence of the son is not attained. The son remains a bond to the father's patronising role in providing everything he needs and therefore silencing him.

The tapster, in the case, is more of the rescue figure, who occupies the space that the father cannot occupy in the raising up of this child and young man. In other words, the tapster assumes a kind of motherhood or mothering in the life of the narrator/character. Tutuola in this anti-realist viewpoint, turns to transgress every norm in the process of talking about the colonial world that he is writing about. In the connection, the tapster, like the father, is in the process of bringing up the youth but the upbringing challenges the identity of the narrator/character as he is constantly silenced. The narrator/character fails to realise himself until death comes to open his eyes to start searching for himself. In fact, the death of tapster is the act that begins and brings 'about a transformation in the Drinkard' (Choudhury 2014: 6); making his first move towards understanding himself yet still thinking that he is going for his tapster.

Travel and Knowing

The decision to travel means a lot of things to different people. The feeling that goes with the thought of traveling is generally built on dualities – exile and discovery, anxiety and excitement, the hope and fear – which begin to define the traveller. It is common to note that travel discourse in postcolonial studies and literature centres around ex-colonised people moving to and from the metropolis and the rural/urban exodus experience. These movements have so much developed discourse that may be interpreted as the canon especially when analysing ex-colonial writers like George Lamming ([1960]1992) where the metropolis continues to be seen and defined as where success comes. This theory of 'the speaking' only in the metropolis and 'silence' in the ex-colony; the myth of Europe where all ex-colonised have as dream tends to blur travels especially precolonial travels represented in myths and folk or oral tradition. Tutuola's *The Palm-Wine Drinkard*, in every right, a pioneering novel, represents travels before and during colonialism and humans in the politics of searching for themselves.

The very first mark of knowing that one finds in the novel is the fact that the narrator/character for the first time tells the reader his name. The narrator/character narrates his first experience out of home thus: 'Then I told the old man (god) that I was looking for my palm-wine tapster who died in my town some time ago, he did not answer to my question but asked me first what was my name? I replied that my name was 'father of gods' who could do everything in this world' (Tutuola 1952:10). Getting to know the narrator/character's name deep into the narrative or at the beginning of his journeys is very important as it shows that the narrator/character is beginning the journey to know himself. Here, the power shifts from the preposition 'I' to noun or noun phrase – one of Yoruba philosophical fortes that is general in most of Africa is that names have meanings whose translation especially into English may end up being whole sentences as is the case of the narrator/character in *The Palm-Wine Drinkard* – which I will reduce just to read as 'father of gods' for purposes of convenience in this work. This shift makes definite the individual that is speaking and the reader has to commune with him more intimately. According to Liz Gunner, 'names …clearly signify a complicated belonging to an intimate identification' (Gunner 1996: 117). Therefore, for 'father of gods' to have a name begins a kind of awakening to both himself and the reader/audience that is following his itinerary. The name 'father of gods' reveals that there is an ongoing crisscrossing between the world of the spirits and the living in African and Yoruba cosmology. 'Father of gods' in this theological world view is most privilege in that he, though living, is a father to all the gods in his town (African Traditional Religion celebrates the worship of several gods; each god having a role to play in the wellbeing of the individual, family, clan and tribe). Since names are also forms of identity, his name directly means that nothing can hurt or harm him since he is the father of the gods. By inference, his name already tells the reader that his mission will be a success and he is going to transform himself and town. His name also justifies the powers he has circumventing and outwitting spirits all through his travels to and from the land of the dead.

The name also reveals that everything in the novel be it character, plot or setting is movable and not static, and this anti-realist structure only enforces the folktale structure that the novel adopts. Nyamnjoh submits in corroboration with my claim that: 'Everyone and everything is malleable and flexible, from humans and their anatomies, to animals and plants, gods, ghost and spirits … A thing can double itself, and the double becomes the thing and the thing the double. Gods are human and humans are gods' (Nyamnjoh 2015: 10). Nyamnjoh's submission is a true presentation on how the novel is wield because, having the name 'father of gods', often times one is tempted to think that the narrator character himself is a god or a spirit. In 'father of gods' conversation with the King the Unreturnable Heaven's Town, we get this:

> The questions that their king asked us went thus: - From where were you coming? I replied that we were coming from the earth. He asked again how did we manage to reach their town? I replied that it was their road brought us to the town and we did not want to come there at all. After that he asked us where were we going to? (Tutuola 1952: 59-60)

There is a strong feeling of what Nyamnjoh describes as double here. In the first place, there is a double reading of heaven. In most of Africa, belief systems hold the earth to be sacred and the gods are on earth, while most monotheist religions like Christianity, Islam and Judaism are sky oriented. 'Father of gods' tells the King of the Unreturnable Heaven's Town that they are coming from the earth. This means that they are somewhere in the skies and this could be seen to be the huge influence of Christianity or Islam in his psyche. In this case, Tutuola in the narrative keep shifting spaces and looking for where to fit. It is very correct therefore for Nyamnjoh to conclude that he Yorubalises English (I mean the colonial culture) and anglicises Yoruba (the Yoruba culture). In this connection, both narrative and character are rightfully described by Newell as hybrids. 'Father of gods' and his wife in the skies – heaven – can no longer be humans; they are spirits and since the king of heaven is a god means that they also possess the quality of gods. Soon we find them performing as mortals who are limited when they finally get to Dead's Town. Here, they are not allowed to get into the town because they are mortals. Interestingly, 'father of gods' does not have any powers to force his way and he resolves to beg until he succeeds in meeting his tapster, Baity. In his conversation with Baity, his tapster, Baity makes him understand that they are different (Tutuola 1952: 99-100) and that he cannot return to the land of the living. While Baity's journey through dead has been a one-way trip, 'father of gods' trip; his search for himself, is built on his experience and knowledge of himself. The duality of personality and of place that governs the narrative world view of *The Palm-Wine Drinkard* further enforces its hybrid nature and in this hybridity, is born an identity as 'father of gods' now understands himself.

Nyamnjoh's argument that 'father of gods' names himself may be valid as he sees the need to do that, especially basing that until he moves, no one ever called him by name. Even when he tells the head of his wife's town his name, the name seems a strange one as it is 'quite ordinarily extraordinary in his capacity to collapse the boundaries between nature and culture, village and town, home and bushes, human and supernatural, plausible and implausible, rational and superstitious, primitive and civilised, African and West' (Nyamnjoh 2015: 13). This submission clearly defines the actions and movements of 'father of gods' blurs frontiers and easily navigate multiple spaces.

The fact that in traveling, 'father of god' gives himself a name also begins the mark of responsibility for him. The first thing that happens to him after the name is that he gets married. In Africa, like most communities in the world, marriage is a ritual to make an adult mature and responsible. In the novel, 'father of gods' marriage transforms him from a drunk to a responsible and hard working person. The wife he gets also becomes a suitable partner for him and counterpart. She assists him and helps him often in a way that they can free themselves when they are in danger. A good example is her role in saving them in Red Town, the land of the red people.

In 'father of gods' travels, he learns to work and to support himself. Here he is very much a round character in the Aristotelian definition of the concept; he evolves from the alcoholic, who does nothing, to a workaholic, who is ready to protect himself and his family. Choudhury writes:

It is seen that after going through an odyssey of hardship, the values of his community are instilled in the drunkard. In the 'Wraith-Island' the drinkard becomes a farmer and plant many kinds of crops – a task which he has never performed while in his native town

…when they are rendered penniless after wilfully abandoning the half-bodied child, the drinkard … successfully runs a ferry business along with his wife for one month. (Choudhury 2014: 6)

In this connection, not only the lifestyle of 'father of gods' has changed, even his personality has changed. He is now described not as one with the carnal body but as one who promotes the ethos of his community. His success and determination transform his selfish intended mission to look for Baity, his tapster, to becoming a leader through the EGG that Baity gives him. He says:

But when I thought that he would not follow us to my town, and again, my wife was pressing me too much to leave there very early, when he came, I told him that we should leave here tomorrow morning, then he gave me an 'EGG'. He told me to keep it as safely as gold and said that if I reached my town, I should keep it inside my box and said that the use of the egg was to give me anything that I wanted in this world and if I wanted to use it, I must put it in a big bowl of water, then I would mention the name of anything that I wanted. (Tutuola 1952: 101)

This is where the greatest ironic twist is in the narrative. We remember that it is lack of palm-wine that makes 'father of gods' to set out to look for his tapster, and with this, it is or may be obvious that if given the opportunity he will do everything to get palm-wine. Suddenly, the tapster tells him he cannot come with him but gives him an option, the egg. So, in place of the tapster comes the egg. The tapster can tap only palm-wine but the egg can provide everything that 'father of gods' need. This implicitly means that travel was worthwhile as his displacement gives him more than what he needs.

Another ironic twist is that he uses the egg to become a community person. The 'father of gods' we find at the beginning is looking for his tapster because he needs palm-wine. Upon his return, he meets his people in a plague which arises because of a conflict between heaven and earth. Upon his return, he is seen at the centre of resolving the faming crisis. He says

I called the rest of the old people who remained and told them how we could stop the famine. We could stopped the famine thus: - We made a sacrifice of two fowls, 6 kolas, one bottle of palm oil, and 6 bitter kolas. Then we killed the fowls and put them in a broken pot, after that we put the kolas and poured the oil in the pot. The sacrifice was to be carried to Heaven in heaven. (Tutuola 1952:124)

Before, that he uses his egg to give food and drink to people. He realises that the giving of food and drinks will not resolve the famine. This in every sense makes 'father of gods' different from the drunk at the beginning of the story. Through his leadership and thanks to his movements, harmony is restored in the town. He ends the story this way 'But when for three months the rain had been falling regularly, there was no famine again' (Tutuola 1952:125).

Conclusion

In this chapter, one's focus was to evaluate Tutuola's The *Palm-Wine Drinkard* as a travel narrative, arguing that travel in the novel leads to self-knowledge and community renaissance. Being largely a discourse on character, the chapter shows that because of the movement theme, the characters, especially seen in the narrator, are round and evolve from their carnal bodies to community productive personalities. Falling within the ambit of postcolonial analysis, this chapter has confidently demonstrated that the novel is an adaptation of folk tradition and like Nyamnjoh and Newell, asserts that the novel does not plagiarise Yoruba folktale and myth, but reinvents myth in a community that is, in itself, changing. Therefore, the study elaborates travel – though physical and mystical in the novel – as understanding the self. In other words, through travel, 'father of gods' gets to understand and to know himself.

Bibliography

Achebe, C., (1975). *Morning Yet on Creation Day*. London: Heinemann.

Chinweizu, Jemie, O., & Madubuike, I., (1980). *Toward the Decolonization of African Literature.* Enugu: Fourth Dimension Publishers.

Choudhury, S., (2014). Folklore and Society in Transition: A Study of The Palm-Wine Drinkard and The Famish Road. *African Journal of History and Culture,* 3-11. doi:10.1897

Gunner, L., (1996). Poetry of Belonging and Unbelonging. In K. Darian-Smith, L. Gunner, & S. Nutall, *Text, Theory, Space: Land, Literature and History in South Africa and Australia* (pp. 115-130). London and New York: Routledge.

Lamming, G., ([1960] 1992). *The Pleasures of Exile.* Ann Arbor: University of Michigan Press.

Larson, C. R., (2001). *The Ordeal of the African Writer.* London: Zed Books.

Lindfors, B., (1999). *The Blind Man and the Elephant and Other Essays in Biographical Criticism.* Trenton: African World Press.

Mbembe, A., (1992). Provisional Notes on the Postcolony. *Journal of the International African Institute,* 3-37.

Newell, S., (2006). *West African Literature: Ways of Reading.* Oxford: Oxford University Press.

Nyamnjoh, F. B., (2015). Amos Tutuola and the Elusiveness of Completeness. *Stichproben,* 1-47.

Nyamnjoh, F. B., (30th June to 4th July 2019). Amos Tutuola as a Quest Hero for Endogenous Africa: Actively Anglicising the Yoruba Language and Yorubanising the English Language. *SAALS Conference on Indigenous Languages in Contemporary African Societies* (pp. 1-7). Pretoria: University of Pretoria.

Silue, L., (2017). Writing Body in Amos Tutuola's *Palm-Wine Drinkard. International Journal of Current Research,* 59402-59405.

Tutuola, A., (1952). *The Palm-Wine Drinkard.* London: Faber and Faber.

Chapter Twelve

Rape and the Nation in Edwidge Danticat's *Breath, Eyes, Memory*

Kelvin Ngong Toh

Introduction

Edwige Danticat's *Breath, Eyes, Memory,* is a defamiliarisation of histories that re-invent the Haitian nation-state from a gendered and diaspora perspective. In the narrative, women narrate their pain, trauma and exilic experiences. These experiences are the result of the construction of a nation-state that is of the colonial model. The Haitian nation-state, that is one of the macro-space of the novel, continues to grapple with issues of the national identity and the traumatic psyche of the people. Olivia Chalkey and Diya Abdo adroitly opine that ' Danticat's *Breath, Eyes, Memory* explores several [...] topics, most prominently exile, sexual violence and war'(Chalkley and Abdo 2017: 19). Nancy F. Gerber goes a little detailed when she submits that:

> Edwige Danticat's first novel, *Breath, Eyes, Memory* (1994), a bildungsroman set in Haiti and the United States, is a searing and beautifully told story of the impact of unspeakable violence on the mother-daughter relationship. In its interrogation of the legacy of rape and violation, the text explores the ways in which patriarchal violence is internalized and perpetuated by women from one generation to the next. (2019: 188)

The outcome of this situation is that 'home' becomes a hostile place and there is need to look elsewhere. This is the central ideology in the novel that I discuss in this chapter.

This chapter, therefore, assesses the Haitian response to rape and its contribution to national construction as represented in Danticat's *Breath, Eyes, Memory*. The chapter is further guided by two research questions: what roles do masculinist violence and imperial oppression play in the construction of the Haitian national identity in the novel? And how have movements, in and out of Haiti, informed the idea of (re)constructing a national ethos? In this chapter, I underscore the fact that Danticate's *Breath, Eyes, Memory* narrates the nation and the woman under terrible oppressive and violent conditions. Hence, exile becomes the only hope for the Haitian in the novel. The chapter is built on the following objectives: it demonstrates that Haiti, in the narrative, is a place of violence. Secondly it proves that the violence in Haiti has made Haitian to exile themselves to the United States of America as represented in the novel and lastly, that exile has led to the creation of a national community in the United States of America. I, therefore, argue in this chapter that Danticat's *Breath, Eyes, Memory* represents the Haitian nation-state that perpetually violates the rights and dignity of people. The violence force people to go into exile and end up creating 'homeland' communities in the land of exile.

Conceptual Framework

Though the concept of rape linked to national construction and culture has few critical interpretation in literary and cultural discourse (Rosello 2010), Danticat's stories, narrated by women of different generations suggest an adequate source for such discussion. Rape is analysed from two perspectives: first as sexual violence committed in the novel by the police on women and second, as political, cultural and economic violence which in the novel is represented by a repressive government and the imperialist, The United States of America. J. K. Gibsen-Graham argues that rape occurs when there is, sexual, ideological and spatial 'penetration' (Gibsen-Graham 1996: 121). The very act of slavery and the colonisation of Haiti by the

French and later American occupation of the 1920s are all signs of outright rape on this first black republic.

This kind of infiltration is what Paulo Freire, in *Pedagogy of the Oppressed,* calls the dehumanisation of the victim. To him, 'Dehumanization, which marks not only those whose humanity has been stolen, but also those who have stolen it, is a *distortion* of the vocation of becoming more fully human. This distortion occurs with history; but it is not an historical vocation. Indeed, to admit dehumanization as an historical vocation would lead either to cynicism or total despair' (Freire 2000: 44). In this connection, both the oppressor and the oppressed share in the meanness of dehumanisation.

This chapter discusses rape as forceful 'penetration' of the weaker gender/masses/State of Haiti as a whole by male/ruled/colonialism from the French and later, the United States occupation. If penetration is forced, it means that it is done without the consent of the victim. Haiti and the feminine gender that constitute the group of those raped in Danticat's novel are suffering from the effects of this colonial and masculinist permeation and infiltration. This concords with Reij Mireille Rosello (2010: 118) who submits when describing *Breath, Eyes, Memory* that, 'rape as a trope is often used to conveniently displace violence along a continuum of supposedly comparable situations where one rape victim is made to stand in for another'

Nation, on its part, comes from the Latin word *nasci* which means 'to be born'. This etymology shows that the idea of belonging for the ideal nation is built on biological roots and has to do with blood relations. This, however, is not what obtains in the modern nation and much more, the nations constructed by the colonial rule –defined by colonial cartography, ideology and history. The nation today goes beyond borders of blood relationships. Benedict Anderson opines that, nations or communities are imagined (Anderson 1980: 15). Anderson's signifiers of the nation points to language and culture. And so, the discussion of the post independent nation constructed from the colonial model, that is built of human right abuse, corruption and tyranny like the Haiti in *Breath, Eyes, Memory*, is fertile ground for national identity to be constructed elsewhere. The nation, in the novel, is one that is defined by an oppressor and a despot. Michael Skey (2011) puts it clearly that people today no longer care about the nation. While I agree with Skey, I argue that the highjacking of the nation by a few monsters in the ruling class in territories that were colonised like Haiti and all of Africa put the idea of a nation in an epistemic disparage. The refusal to think or reject the nation is a form of resistance to what people are forced to believe and live. This makes it that when resisted openly, the people are brutalised. The bloody war in Cameroon since 2016 is because Anglophone Cameroon (not English speaking Cameroon) interrogates the 'nation' that excludes them. Anderson 's notion of the nation becomes a lush for the blurring of boundaries for national identity and endorses belonging without considerations to territory.

The nation, as discussed in this chapter, and as perceived today has evolved from the sanguine space to a more federalised community that shares common desires (Renan 1990). It becomes a psyche construct that people share at a particular time and space with or without any faithful allegiance to geographical mappings. Therefore, the sacredness of the nation and the form of the nation, as most post independent despots hang on today, can only be achieved when the people of the 'place' feel the sense of belonging and are respected. What most nations today see as forms or markers of their nationness are based on what Michel-Ralph Trouillot, in *Haiti: State against Nation: The Origins and Legacy of Duvalierism*, calls 'a political claim made on the basis of culture and history' (Trouillot 1990: 26). This claim further substantiates my view that the nation, within the context of this chapter, is not seen exclusively from the standpoint of a geographical map. It suggest the sense of 'being' and belonging to cultural identity and historical pride.

The postcolonial theorisation of nation, *nationness* and nationalism are the tools used for analyses in this chapter. Bill Ashcroft, Gareth

Griffiths and Helen Tiffin have discussed the nation as a 'shared community…that has enabled post-colonial societies to invent a self image through which they could act to liberate themselves from imperialist oppression' (Ashcroft, Griffiths and Tiffin 2011: 117). The theorising of the nation does not only emphasise the coming together of a group with a common goal; it is not just an imagined community as Anderson puts it, nor just a 'soul' as Ernest Renan subscribes to in 'What is a Nation?' It is the creation of a self image that is effaced by the colonial invader. It has to do with the reconstruction of a deconstructed social space with a decolonising spirit of returning the gaze to imperialism (Chakrabarty 2000). The 'postcolonial' nation is both territorial and ideological especially as colonial victims have been displaced. To Ashcroft, Griffiths and Tiffin, 'Settler colony cultures have never been able to construct simple concepts of the nation, such as those based on linguistic communality or racial or religious homogeneity. Faced with their mosaic reality, there have, in many ways, been clear examples of the *constructedness* of nation' (Ashcroft, Griffiths and Tiffin 2011: 117). The postcolonial *nationness* is seen in the light of what Michel Foucault calls a 'discoursive formation' which interrelates with what Homi K. Bhabha describes as 'a kind of 'analytic pluralism' as the *form* of critical attention appropriate to the cultural effects of the nation' (Bhabha 1990: 4) and finally, what Tomothy Brennan calls the 'gestative political structure which the Third World artist is consciously building or suffering the lack of' (Brennan 1990: 46-47). The nation in the chapter is any locale to which people feel the sense of belonging and recognition especially if coming from the traumatic past of colonialism and masculinised aggression. It is not dictated upon by a corrupt, aging and egocentric ruling class of greedy and thieving elites.

The Nation in Violence

This section underscores the fact that *Breath, Eyes, Memory* represent a Haitian nation that has a history of violence. As a consequence, her citizens are always looking elsewhere for security. The major narrative form being the ulterior narration where 'events [are] narrated only after they happened' (Rimmon-Kenan 2002: 89) stresses the centrality of the child narrative technique. Here, the narrator carefully links Haiti and the United States – the dominant spaces in the narrative – as locales that shape the destinies and aspirations of the characters. This territorial expansion, as well as cultural and linguistic extension, advances the transnational diaspora culture of the Haitian people.

The narrative recounts the life of a family (dominantly of women) in Haiti at a time when *'la dictature duvaliériste se durcit et bascule dans l'horreur'*(Dominique 1998: 12). The representation of these women reveals that the Haitian nation, like the women in this Caribbean island have a painful and traumatic past as well as present. The traumatic experience begins with slave trade where these Afro-Caribbean people are forcefully cut off from their motherland and are subjected to the worst dehumanisation and uprooting from the homeland, culture and history. The nostalgia of the loss of the African heritage is always being expressed though it is hard to get to that longed for past. Tante Atie, a major character in the novel, tells the story to her niece, Sophie Caco, the main character, who recounts to us, with the nostalgia that one feels in her tone, the history of their origin. She says:

> She told me about a group of people in Guinea who carry the sky on their heads. They are the people of Creation. Strong, tall, and mighty people who can bear anything. Their Maker, she said, gives them the sky to carry because they are strong. These people do not know who they are, if you see a lot of trouble in your life, it is because you were chosen to carry part of the sky on your head. (Danticat 1994: 25)

The picture painted in this quote justifies the Haitian's feeling of her lost past. One thing we get from the quote is the debate that remains fresh on the divine suppression of the black race and its Judeo-Christian justification of slavery and slave trade. Tante Atie makes her niece believe in the traditional tale that God or the gods are responsible for the black man serving the white man because the black man is strong. This theological position has governed the mind-set of most slaves in the Western hemisphere so much so that, it is transmitted even to the young as Tante Atie is doing here. There is some regret in the narrative tone because, from every indication, these blacks were forced to leave their homeland through capture and subjected to the most inhuman slavery in human history. Home, in the quote, is Guinea which is an extended metaphor for the African motherland.

Th tone in the tale reveals elements of the nation in that though it comes from the reported speech technique, the speaker, who is in Haiti physically, has built a nation in a Guinea that is past and lost. That is why she accepts the task of being the carrier of the sky. The physical nature of this nation has been taken away from this speaker even before she is born in Haiti. The nation, as an imagined community, is relevant and transgresses the utopia of territorial construction. However, the metaphor of carrying the sky lingers both in the Guinean space like in the Haitian spaces as these women all bear the burden of their feminine 'self' in a dominantly patriarchal and capitalist constructed State of Haiti and the United States of America. More importantly, what Tante Atie tells Sophie is also part of *herstory* that is constructed as her forebears were forcefully carried from Africa to the Caribbean. According to C. L. R. James,

> The slaves were collected in the interior, fastened one to the other in columns, loaded with heavy stones of 40 or 50 pounds in weight to prevent attempts at escape, and then marched the long journey to the sea, sometimes hundreds of miles, the weak and sick dropping to die in the African jungle. Some were brought to the coast by canoe, lying in the bottom of boats for days on end, their hands bound.(James 1989: 7)

From what James writes, one sees violence orchestrated against these blacks. From an analytical perspective, these black Haitians are supposed to carry this sky of slavery and deracination that the slave holder and colonialist had willed for them. This image of the sky depicts the encumbrance that is made bare in the lives of black Haitians as slaves, with no sense of self worth.

Besides slave trade and slavery, Haiti suffered under the occupation of the United States of America between 1915 and 1935. This period of occupation can be seen as intrusion into an independent State by the United States of America. The reason for this aggression on Haiti may not be very relevant here. My aim is to show that, at this stage, again, the Haitians under-went another rape from a foreign invader. American activities in Haiti were a blatant abuse of the human rights, freedom and democracy. In *Breath, Eyes, Memory* one Haitian living in the United States of America says that 'Never the Americans in Haiti again,' shouted one man. 'remember what they did in the twenties. They treated our people like animals. They abused the *konbit* system and they made us work like slaves' (Danticat 1994: 54). From the statement, one can deduce that they are susceptible to another possible occupation by the United States of America.

From this dialogue, Haitians became slaves in their own country, working for an invader. It seems clear that United States's forceful intrusion only enforces their notion of the global world which Gibsen-Graham describes as 'The dynamic image of penetration and domination.' Such activity as she stresses is 'linked to a vision of the world as already or about to be wholly capitalist – that is, a world 'righfully owned' by capitalism' (Gibsen-Graham 1996: 121).

However, there are differences about the occupation of the United States of America as some Haitians in the diaspora prefer the occupation to the poor governance that they find back home. This is what another character in *Breath, Eyes, Memory* thinks. 'Roads, we need roads,' said another man. 'At least they gave us roads' (Danticat 1994:

54). From what one gets from this debate, *nationness* is built on the ambiguities that reveal the different perceptions a people have for their nation. What this means is that Danticat's *Breath, Eyes, Memory* advocates a nation in a polarised and federalised form. Unfortunately, the State of Haiti is governed by a despot who never gives room for free thinking. These people are speaking as Haitians in the diaspora, longing for a homeland.

The outcome of dictatorial rule in Haiti, the continuous violation on the people is artistically represented by Danticat in the novel in the Caco family. The family tradition of testing the girl child, where a mother inserts her finger into the female child's vagina to ensure her virginity for a decent life. As we get from the narrator, the practice has become a culture. This activity is seen as rape on the human body. If we go back to our concept of the nation which emanates from the Latin word 'to be born,' then the relationship between mother/daughter(children) is the starting point for the construction of the nation. Ironically, Danticat's *Breath, Eyes, Memory* reveals daughters who run away from home, nation and culture. Danticat, in this family metaphor, discusses how the Haitian diaspora in North America and Europe is growing as the people exile themselves for freedom and green pastures. Martine, Sophie's mother, tells Sophie about her (and her sister's) testing experience in these words:

> When I was a girl, my mother used to test us to see if we were virgins. She would put her finger in our private parts and see if it would go inside. Your Tante Atie hated it. She used to scream like a pig in a slaughter house. The way my mother was raised, a mother is supposed to do that to her daughter until the daughter is married. (Danticat 1994: 60-61)

The authority of the mother as a superior makes her an oppressor and rapist to the daughter who naturally represents the victim . The penetration of fingers into the girl's private is nothing less than rape orchestrated by the mother. This is because it is practised without the consent of the female child. Martine's description of Atie's hatred for the testing shows that the violence on the rights of the victim is real. The imagery of the slaughterhouse and the screams of the pig reveals the traumatic experience that the young woman undergoes and by extension the Duvalier horrific rule in Haiti.

The act of testing leads to rebellion which is another historical characteristic of the Haitian State. Rebellion is seen by the victim against the authority and in this case, the daughter against the mother. Sophie decides to force an object into her private to stop her mother from testing her. She vividly describes the scene in these words: 'My flesh ripped apart as I pressed the pestle into it. I could see the blood slowly dripping onto the bed sheet. I took the pestle and the bloody sheet and suffered them into a bag. It was gone, the veil that always held my mother's finger back every time she tested me' (Danticat 1994: 88). Sophie's action is a response to her mother's constant violence against her freedom to own and control her body. This, as already noted, is a prolonged representation for the individuals in the Haitian State that have no freedom of their own. The result of this act of violence is the separation between mother and child, nation and citizen. It is not surprising that when Martine, Sophie's mother, realises that she has lost her virginity before marriage, there is a rupture between them leading to Martine's sending her daughter out of the house. 'Go,' she said with tears running down her face. She seized my books and clothes and threw them at me. 'You just go to him and see what he can do for you' (Danticat 1994: 88).

This rupture between mother and daughter is also seen in Martine's departure from Haiti due to rape. She does not feel like returning to the island where she is born. This is because home/nation is not free and hardly does one belong all through the narrative. Her continuous nightmares make that she feels the horror of returning to the land where she is raped by the very forces that are supposed to protect her. Martine's movement to the United States of America only demonstrates that the nation, under rape, has its toll more on the female who suffers a double rape. Therefore, her escape from 'home' begins her search for a 'home' elsewhere. Louis-Phillipe Dalembert has argued that the Haitian is always moving either running from political repression or looking for where to cope with hardship economically (Dalembert 1998: 40) and so, belonging and nationness is sought elsewhere.

Just as children internally rebel against their parents as seen above, there is an open and wide rebellion against government by the youth. This is because the government seems not to meet the demands of the youth. Set during the period of the dictatorship of the Duvaliers in Haiti, the events of the novel deal with the turmoil of the period that is often described as the most insecured in Haitian history. According to Priska Degras in, 'Enfances', 'Le mal y également puissant et s'avance notamment sous les traits des tontons-macoutes et autres miliciens qui soutiennent les dernier jours de la dictature Haitianne'(Degras 1998: 104). In a discussion between Tante Atie and the driver who drives them to Port of Spain, Haiti's political headquarter, for Sophie to travel, we get this: 'There is always some trouble here' the driver said. 'This time around it's crazy young people trying to fight the soldiers and government officials who would rather curse them with their last breath than give in to their protest' (Danticat 1994: 33). This situation shows that Haiti is a country where the people's protection cannot be guaranteed. The government officials and soldiers can be seen as heartless people who support the despot. That is why they cannot listen to the young people even when they protest. Even to get to the point of protest shows that there is disharmony between the ruled and the ruler and the ruled have no other way to be heard than to rebel.

In the words of the driver, one feels the dictatorship of the Haitian government. The driver describes the young people as 'crazy young people.' This is because with the despotism of the regime, only a mad man will have the temerity to go out to protest. This stems from the fact that it is suicidal to openly criticise the action of a despotic government like that which governs the Haiti in this narrative. It is not surprising that this dictatorship repressses and responds to the young people's rebellion with their might and in all brutality. Their response is vivid and most dramatically realised through the first person narrator who tells the story:

> Some of the students fell and rolled down the hill. They screamed at the soldiers that they were once again betraying the people. One girl rushed down the hill and grabed one of the soldiers by the arm. He raised his pistol and pounded it on top of her head. She fell to the ground, her face covered with her own blood. (Danticat 1994: 34)

From this action, so vividly described, it is realised that these protesters are students. In the text, the soldiers seem to defend the government against the 'people' in the most repressive manner while the students are considered patriots who are fighting for the commonwealth. Here, there is a dialectical view with regards to who is constructing the nation and the patriot can only be interpreted from which side of the divide that he/she is found.

The role played by the female student in the struggle to regain the nation, that is, being raped by government and its militia men is very important. The principal focus of *Breath, Eyes, Memory* is on women who, in their own way, are struggling to build the Haitian nation. The soldier's brutality on this student, fighting for her rights, shows that the women of Haiti understand that they have a role to play as far as national construction is concerned. In other words, though the nation is constantly under the totalitarianism of the government in place, women can fight to reclaim it and make Haiti a better place for their offspring and also for themselves.

In this section, the focus has been to discuss violence as part of the national character of the nation of Haiti that Danticat presents in *Breath, Eyes, Memory*. It is discovered that violence in the novel is carried out both at the level of the family and the nation. This renders the people in this locale uncertain about themselves. The woman's position in this history of violence is very precarious as she suffers all the indignities of the brutal man, state and capitalism. Therefore,

Haiti becomes an unsafe locale for its citizens. While these weak people, for the most part, choose to fight back with violence from a purely Fanonian view, others seek comfort and security elsewhere.

The Nation Elsewhere

This section justifies the claim that Haitians in *Breath, Eyes, Memory* have, in their effort to free themselves, constructed a dream national identity in the United States of America. In this section, I argue that the 'nation' is no longer a territorial construct but a deterritorialised one. This means that when it comes to nationalising, cartographic mappings no longer take precedence. This nationalising tendency has been fostered by the free world, the free economy ideology and the technological outburst that have made the discourse of the global world. George Steiner refutes the idea of nation as territory especially when it comes to the construction of the Jewish nation. He considers the Jewish patrimony in the Torah. He writes, 'the 'land of the fathers,' the *patrimoine*, is the script' (Steiner 1985: 5). Steiner's vision of the construction of the Jewish nation in the Torah indicates that the strength of the Jewish *nationness* lies in the belief system of the people and in their strong sense of belonging to Judaism wherever they are found. The Jews, as it is known, have one of the largest diaspora communities today in the world. In Danticat's *Breath, Eyes, Memory* the *patrimoine* is seen in the language and transnational belief of the people. Danticat's novel has characters in search of a place to heal the wounds of rape. This explains why in this section, I defend the contention that the nation and freedom could be accomplished in the diaspora.

When news comes that Sophie Caco has to leave Haiti for the United States of America, she is greatly admired by her people. This confirms one of the ideas of postcolonial conditions where Europe and the West in general are regarded with the supremacy myth. Fanon and George Lamming have discussed this myth of the superiority/inferiority complex that has been constructed in the minds of the Caribbean in their effort to deconstruct this myth. Lamming writes that 'It begins with the fact of England's supremacy in taste and judgement: a fact which can only have meaning and weight by a calculated cutting down to size of all of non-England. The first to be cut down is the colonial himself' (Lamming 1995: 14). This supremacy of the West governs the psyche of the Haitians in this narrative so that going the United States becomes a mark of achievement as we get comments like '[T]his is very good news,' said the accompanying voice. 'It is the best thing that is ever going to happen to you' (Lamming 1995: 14). This declaration reveals that the characters have no sense of belonging where they are and because of this, they see the need to negotiate place elsewhere so as to feel that sense of belonging. The adjectives 'good' and 'best' reveal that the myth that Lamming discusses is very strong as everything from the West carries the superlative to justify Western supremacy. Tzvetan Todorov has argued that 'C'est le pays auquel j'appartiens qui détient les valeurs les plus hautes, quelles qu'elles soient, affirme le nationaliste, non, c'est un pays dont la seule caractéristique pertinente est qu'il ne soit pas le mien dit celui qui professe l'exotisme.' (Todorov 1989 : 355). Danticat's characters dominantly fall in the category of Caribbean people driven by the myth that Lamming and Todorov discuss and therefore, it seems very normal for the characters to envy and admire Sophie for leaving. That is why the speakers perceive departure from Haiti as the best decision for any Haitian though up to this point, leaving does not mean anything to the child narrator, Sophie.

While the child, Sophie, leaves Haiti with little resistance, the boy in the plane cries. His crying reveals that he is being taken off his roots. From the narrative, we learn that the difference in reaction between these children is governed by the difference in status between the boy and Sophie. In the dialogue in the plane, we get more information about the boy:

…What is the matter with him?' the man said in French. 'His father died in that fire out front. His father was some kind of old government official, *très* corrupt,' she whispered. '*Très* guilty of crimes against the people.' 'And we are letting him travel?' He does not have any more relatives here. His father's sister lives in New York. I called her. She is going to meet him there.' (Danticat 1994: 37-38)

In this discussion, the country's leadership is first of all corrupt and the boy's father is among the ruling class that is corrupt. As one of the speakers put it, corruption is already a crime against the people. It is therefore not surprising that he becomes the victim of the people. The father of the boy becomes the kind of person that Giorgio Agamben calls 'the sacred man' who is:

> [T]he one whom the people have judged on account of a crime. It is not permitted to sacrifice this man, yet he who kills him will not be condemned for homicide; in the tribunitian law, in fact, it is noted that 'if someone kills the one who is sacred according to the plebiscite, it will not be considered homicide.' This is why it is customary for a bad and impure man to be called sacred. (Agamben 1998: 47)

The father that the hostess discusses about reflects Agamben's description. He is first of all condemned by the people and that is why he is killed. He is corrupt and therefore considered as one of the rapists of the nation as he becomes a parasite tapping wrongfully on the resources of the State. The people decide to eliminate him. In this case, the profanation of what is 'sacred' becomes the duty of the people. This is because when it comes to the ruled/ruler divide, the ruler is considered 'pure' and 'sacred.' Yet, as Agamben puts it, most of such people are mean, corrupt and most unpatriotic. So, in Agamben's discourse, the society makes these rulers 'pure' and unattained by the people. But when the people considered profane rise against the sacred people and profane them by killing them, it is considered as the victory of the people. The father of the boy, who belongs to the 'pure' class, has activities that are so hostile that the people have to rise against him. Though the narrative duration here is greatly accelerated because of the limited narrative point of view, we can infer that the destruction of the boy's father shows the people's rejection of the rulers in Haiti.

Also, as the hostess says, the boy is being taken by his aunt to the United States. This shows that the lady [aunt] is looking for a better security for her nephew who may have to pay for his father's sins. Still, the hostilities of this man makes a typical Fanonian violence become the inevitable response to his acts and so his death is partly victory for the people.

In *Breath, Eyes, Memory*, the villagers are described as very poor. Therefore, those with relatives who have travelled out of the country are seen as the source of redemption for those back home. Tante Atie tells Sophie:

> Here in Croix-des-Rosets, most of the people were city workers who laboured in baseball or clothing factories and lived in small cramped houses to support their families back in the provinces. Tante Atie said that we were lucky to live in a house as big as ours, with a living room to receive our guest, plus a room for the two of us to sleep in. Tante Atie said that only people living on New York money…could afford to live in a house where they did not have to share a yard with a pack of other people.(Danticat 1994: 11)

This contrast expatiates why each Haitian, as presented in the text, longs to travel to New York. New York symbolises wealth and comfortable living while Croix-des-Rosets and the Haitian villages are rippled with poverty as the people live 'in huts, shacks, or one-room houses that, sometimes, they had to build themselves' (Danticat 1994: 11). This representation of Haiti, compared to that of the United States of America, reveals that the Haitian diaspora are free to express themselves in the United States and also, can make a happier and better life in the United States.

In this case, remittancy becomes evident as the Haitians who have settle in New York begin to work hard to salvage the poverty back in Haiti. Tante Atie tells Sophie that it is New York's money that helps them have a house of their own. Kezia Page submits in 'What If He Did Not Have a Sister [Who Lived in the United States]?': Jamaica Kincaid's *My Brother* as remittance Text' that ' Remittance represent a significant means of foreign earnings or inflows to Caribbean nations' (Page 2008: 190). So, we hear the speaker say 'The streets along Flatbusg Avenue reminded me of home. My mother took me to Haiti Express, so I could see the place where she sent our money orders and cassettes from… People stood on line patiently waiting their turn' (Danticat 1994: 50). This explains why most Haitians, as seen in *Breath, Eyes, Memory* go out of the country and/or be there and have nothing to do with the affairs of the homeland. Their only contact with Haiti is seen in their assistance to their relatives back there. From Martine's psychological state, she only thinks of home because of her mother, child and sister. When Tante Atie makes a statement like 'Did they have to do it today…We cannot miss our appointment' (Danticat 1994: 33). Tante Atie, with this question that is not answered by the driver only confirms Haitians' attitude towards their country. The Island is a place of chaos and disorder. This woman's only problem is that the disorder should not hinder her private plan of sending her niece to the Unites States. This private feeling, coupled with her chiding tone, shows that she has no feeling and concern about what is happening to the Island. Tante Atie may be seen as those Haitians who go into exile themselves and would prefer their individual safety because they find nothing good at home. To end this section, It seems likely that the absence of peace, and the callousness of the regime in place in Haiti, as presented in *Breath, Eyes, Memory*, towards the people has pushed them to look elsewhere with the hope of getting psychological, emotional and economic restoration.

Diaspora Home

In this section, I argue that Danticat's notion of the nation, in the novel, goes beyond geopolitical space and has to do with people's ability to belong where they find themselves. From this perspective, it seems to me that the Haitian nation and its literature have been constructed in the diaspora. Romuald Fonkoua in 'Une Nouvelle Génération aux Caribe. Rupture et Continuités' argues that: 'Ecrire les Caribes est une entreprise qui se limite guère à l'enfermement géographique. Au contraire! De même qu'hier les écrivains pensaient ces îles à partir de l'Afrique …de l'Europe… ou des Ameriques … de même, aujourd'hui, c'est à travers ces espaces du monde que les écrivians pensent les îles' (Fonkoua 2007: 77). Fonkoua's assertion here, lays claim to the fact that the nation can be constructed irrespective of where the people come together to imagine it. This claim holds true in Danticat's *Breath, Eyes, Memory* in which the idea of the nation shifts from a location to where people become pyscho-ideologically accepted. It is my argument that such communities are nations that are imagined and constructed by people based on ideology, language, and race or ethnic affiliation. This view is corroborated by Roger Rouse in his article entitled 'Mexican Migration and the Social Space of Postmodernism' where he posits that: 'We live in a confusing world, a world of crisscross economics, intersecting systems of meaning and fragmented identities. Suddenly, the comforting modern imagery of nation-state and national languages, of coherent communities and consistent subjuctivitities, of dominant centres and distant margins no longer seems adequate' (Rouse 1991: 8). The argument here is the deterritorialisation of subjects and the freedom to construct identities where one finds oneself. A significant part of Danticat's narrative is set out of Haiti – in The United States of America. The Haitians in this country are negotiating their identity in such a way that their community seems to be no different from what is in Haiti. Sophie says that 'The Streets along Flatbush Avenue reminded me of home'(Danticat 1994: 50).

Sophie Caco's statement reveals that territorial construction has been transported and here we are reminded of Arjun Appadurai's concept of *scape* and most especially the *ethnoscape* which he defines as 'the landscape of persons who constitute the shifting world in which they live: tourists, immigrants, refugees, exiles guest workers, and other moving groups and individuals constitute an essential feature of the world and appear to affect the politics of …nations to a hitherto unprecedented degree' (Appadurai 1996: 33) are, for the most part, immigrants who have different reasons for living in New York. Their ability even to transform this street in a Haitian homeland justifies the claim that 'there are no relative stable communities'(Appadurai 1996: 33). In New York, these people work hard to earn their living. Some work as money exchange and courier agents (Danticat 1994: 50) others in beauty salon (Danticat 1994: 51) and others still doing odds jobs as working in nursing homes like Martine (Danticat 1994: 51). This community seems to grow strong because they do not feel that they are Americans and thereby, the task is to build a strong Haitian community. Arjun Appadurai adroitly submits that:

> Because they are so often the product of force as well as voluntary diasporas, of mobile intellectuals as well as manual workers, of dialogues with hostile as well as hospitable states, very few of the new nationalisms can be separated from the anguish of displacement, the nostalgia of exile, the aspiration of funds, or the brutalities of asylum seeking. Haitians in Miami, Tamils in Boston, Moroccans in France, Moluccans in Holland are the carriers of these new transnational and post national loyalties. (Appadurai 1996: 165)

The construction of an imagined nation/home with its own nationalism is built along these lines in Danticat's novel. It is therefore justifiable why Haitians in the novel, though not happy with American invasion of their home-country, still can settle in the United States to negotiate themselves.

Conclusion

In this chapter, rape has been discussed as the forceful 'penetration' from a stronger force (male and colonial as well as imperialist States) on the weak, (female and Third World States) which has led the victim to reconstruct previous ideologies. Thus, producing not only strong diasporas but putting to question the very essence of the nation as a concept and political structure. With this, the chapter discusses the Haitian responses to rape and its contribution to national construction in Danticat's *Breath, Eyes, Memory*. With the postcolonial theory as a principal tool of analysis, The chapter has revealed that Danitcat's *Breath, Eyes, Memory* does not only depict the history of Haitian women being silenced by patriarchy and a harsh political and economic situation, but presents postnational constructions put in place by the transnational relationships that govern the textual structure of the narrative. Danticat's women in the novel have shown sufficient evidence that the postcolonial Caribbean woman can cease and create her centre as she castigates the wrongs of patriarchy and misrule.

Bibliography

Agamben, G., (1998). *Homo Sacer: Sovereign Power and Bare Life*. Stanford: Stanford University Press.

Agamben, G., (2000). *Means without End: Notes on Politics*. London: University of Minnesota.

Anderson, B., (1980). *Imagined Communities: Reflections on the Origin and Spread of Nationalism*. London: Verso.

Appadurai, A., (1996). *Modernity at Large: Cultural Dimensions of Globalization*. Minneapolis: University of Minnesota.

Ashcroft, B., Griffiths , G. & Tiffin, H., (2011). *The Post-Colonial Studies Reader*. 2 ed. London and New York: Routledge.

Bhabha, H. K., (1990). *Nation and Narration*. London and New York:

Routledge.

Brennan, T., (1990). The National Longing of Form. In: *Nation and Narration*. London and New York: Routledge, pp. 44-70.

Chalkley, O, & Abdo, D., (2017). Mortar and Pestle, Orange and Navel: (M)otherhood, Exile, and Cultural Reproduction in Edwidge Danticat's *Breath, Eyes, Memory* and Hanan Al-Shaykh's *The Story of Zahra*. *Explorations.* pp.19-27.

Dalembert, L.-P., (1995). Exil et Diaspora: Une Littérature en Migration. *Notre Libraire*, pp. 40-45.

Danticat, E., (1994). *Breath, Eyes, Memory*. New York: Vintage.

Degras, P., (1998). Enfance. *Notre Libraire*, pp. 102-107.

Dominique, M., (1998). Haiti Littéraire: Position et Proposition. *Notre Librairie*, pp. 11-18.

Fanon, F., (1968). *The Wretched of the Earth*. New York: Grove.

Fonkoua, R., 2007. Une Nouvelle Génération aux Caraïbe. Ruptures et Continuites. *Culture Sud*, pp. 77-82.

Freire, P., (2000). *Pedagogy of the Oppressed*. New York and London: Continuum.

Gerber, N. F., (2019). Binding the Narrative Thread: Storytelling and the Mother-Daughter Relationship in Edwidge Danticat's *Breath, Eyes, Memory*. *Academy of Clinical and Applied Psychoanalysis.* pp. 188-199.

Gibson-Graham, J. K., (1996). *The End of Capitalism (As We Knew It): A Feminist Critique of Political Economy*. Oxford: Blackwell.

James, C. L. R., (1989). *The Black Jacobins: Toussaint L'Ouverture and the San Domingo Revolution*. New York: Vintage.

Lamming, G., (1995). The Occasion for Speaking . In: *The Post-Colonial Studies Reader*. London and New York: Routledge, pp.12-17.

Page, K., (2008). What If He Did Not Have a Sister [Who Lived in the United States]?: Jamaica Kincaid's My Brother as Remittance Text. In: *Jamaica Kindcaid*. New York: Bloom's Literary Criticism, pp. 189-206.

Rath, S. P., (2000). *Home(s) Abroad: Diasporic Identities in Third*

Space.[Online]Available at: english.class.ncsu.edu[Accessed 15 May 2014].

Renan, E., (1990). What is a Nation. In: *Nation and Narration.* London and New York: Routledge, pp. 8-22.

Rimmon-Kenan, S., (2002). *Narrative Fiction.* London: Taylor and Francis Froup.

Rosello, R. M., (2010). Marassa with a Difference, *Breath, Eyes, Memory. Language Learning.* pp. 117-128.

Rouse, R., (1991). Mexican Migration and the Social Space of Postmodernism. *Diaspora: A Journal of Transnational Studies,* pp. 8-22.

Said, E., (1999). *Culture and Imperialism.* New York: Vintage.

Samway, P. S. J., (2003). *A Homeward Journey: Edwidge Danticant's Fictional Landscapes, Mindscape, Genescape and Signscape in Breath Eyes Memory.* [Online]Available at: www.highbeam.com [Accessed 14 May 2014].

Skey, M., (2011). *National Belonging and Everyday Life: The Significance of Nationhood in an Uncertain World.* London: Palgrave.

Steiner, G., (1985). Our Home, the Text. *Salmagundi,* pp. 5-25.

Todorov, T., (1989). *Nous et les Autres: La Réflexion Française sur la Diversité Humaine.* Paris: Edition du Seuil.

Trouillot, M.-R., (1990). *Haiti: State against Nation.* New York: Month Press Review.

www.ingramcontent.com/pod-product-compliance
Lightning Source LLC
Chambersburg PA
CBHW050530300426
44113CB00012B/2032